DRAGON IN THE KREMLIN

DRAGON IN THE KREMLIN

A Report on the Russian-Chinese Alliance

by Marvin L. Kalb

E. P. DUTTON & CO., INC. NEW YORK

TO MADY

FIRST EDITION

Published simultaneously in Canada by CLARKE, IRWIN & CO., LTD. OF TORONTO

Library of Congress Catalog Card Number: 61-6004

Contents

Foreword

Over the last few years, many disagreements have come to the surface of the Russian-Chinese alliance. They have focused world attention on this unusual coalition of friendly enemies. This is a book about the alliance. Although I have read most of the pertinent material and have talked with most of the right people, I have no illusions that this is a definitive book. I have attempted in it merely to bring us up to date and to raise some important questions. If this book succeeds in stimulating an awareness of the dangers the alliance poses for us, I shall consider it a success.

So many kind people have helped me with the book that it would be impossible to thank them all. But I should especially like to thank Marshall D. Shulman of Harvard; Alexander Dallin, Henry Roberts, Allen Whiting, C. Martin Wilbur, and O. Edmund Clubb of Columbia; Sig Mickelson and John F. Day of CBS News; William Ackerman of the CBS Foundation, which awarded me a CBS News and Public Affairs Fellowship for the academic year 1959–1960; Henry Graff, Director of the Fellowship program at Columbia; the Ford Foundation, which awarded me a travel grant so I could conduct an interview project; Rose Bell Green, who painstakingly copyread and edited the manuscript; and, finally, my wife, Mady, who was colleague, travel companion, editor, and a constant source of encouragement.

One separate note: all of this book, except for one section of the last chapter, was written before I was appointed Moscow Correspondent for CBS News. Therefore its conception and its views are entirely unconnected with CBS News. If there are any errors, they are mine. If there are any misconceptions, they are mine.

Marvin L. Kalb

New York City
December 28, 1960

DRAGON IN THE KREMLIN

CHAPTER ONE New York

ON DECEMBER 16, 1949, A LEGEND ARRIVED IN MOSCOW. TALL, proud, and taciturn, the legend was already an *ism,* a triumphant twentieth century *ism* that had inspired a mass Communist revolution in the most heavily populated nation on earth. The *ism* was Maoism, and the legend belonged to a dedicated Chinese revolutionary named Mao Tse-tung.

Like a Chinese scroll, the legend and the man were shrouded in historical mist. A few facts and some statistics were known. Mao was the leader of the Chinese Communist Party, which two months earlier had raised its red flag over the ancient capital of Peking. He had defied Marxism and Moscow by pegging his political and ideological destiny to the teeming Chinese peasantry. He had survived the Long March—an incredibly arduous six-thousand-mile trek through mountainous terrain; established a network of village soviets in northwestern China; created a huge army of fighter-revolutionaries who skillfully blended traditional Chinese guerrilla tactics with the strategy of modern warfare to defeat the dispirited Chinese army of Nationalist President Chiang Kai-shek; and brought a unifying plan for disciplined economic and social revolution to China for the first time in over a thousand years. In addition, he was a chain smoker who liked women.

These were the known facts, and the paucity of data only fed the legend. So it was not surprising that Moscow sighed, almost audibly, when Mao arrived, and the lofty legend was cut to the size of mortal man.

An enterprising Tass reporter asked the man, who was then making his first trip out of China, "For how long, Mr. Mao Tse-tung, have you come to the USSR?"

Mao, apparently miffed at not having been called Comrade,

replied coldly, "I have come for a few weeks." Then he added: "The length of my sojourn in the USSR depends on the period in which it will be possible to settle questions of interest to the People's Republic of China."

Mao stayed for ten weeks, and, on February 14, 1950, the Russian-Chinese alliance was born.

Two friendly enemies had agreed to shake hands so that they could shake the world. Now, more than a decade later, the world does shake, with either a terrible fascination or a hopeless dedication, as populations are brandished like swords and rockets rattled like toys. Moscow and Peking control a billion people who inhabit one-fourth of the globe. Together they command the allegiance of every Communist Party except that of Tito, the redoubtable Yugoslav. Moscow has stockpiled atomic and hydrogen bombs, and her rockets can deliver them—anywhere on earth. Peking scowls at Asia and intrudes into India and Indonesia, as she trains her modern 3,000,000-man army to razor-sharp perfection. Peking does not speak to her people or the world without referring to Moscow, and Moscow plugs for Peking with increasing frequency.

This alliance, born in revolutionary war and baptized by solemn Marxists, has been etched across the diplomatic map of the world in indelible red ink, and "The Alliance" has become a familiar, if frightening, term in the Foreign Offices of every major capital. It possesses extraordinary powers of destruction; it has a seemingly endless supply of manpower; and it believes in a political creed that professes to have all the answers.

Yet what is known about this alliance?

Are the ties that bind Moscow and Peking really as "indissoluble" as Chou En-lai and Nikita Khrushchev proclaim? Are the Moscow smiles and Peking frowns two faces of a single, well-integrated foreign policy, or are there two distinct foreign policies in the alliance? Are the Russians concerned about a "yellow peril"? Does Khrushchev mind the establishment of communes in China? How soon will China develop its own atomic bomb? And is it possible that Chinese truculence will accidentally or deliberately trigger a hydrogen war?

There are no easy answers to any of these questions. In fact, of all the coalitions of modern times, the Russian-Chinese alliance emerges as the biggest question mark that has been carved into the husk of history—and the most powerful. Rarely, it appears, has the West faced so alarming a combination of ideological, military, political, economic, and psychological forces with so pathetically little information.

* * *

It was in the fall of 1958 that I realized how little we knew about the alliance. The Chinese had just embarked upon the most incredible social revolution of the century. More than 500,000,000 peasants were being forced into "people's communes," and Peking's propagandists were already championing the "commune" as the "primary unit of Communism."

Some underdeveloped nations were shocked; others were thrilled. Perhaps, they reasoned, China had evolved a magic formula for transforming backward countries into mechanized giants. Western capitals were openly revolted by Peking's "inhumanity." Moscow, which usually cheers the production of every toothbrush in "fraternal China," was frigidly silent. In a strangely neutral tone, *Pravda* mentioned the communes, but there were no cheers and no boos.

This Soviet reaction was so unprecedented that it touched off speculation about a major fissure in the alliance. Specialists took sides, selected their facts, marshaled them like an army, and wrote stories illustrating four viewpoints: first, that Moscow and Peking were firm allies committed to a common cause that overrode all petty squabbles; second, that Moscow and Peking had differences, just as Washington and London had differences, but that nothing would come between them; third, that Moscow and Peking had major differences stemming from race, history, and ideology that would inevitably drive them apart; and, fourth, that there really was not enough information to make an intelligent estimate of the apparent difficulties that had begun to envelop the Russian-Chinese alliance.

I agreed with the fourth view.

In early November I had been asked by the Brookings Institution to deliver a talk in Washington about the Moscow-Peking axis. I consented—after warning the Institution that I might be raising more questions than I would be answering.

For the next month or so, I read most of the newspaper, textbook, and magazine accounts of this strange alliance. As I slowly became aware of how little was known about the alliance, I knew that I would have to reach back into history for the answers to some of today's enigmas. I was grateful that I had taken my Ph.D. orals at Harvard in Russian and Chinese history and that I could also call upon personal experience. I had been in Moscow for the State Department in 1956–1957. I recalled that Russians didn't talk very much about China. Everyone recognized that Peking was the junior partner in the alliance—though now, it seemed, China was beginning to play an ever more important role in the alliance and in the bloc.

This was the heart of the theme I brought to Washington, and, as I suspected, it raised more questions than I could answer. That morning, in early December, 1958, the newspapers ran banner headlines of a Hong Kong story that made me scrap my neat outline. Actually, the story was the first of several that seemed to portend major political and economic changes in Communist China. The Chinese announced that two key decisions had just been made at an important Party meeting in Wuhan. First, Mao Tse-tung would relinquish his job as Chairman of the Chinese Government; and, second, the communes would not be pressed upon urban areas for the present time. The Chinese referred to the communes as "the primary unit of the future Communist society," but Peking admitted that they needed more efficient management. Echoing Stalin's 1930 speech, the Chinese conceded that they had become "dizzy with success."

Did this December resolution mean the Chinese would soon abandon the communes? Why did Mao step down from the post of Chairman?

I did not know the answers, but my curiosity about the story was aroused to fever pitch.

When I returned to New York, I devoted most of my time to a

more concentrated study of the Russian-Chinese alliance. Among other things, I read Allen Whiting's excellent articles; Peter Tang's books on Communist China; Robert C. North's *Moscow and Chinese Communists;* John K. Fairbank's updated classic on Chinese history, *The United States and China;* Henry Wei's *China and Soviet Russia;* and, perhaps most valuable, the superb collection of essays by Professors Harold Boorman, Alexander Eckstein, Philip E. Mosely, and Benjamin Schwartz published under the auspices of the Council on Foreign Relations and entitled *Moscow-Peking Axis.* I read newspaper clips from the *New York Times,* the *New York Herald Tribune,* the *Christian Science Monitor,* the *Manchester Guardian,* the *Observer.* I studied the Soviet press in greater detail, searching for references, direct or oblique, that might shed some light on the alliance; and I read translations of the Chinese Communist press.

The more I read, the more I learned how little was known. It was almost as though two red giants were poised to smash us, and we did not even take the preliminary precaution of getting out of the way.

In the last few years American scholars and journalists have attempted a few ground-breaking efforts aimed at illuminating some of the dark corners of the Mao-Moscow relationship. Several universities have instituted Asian Studies programs to train specialists in Chinese affairs. Our magazines have recently become more aware of the fact that, as Mao himself might put it, a "yellow wind" has begun to stir around our Asian flanks. Even the Russians have suddenly become aware of the Chinese Goliath who is called an "eternal friend" but who nevertheless awakens faint recollections of invading Mongol hordes. Recently, Moscow University instituted a special program on Chinese history, culture, and language; apparently Russia has an even greater need for China experts than we do, since its universities are not blessed, as ours are, with the sons of missionaries who have been raised on the Chinese mainland.

Still, from a Western standpoint, there is an unprecedented and dangerous shortage of information about the Russian-Chinese alliance. There are some good reasons.

First, there is a general uneasiness in Washington about discussing China. Our popular image of that aroused giant, which has never been too sharp, is still fuzzy around the edges, and it has been distorted by improbable Hollywood pictures of pigtailed peasants and skinny, bearded scholars. The State Department has liberated itself—at least partially—from the pervasive influence of the China Lobby, but it still refuses to recognize the realities of America's deep involvement in Far Eastern politics—an involvement that inevitably brings us face to face with Peking.

During the Korean War the United States had 125,000 casualties—a fact that made us blind to the clear dangers and opportunities presented by Peking's alliance with Moscow. A Des Moines family that has lost a son on the frozen battlefields of an Asian nation fighting Chinese Communist troops surely opposes any diplomatic and commercial ties with Peking, and the local politician with a crafty eye on Congress would hardly sponsor even a civil relationship with Mao.

Second, China does not want to be known; it prefers the freedom of anonymity to the responsibility of recognition. Mao is engaged in the most far-reaching social revolution of modern times. His peasants are still being herded into communes, and 650,000,000 people labor with a verve and ambition that amaze "old China hands" in Hong Kong. As one of them told me: "China is guilty not only of un-Chinese behavior but also of un-Asian dynamics." Mao, who at one time showed some inclination to allow reporters into his country, now feels that China is too involved with social revolution to put its best foot forward. He would prefer that for the present, Western reporters snoop elsewhere in the Communist bloc. Therefore he has forbidden American correspondents to "cover" the Chinese mainland. I tried to get into China in 1957 and again last year when I was gathering material for this book. Each time I was rejected, which was not a surprise, just a disappointment. After some of the revolutionary dust has settled, chances will undoubtedly become better for on-the-scene coverage of the China story.

The tragedy of the current situation is that we have come to live with so little information about China for so long a time that we may have grown comfortable in our ignorance. We may be accepting rumor for fact and contemplating policy in the framework of pat generalizations engendered by an atmosphere of national jitters.

Third, all important problems behind the somewhat porous Curtain are shrouded in the deepest secrecy. The Byzantine mystery that has always surrounded the Kremlin continues to envelop the Communist world. This is especially true of the Moscow-Peking alliance. A topic of extreme sensitivity, it is cushioned in diplomatic niceties that add up only to impressive clichés. "Firm friendship" and "indissoluble unity" are the glib descriptions of this unusual relationship that decorate many a public communiqué between Russia and China. Moreover, neither Khrushchev nor Mao hold press conferences to explain their frequently baffling attitudes toward each other. It seems that these two Communist titans are delighted that our appreciation of their alliance is so inadequate, and it is highly unlikely that they will help us.

Fourth, there is the complexity of Moscow's relations with Peking. If China were Bulgaria, it would be so much easier to write about the Moscow-Sofia alliance. Bulgaria is a small country. Its government is Communist largely because the Soviet Union contributed generously to make it Communist. It would not do anything without first checking with Moscow, and it would do whatever the Kremlin desired. But China is not Bulgaria. Ever since Mao rode to power in October, 1949, on the breaking waves of ideological dedication and Nationalist inefficiency, the Russians have realized that they have incorporated an important but rambunctious ally into the Marxist family of nations. China has never been an ordinary satellite.

Moscow cannot put China in its hip pocket as a handy flask of raw materials and manpower resources. China has 650,000,000 people, and Peking rarely permits Moscow to forget that its population is increasing by 16,000,000 a year. In addition, Mao did not have to depend upon Soviet support to destroy Chiang Kai-shek and to raise his red flag over the ancient capital of Peking. His own troops conquered China. Mao was never the sniveling "patriot" who sat out the war studying Marxism in Moscow. He led his victory, and his victory gave Moscow the opportunity to speak of a "Communist bloc of one billion people." Before 1949, Moscow led a nation, not a bloc. After 1949, Moscow not only had its bloc; it also had a new race of Communists and a new region for Communism.

Clearly, Moscow saw the enormous advantages of the Russian-Chinese alliance, but it has never forgotten that the Chinese Communist Party achieved its present peak mostly on its own power. Mao realizes that China's power does not equal Russia's, but, like all nationalists, Mao is extremely conscious of his and China's dignity. To Edgar Faure, the French politician who visited him in 1957, Mao said: "China is an independent state. She is absolutely independent of the Soviet Union. If we have asked for experts and machinery from the Soviet Union, it is because we have need of them. We cannot do without them. But the men who have come will go away again once their work is finished. And we shall pay them for all that we have taken."

Mao is the kind of Communist who knows his history, and the history of pre-1949 Moscow-Mao relations can cast highly illuminating lights on many obscure aspects of the Moscow-Peking axis.

* * *

In November, 1917, when Russia's Communists seized power in Leningrad and Moscow, unfurling a banner of proletarian revolution that sent a chill through the West and a hope through Asia, Mao Tse-tung was a librarian's assistant in the National University of Peking, known throughout China as Peita. Mao did not earn very much at Peita, but he did not mind. His rewards were spiritual, for Peita was the hotbed of intellectual and literary ferment in China.

Mao heard his friends discuss Sun Yat-sen's republican revolution of 1911—a revolution that awakened China from centuries of slothfulness—and he shared their disillusionment that China was still convulsed in economic chaos and administrative corruption.

All over the world, Chinese intellectuals, who traditionally shunned violence, searched for an ideology that could help China. Some of them, in Europe, were fascinated by Lenin's Bolshevism in Russia. They remembered their history, and they agreed with Lenin that "imperialism" and "colonialism" had to be crushed.

On July 1, 1921, the First National Congress of the Chinese Communist Party opened in Shanghai. The leader of the Party was Ch'ên Tu-hsiu; a delegate from Hunan was Mao Tse-tung, formerly the librarian's assistant at Peita.

Mao had become a Communist.

For the next six years the Chinese Communist Party was under Ch'ên's control. Stalin ordered Ch'ên to co-operate with the Kuomintang in an unusual test-tube experiment in social revolution. The Kuomintang, once Sun's party, had fallen under the power of Chiang Kai-shek, an ambitious young officer who had been trained in Moscow. But in April, 1927, Stalin's plans backfired. Chiang turned on the Communists, almost destroying their movement—particularly in the urban areas.

Many fled to Moscow; others defied Moscow and withdrew to the remote mountainous regions of southern Kiangsi, where they slowly came under Mao's influence. A Hunanese peasant intellectual, Mao quickly realized that Chinese Communism would have to depend on the peasants. Dropping Moscow's emphasis on the proletariat, he instituted a series of revolutionary reforms that turned disaster into victory.

First, he distributed the land in Kiangsi to the peasants—a popular act that brought him fresh adherents from neighboring Hupeh and Fukien provinces. Second, he put Chu Teh, a friend, in charge of the Red Army. In 1928 the Red Army consisted of 10,000 ragged peasants and 2,000 rifles. By 1932 this scattered group had been tailored into a disciplined army of 100,000 troops. Finally, he converted Kiangsi into a Soviet province under exclusive Communist control.

Chiang launched a major offensive against Mao in 1933; he even succeeded in encircling Communist troops in Kiangsi. Victory appeared within his grasp, but Mao, a brilliant strategist, managed to escape Chiang's encirclement—with his army intact. The Communists then made their way through the mountains to northwest China—a historic trek known as the Long March. Once Mao had organized his soviets in Yenan, he again divided the land and helped the peasants. In a nation of peasants, this was simple and clever.

Mao always wanted to be known as a popular figure; and when the Japanese resumed their attack on China, Mao ordered his army into battle against "the foreign invader." When the Japanese were finally defeated in 1945, Mao resumed his fight against Chiang. Four years later, Mao won.

His days in Yenan were described by Edgar Snow in *Red Star Over China,* a classic in history and journalism. Snow had a wonderful opportunity to observe the Chinese Communists in their own back yard, and he saw how much Mao borrowed from the Russians. But, Snow reports, "in all this borrowing, there was much adaptation; few Russian ideas or institutions have survived without drastic changes to suit the milieu in which they operate." This kind of "adaptation" certainly did not please Stalin, who at this time was plunging Russia into the blood bath of the 1936–1938 purges.

Did Russia control the Chinese Red Army, as many observers claimed? Snow: "The Soviet movement and the Chinese Red Army began spontaneously, under purely Chinese leadership, and they did not in fact get much applause from Russia."

Did Russia finance Mao? Snow: ". . . the financial help given to the Chinese Reds by Moscow or the Comintern during this decade seems to have been amazingly small. . . . It seems to be rubbish to assert that Russia has been propping up the Chinese Reds."

In 1940 Mao wrote a pamphlet called *China's New Democracy.* It is an attempt to answer the question: Whither China? If Mao were a Stalinist, even then, it seems hard to imagine that he would have authored this idea:

"This Republic of the New Democracy is different on the one hand from the old Western-style capitalist republics that are ruled by capitalists and are already out of date. On the other hand, it is also different from the newest Soviet-style socialist republic, that is ruled by the proletariat. Nevertheless, in a certain historical period, the Soviet-style Republic cannot be fittingly practiced in colonial and semi-colonial countries, the national polity of which therefore must be of a third type—that of the New Democracy. This is a national polity for a certain historical period, and is therefore transitional in character, but it is a form indispensable and unalterable."

There has never been any real question about what Mao had in mind. He was telling Moscow that he had his own ideas about building Communism in China, and he was suggesting in a typically Chinese way that Stalin ought to be wise enough to let him alone.

Just as Mao had little faith in Stalin, Stalin consistently underestimated Mao's power. During the Second World War he told United States Ambassador Averell Harriman: "The Chinese Communists are not real Communists; they are 'margarine' Communists." And Donald Nelson, one of America's two representatives to Chungking, according to *United States Relations with China,* told of a talk he had with former Soviet Foreign Minister Molotov. "Although he said," Nelson wrote, "that the Soviet Government had unjustifiably been held responsible for various happenings in China during recent years, Molotov stressed that it would bear no responsibility for internal affairs and developments in China. Molotov then spoke of the very impoverished conditions of the people in parts of China, some of whom called themselves Communists but were related to Communism in no way at all."

There is also the unconfirmed story V. Dedijer tells in his biography of Tito, *Tito Speaks*—that Stalin proposed the dissolution of the Chinese Red Army at the end of 1945. He is reported to have told Yugoslav Politburo member Edward Kardelj: ". . . after the war, we invited the Chinese Comrades to come to Moscow and we discussed the situation in China. We told them bluntly that we considered the development of the uprising in China had no prospect, and that the Chinese Comrades should seek a *modus vivendi* with Chiang Kai-shek, that they should join the Chiang Kai-shek government and dissolve their army. The Chinese Comrades agreed here with the views of the Soviet Comrades, but went back to China and acted quite otherwise."

Clearly, Stalin did not have the highest hopes for the Chinese

Communists. His pessimism arose partly from the bitter memory of his 1927 miscalculation and partly from his misreading of Mao's strength and Chiang's weakness. In any case, for a time he actively supported Chiang with military and economic assistance.

* * *

When the Chinese Communists triumphed in October, 1949, it was clear that China had no course but to enter into an alliance with the Soviet Union. Only a few months earlier, Mao had explained in a document called *On the People's Democratic Dictatorship* that "you lean to one side." He believed that the Chinese people "either lean to the side of imperialism or the side of socialism."

He concluded: "To sit on the fence is impossible."

A Marxist realist, Mao knew that a Communist China needed the help of a Communist Russia. So, when Mao left China in December, 1949, for Moscow and one of the most memorable summit conferences of the twentieth century, his aim was clear. He wanted an alliance with Stalin, but Mao, the modern mandarin, would not kowtow.

Mao, who was in Russia for ten weeks, did not kowtow. Tough deliberations finally produced three Sino-Soviet agreements.

The first was a Treaty of Friendship, Alliance, and Mutual Assistance, which was basically a Russian promise to come to China's support in the event of a Japanese threat. Since both Moscow and Peking realized that Tokyo was being checkreined by Washington, the treaty added that Russia would rush to China's aid if the mainland were attacked by Japan "or any state that may collaborate with Japan directly or indirectly."

The second treaty concerned Manchuria, a border area in which Moscow and Peking have been traditional rivals. It was agreed that the Chinese-Changchun Railway would continue to operate under joint Sino-Soviet administration. Ironically, this was the same arrangement that Stalin had reached with Chiang in 1945, after the Soviet Army had looted Manchuria's industry. It was also agreed that Port Arthur, a naval base, would continue to serve

Russian and Chinese ships but that Dairen, another port, would fall exclusively under Peking's control.

The third treaty outlined the measure of Moscow's economic support of Communist China. The equivalent of $300,000,000 was granted to Peking to be repaid in ten equal annual installments beginning in 1954. This loan carried an interest rate of 1 per cent a year, and it was to be administered over a five-year period. Thus the Russians said they would give the Chinese, their newest and most important ally, $60,000,000 a year, which by any standard was not a large sum.

Mao and Stalin also declared that the Mongolian People's Republic was an independent nation. Later, in the spring, they agreed—Mao, with some reluctance—to establish a network of Sino-Soviet joint-stock companies in Sinkiang and Manchuria. One company would also be set up in Dairen to "build and repair" ships. The provision on joint-stock companies was reported briefly at that time in the Chinese press, but was not mentioned again until the end of 1954. It was not fashioned to win friends and influence people in a nation that had just fought a revolutionary war against all forms of "foreign" control.

When Mao returned to Peking, he received wildly enthusiastic acclaim. At least, that was what the Chinese Communist press reported. Now Mao was free to press forward with the urgent domestic tasks of political unification and economic rehabilitation. But in June, 1950, the Korean War erupted on his northeastern flank, and, later in the year, he ordered his troops into battle against the United Nations. China's gargantuan job of domestic reform was forced to wait.

Was the Korean War Mao's brainstorm? Or was it Stalin's? Or was it a joint inspiration?

These are questions that are doomed to remain questions. As Howard L. Boorman puts it, "Caution suggests that the interpretation of the diplomatic history of the Korean War be left to the future, since the present evidence is as overabundant as it is incomplete."

In any case, by the middle of 1952, Mao apparently felt that the war had stopped paying dividends. The United Nations had condemned China's "aggression," and the United States had given clear proof that it was prepared to oppose the further expansion of Communism. China again turned to its internal problems.

In September, 1952, Chou En-lai flew to Moscow. His purpose was to reach a new understanding with the Russians on the Chinese-Changchun Railway in Manchuria. He did; the Russians finally agreed to give China full control of the railway.

Chou returned to Peking, just as Liu Shao-chi departed for Moscow to represent the Chinese Communist Party at the nineteenth Congress of the Soviet Communist Party. For Liu, this was a return trip, for he had studied there from 1920 to 1922. He stayed in Moscow for three months—an unusually lengthy stay during which he undoubtedly conducted serious negotiations. But no communiqué was published, and his visit remains a big question mark.

* * *

Soon after Liu returned to Peking, Stalin died, and the Russian-Chinese alliance entered a new phase. Mao was suddenly catapulted into the glorious but uncomfortable role of the greatest theoretician in the Communist world, and, according to one report, even the Russians acknowledged his commanding stature as Marxism's Number One thinker. Moreover, Moscow's new leaders realized that an era had ended. How would their people respond? How would Mao respond?

The Russian people's response was a mixture of bewilderment, fear, and uncertainty; Malenkov and Molotov both promised the people a better life, and they glorified the Red Army as the "savior of Russia and eastern Europe." Implicitly, they appealed to the army to help the Party "ward off public disarray."

The Chinese responded with warm praise for Stalin and Russia. On March 6, 1953, Mao stressed the "maximum resolution" of the Chinese people to "unite closely and forever with the great Soviet people" and "to consolidate and strengthen the world camp of peace and democracy headed by the Soviet Union." Western observers speculated that the alliance was severely strained, but Chou En-lai, in November, 1953, ridiculed "any calumny or any attempts" by "imperialist warmongers" to "create discord" and "disturb" the "indestructible solidarity" of the Moscow-Peking alliance.

The Russians were visibly pleased. At Stalin's funeral they treated Chou with extraordinary solicitude. He walked with Khrushchev, Beria, Malenkov, and Molotov behind Stalin's bier—an honor rarely accorded a foreign Communist. In speeches, the Russians praised Mao and the "great Chinese people" with a frequency that raised many a diplomatic eyebrow in Moscow. They also quickly agreed to give the Chinese more money, more aid, and more honor.

Throughout 1954 Russia bundled its Chinese ally in warm, friendly praise, glorifying Mao and extolling Maoism. In October, 1954, Nikita Khrushchev, the energetic, intelligent First Secretary of the Soviet Communist Party, journeyed to Peking. He was accompanied by Nikolai Bulganin, Soviet Minister of Defense who was soon to become Premier. Both Russians congratulated Chou En-lai on his slick diplomacy at Geneva and applauded China's economic progress.

Before the two Soviet leaders returned to Moscow, they signed a battery of seven communiqués that all contained a simple message. Paraphrased, it might have read: "Dear Mao, let us please forget that there was ever any disagreement between you and Stalin. The old tyrant is dead, so let's bury the hatchet and strengthen the alliance. Remember, the world is still full of capitalists, and we've got to stick together to beat them. Sincerely, B and K."

First, Khrushchev and Mao reaffirmed the general principles of the 1950 Treaty of Friendship, adding that in the future both governments would consult each other on mutual problems.

Second, Khrushchev and Mao agreed to co-ordinate Communist policy in Asia, and Khrushchev heartily endorsed the "five principles" of peace and friendship that Chou and Nehru had christened earlier in the year.

Third, Khrushchev and Mao said that Japan was a "menace" to peace in Asia—particularly since Japan was "under the heel" of the United States. Still, they added, if Japan wanted to change its policy and trade with China, Mao would not object.

Fourth, Khrushchev conceded that Port Arthur did belong to

China, and he promised that Soviet troops would be withdrawn by May, 1955.

Fifth, Khrushchev understood that Mao did not like those joint-stock companies in Manchuria, Sinkiang, and Dairen, so he agreed to sell all of Russia's shares to the Chinese "as soon as practicable."

Sixth, Khrushchev and Mao decided it would be a good idea if they would sign an agreement on technical and scientific co-operation between the two countries.

Finally, Khrushchev and Mao expressed their "full agreement" that a railroad should be built through Sinkiang, linking Alma-Ata with Lanchow.

It was clear to Mao that Khrushchev wanted to be a good friend; and, if there was still any doubt, the bouncy Russian leader extended an additional long-term credit to the Chinese, promising to build 156 industrial complexes in China.

At the summit conference in July, 1955, Bulganin plugged steadily for Peking's right to Formosa and a seat in the United Nations. Mao should have been pleased. His "big brother" was fighting for China's interests at the world's councils.

In February, 1956, Khrushchev surprised Russia, China, and the West with a strong attack against Stalin. He called the former dictator a "tyrant" who "ignored" the Red Army in 1941 and almost "destroyed the Motherland." Russia recovered from its initial shock, and de-Stalinization swept through the land. The Lenin Testament was published. Tito was welcomed in Moscow. Soviet writers rediscovered the "individual." Tensions eased, and students rebelled.

The legend of Stalin was defaced.

In Peking the legend persisted. It took Mao about three months to respond publicly to Khrushchev's "secret-speech" attack on Stalin; and when he did his emphasis differed from Moscow's. Khrushchev had stressed Stalin's "mistakes"; Mao stressed his "contributions." This basic difference still lingers in official Communist pronouncements.

The Chinese said—and say—that their Communist Party did not develop a "personality cult." Mao, they claim, has yet to commit a "basic" mistake. He leads the Communist Party because he is "wise" and "farsighted," not because he is a "tyrant." Before the Russians or the Chinese could ponder this difference in nuance, Mikoyan, the durable Armenian, rushed to Peking to promise the Chinese Soviet assistance on an additional fifty-five industrial projects.

In October, 1956, two revolutions exploded in Russia's back yard. One was peaceful. It produced Gomulka and Wyszynski, the Commissar and the Cardinal, and Poland gave birth to a strange heresy—a Catholic country dominated by a Communist Party that permitted degrees of intellectual and economic freedom. The other was bloody and violent. It produced hatred and Kádár, and Hungary was hurled back to the Soviet lion while the world watched in revulsion.

The Kremlin's East European Empire was shaky, and Khrushchev's grip was slipping. Molotov called for Khrushchev's expulsion from the Soviet Communist Party, but the nimble Nikita side-stepped punishment. Warsaw would not listen to Moscow, but it would, it seemed, listen to Peking; and Peking wanted "unity" and "solidarity." Thus, Khrushchev managed to reassert his control over the Kremlin and eastern Europe. In January, 1957, he publicly thanked the Chinese. Symbolically and politely, the Chinese bowed. "The camp of peace is headed by the Soviet Union," Peking shouted. "The camp of peace *is* headed by the Soviet Union," Moscow echoed.

For the next two months, while Russia was busy explaining the "real" reasons for the Polish and Hungarian revolutions, Mao lectured the Chinese Communists on a new theory about which he had been thinking for nearly a year. In two speeches before the Party faithful, on February 27th and March 12th, Mao summarized the lessons of Hungary, and his summary contained the core of a bold addition to Communist ideology. Mao charged that Stalin and, by implication, Khrushchev did not understand the "proper" relationship between the "rulers" and the "ruled" in socialist society. Mao claimed that "contradictions" can exist between these two groups; Stalin had theorized that "contradictions" could exist only in capitalist societies. This "misunderstanding," Mao insisted, "led to a rule of terror in the Soviet Union and the liquidation of thousands of Communists."

Thus, the lesson of Hungary was clear. If the workers of Budapest had had a legal outlet for their "antagonism" against the government, they could have "eased" their hostility. They would not have revolted; they would have discussed their social and economic unhappiness, and the Hungarian Communist Party would have taken the necessary steps to ward off the popular explosion.

This will not happen in China, Mao implied, and, with a poet's flair, he uncorked a heady ideological bottle with the words: "Let a hundred flowers bloom, let a hundred schools of thought contend." He urged his huge country to talk, argue, debate. Don't be afraid, he said; we know you may disagree with some of our policies; but we recognize "contradictions," so "bloom" and "contend."

Mao's new doctrine on contradictions was powerful stuff; and when it finally appeared in *Pravda,* on April 15th, it was accompanied by a loud chorus of official Soviet silence. Mao had philosophized: "There need be no fear that the policy of a hundred flowers will yield poisoned fruit. Sometimes it is necessary even to have this poisoned fruit to know what it is that we are fighting against." After Hungary, Khrushchev was not at all sure.

In early June, Khrushchev appeared on a Columbia Broadcasting System news program, in which he denied categorically that "contradictions" existed in the Soviet Union.

Actually, by June, Mao himself was beginning to have second thoughts about his blooming flowers and contending schools. Students were reliably reported to have formed opposition political parties; illegal newspapers suddenly sprouted in provincial universities; and the peasants became bold enough to ignore local Party directives. Mao apparently was surprised by the profound gulf that separated his Party from his people. When some minor uprisings took place in various parts of his domain, Mao suspended his experiment in limited freedom; and the spike of dictatorship was again driven through the heart of China.

In Moscow, Khrushchev solidified his personal power by "exposing" the "anti-Party clique of Malenkov, Molotov, Kaganovitch, and Shepilov." These Bolsheviks were assigned to minor jobs in the Soviet hierarchy. Defense Minister Zhukov, hero of the Second World War, was then accused of "trying to subvert Party control in the Red Army," and he too was purged. In 1958 even Khrushchev's old side-kick Bulganin was purged, and Moscow ideologists conveniently lumped him with the "anti-Party clique."

Western propagandists might have had a field day tracing the rise of Khrushchev's "personality cult," but they never had a chance. On October 4, 1957, the Soviet Union fired a Sputnik into orbit around the earth, and the age of space was born. A month later another Sputnik was launched—this one, twice as heavy as the first. Western scientists were stunned; the Sputniks meant Russia had the rocket power to shoot ICBM's at the United States with "reasonable" accuracy.

The irritating persistence of Moscow's rocket successes bolstered Khrushchev's power and brought Soviet diplomacy a new measure of strength and authenticity. Western statesmen began to treat Khrushchev with more respect. When the Soviet leader boasted that Russia would overtake America in economic output by 1965, Washington did not pooh-pooh the claim. Instead, economists pointed to Moscow's booming rates of economic growth and our occasionally faltering progress, and they suggested that Khrushchev might be right. Our military strategists who had seemed perfectly delighted with our "defense posture" a few months earlier began to call for a "reappraisal" of our military concepts.

Even our psychology underwent a gradual shift. We had been opposed to summit meetings; now we favored a whole series of them. We had been frightened of "pinks" and "reds," and our businessmen wouldn't "touch" a deal with Moscow; now it had become unfashionable to say that Russia was still a dictatorship.

Khrushchev had been able to convince eastern Europe of his policy of peaceful coexistence; he has been less than successful in convincing the Chinese. In July, 1958, Khrushchev almost had a summit meeting; in fact, he was scheduled to arrive in New York on August 12th. The summit meeting was not held, and on August 4th it was announced that Khrushchev had been in Peking to discuss "problems" with Mao. It was also announced that Khrushchev would not attend any meeting with Chiang Kai-shek in the Security Council.

Before anyone had a chance to figure out this puzzling diplomatic switch, the Chinese began a heavy bombardment of Quemoy and Matsu—an action that sped our powerful Pacific Fleet into the Formosa Strait. Clearly, Mao was playing with brinksmanship. Why?

In late August the Chinese supplied part of the answer—the communes.

The communes, as we know, touched off a lively debate about the Russian-Chinese alliance—a debate that became more heated when Anastas Mikoyan, First Deputy Premier of the Soviet Union, criticized the communes during a bull session with students at the University of California at Los Angeles in January, 1959. Mikoyan said that Russia had tried communes in 1918 but had found that they were unsatisfactory in an economy of scarcity. It was impossible, he explained, to establish the principle of "from each according to his ability, to each according to his needs" until a highly developed economy had evolved.

Although Khrushchev had called the communes "old-fashioned" and "reactionary" during a talk with Democratic Senator Hubert Humphrey of Minnesota in November, 1958, Mikoyan denied that there was any disagreement between Moscow and Peking about the communes.

The First Deputy Premier returned to Moscow in time for the twenty-first Congress of the Soviet Communist Party. Before fifteen hundred assembled delegates, Khrushchev denied that he had told Humphrey anything "derogatory" about the communes. Then, he told the delegates, Chou En-lai included, that all "socialist countries will more or less simultaneously pass into Communism." "We cannot," he added, "carry out hurriedly and rashly what is immature, as this will distort and undermine our cause."

On February 5, 1959, the Chinese publicly agreed with Khrushchev: The Soviet Communist Party has set a "brilliant example for all socialist nations," and they will "more or less simultaneously" reach Communism.

As the Chinese mouthed these platitudes, Chou En-lai and Nikita Khrushchev signed an economic agreement pledging $1,250,-000,000 of aid to China over an eight-year period. Khrushchev also agreed to help the Chinese build an additional thirty-one industrial plants.

On February 14, 1959, the Russians and the Chinese celebrated the ninth anniversary of their alliance; and as Western observers toyed with the notion that Khrushchev had used Russia's wealth to forestall a possible Chinese defection, *Pravda* and *Jen Min Jih Pao* claimed that the alliance was stronger than ever. They discounted all speculation about any difference of opinion, and asserted that Khrushchev and Chou had attained a "complete identity of views."

I had the feeling that they were "protesting" too much. Shortly after the anniversary celebrations, *Pravda* began to "explain" Khrushchev's new dictum on the simultaneous admission of socialist nations to Communism. Apparently, Khrushchev had not meant "simultaneous" in a literal sense. For Russia was described as the most industrialized socialist nation, and it was claimed that it would reach Communism before any other bloc power.

Pravda's "explanation" fired my curiosity about the alliance. I felt that there had to be some way of getting more information about it than I had been getting from the books, the articles, the newspapers, and the communiqués. One day, in April, 1959, I received a letter from my brother, Bernard, a *New York Times* correspondent in Indonesia, in which he mentioned that several Indonesian diplomats had recently returned from a swing through China—some of them with fascinating experiences.

This letter gave birth to an idea. There were probably many people all over the world who had had a chance to visit China and/or Russia—diplomats who had served in Peking or Moscow; journalists who had covered the Communist world; scholars who had analyzed its problems; businessmen who had exchanged checks and ideas with the Communists; and government people who had to deal with the alliance.

If I could talk to them, I would be tapping a valuable source of information—one that had not yet been tapped. And I could also find out how the alliance affected different parts of the world.

Now, where would these people be? In London, surely. The British have a consulate in Peking; also, many of Africa's young revolutionaries congregate in London to map their continent's future. Paris, possibly. And Munich would be valuable because it is the site of Radio Free Europe, which has an excellent file on Communist affairs. Vienna, I knew, was valuable as the listening post for eastern Europe—and I would also try to get into Warsaw and Moscow. Then, southeastward, for visits to India, Thailand, Indonesia, Singapore, and Hong Kong; and I would visit Formosa and, of course, Japan.

I managed to get a leave of absence from CBS News and some financial assistance from the Ford Foundation for this round-the-world check on a diplomatic mystery armed with hydrogen weapons.

I left in early June, 1959.

First stop—London.

CHAPTER TWO London

IT WAS TWO YEARS SINCE I HAD LAST BEEN IN LONDON, AND THE ride to downtown Kensington from the airport was crowded with new impressions. London, as usual, was dressed in morning coat and bowler hat to greet us. A sweet June shower was falling, but, as our giant double-deckered bus lumbered through heavy traffic, my wife and I were so filled with excitement and anticipation that we did not mind nature's damp reception.

Futuristic factories sat along broad avenues, and, intermittently, small Tudor-styled homes with neat gardens enlivened the gray landscape. Children played in the rain, and their laughter seemed the proper accompaniment for England's tune of economic prosperity. We hoped that London would gush with impressions, information, and interpretation about the Russian-Chinese alliance, just as it gushed with consumer abundance. There were good reasons for optimism.

We had been told in New York that some of the most fertile minds on the subject were in London—one group in the Foreign Office, another in the journalistic community, and a third in the academic world. I had the feeling that since the British staffed a consulate in Peking, I might be able to learn some firsthand information about internal Chinese developments and the alliance. Furthermore, the British have always impressed me as having a much more sensitive ear for diplomatic double talk than Americans, and I wanted to ask them about three pivotal moments in the alliance. The first involved China's role in the Polish Revolution of 1956; the second, why Khrushchev met secretly with Mao in August, 1958; and the third, the communes.

From our small hotel on Basil Street, we started to make appointments. Richard Lowenthal, the *Observer*'s profound analyst of the Communist world, was first on the list. I called his home, and his wife told me that he was in Berlin, lecturing at the Free University. But, she added, he planned to return to London the next day, and she invited us to dinner.

For some reason, I had expected Lowenthal to be very *British*. His written English is flawless, and his interpretations are so pithy that I thought I detected the influence of Eton and Oxford behind every flight of intellectual fancy. I was wrong. Lowenthal is a compact bundle of Central European brainpower. His large brown eyes seem to pop from beneath a broad forehead topped by a shock of light brown hair. He speaks with a German accent, and his sentences are constructed with charm and imagination.

We were not the only guests. Mrs. Lowenthal had also invited Dr. Werner Klatt, a tall, vital German economist who works for the Foreign Office, and Dr. William Griffith, a stocky Harvard Ph.D., wearing horn-rimmed glasses, who once captained the political section of Radio Free Europe. After ten minutes Dr. Griffith was Bill, but Dr. Klatt was still Dr. Klatt. Both men were keenly interested in the Moscow-Peking alliance. Dr. Klatt's interest was obviously economic, but it was colored by a broad appreciation of China's cultural heritage. "Still," Dr. Klatt remarked, "who would have thought that Hitler could develop in the land of Bach and Beethoven?" Bill's interest was political. Under his direction, Radio Free Europe had developed a superb file on the alliance, and he appeared to be especially interested in Peking's role in eastern Europe. Lowenthal's interest was all-embracing. He had once been a Communist, and he has not lost his dialectical ability to build the details of any situation into an imposing whole.

Before, during, and after dinner, we talked about the alliance. I wanted to find out exactly what China's role was in the East European upheavals of 1956. We knew that Chou En-lai was selling "peace and friendship" to Southeast Asia when Moscow ordered the Red Army to destroy Hungary's revolution. We knew too that Chou attacked "great-power chauvinism," and promised little Cambodia that China would never use "force" to gain a political objective. In January, 1957, as the West expressed its indignation at Russia, Chou arrived in Moscow for high-level talks with a Politburo that was divided into competing factions. Khrushchev believed in the "thaw"; Molotov believed that the "thaw" had caused the Hungarian upheaval and that Russia desperately needed a return to Stalinism. Chou then went to Warsaw and Budapest, where he advocated bloc solidarity.

Why did Chou go to Moscow? Did Khrushchev ask for his help? Or, did Chou, a skilled negotiator, volunteer his special services to mediate Moscow's dispute with eastern Europe? Finally, what did Chou's role in this dispute signify about China's position in the bloc?

So far as Lowenthal, Klatt, and Griffith were concerned, the answers to these questions could be found in the murky maze of inter-Party relationships. For example, Griffith pointed out that it was not necessary for Chou to get an invitation with Krushchev—nor, for that matter, for Chou to "seize the initiative," as I had suggested, to mediate this dispute. The Soviet Communist Party, Griffith said, is always in close touch with the Chinese Communist Party—on an economic, political, or military level. The slightest nuance can be transmitted along these lines of communication which are eminently capable of conveying a carefully planted hint asking for Peking's support. Chou understood, and quickly made plans to visit Moscow.

Lowenthal, who remembers how Communist parties communicate, heartily agreed with Griffith. "There is no RSVP in a Communist invitation," he remarked. Then Lowenthal raised Griffith's analysis to a new level of interpretation. The Chinese Communists, he said, were particularly concerned at that time about the unity of the bloc. Peking wanted Moscow to tighten its grip upon eastern Europe. Mao understood, Lowenthal continued, that the industrialization of China required Moscow's help. The disintegration of the bloc—"a real possibility in November, 1956"—would have adversely affected China's chances for economic security, since Russia would have been totally absorbed in recapturing its empire.

Dr. Klatt agreed that China's concern about industrialization prompted her to rush to Moscow's support. But, he added, the Chinese were not completely dependent upon Soviet aid, and, in fact, were getting along with less all the time. Still, their ideological obsession with industrialization had become such a fixed orientation that it seemed to dominate all other matters.

It was at this point that Lowenthal introduced the usually inhibiting topic of Chinese psychology, which, he said, was not "inscrutable." For thousands of years, the Chinese have considered themselves the most sophisticated and cultivated nation on earth. Even when the empire was beginning to disintegrate under the impact of foreign exploitation and domestic corruption, the emperor still believed that he was superior to all other rulers. In the 1790's, Lowenthal wryly recalled, Lord Macartney of Britain came to Peking to open negotiations on trade with the emperor; but he was told that if he wished to talk with the emperor he would have to speak from a kneeling position after three kowtows and nine prostrations.

During the nineteenth century Western nations, including Russia, succeeded in extracting major economic concessions from the faltering central government. These concessions ignited a bitter nationalism. Chinese revolutionaries began to despise their nation's backwardness, and they shouted hot epithets at Western incursions. They wanted to assert Chinese independence and destroy the "red-nosed devils." Even the Communists, Lowenthal observed, shared these sentiments.

When Mao went to Moscow in 1949, he remembered that it was Stalin, the Georgian leader of Russia, who had almost single-handedly destroyed the Chinese Communist Party in 1927. Certainly, Lowenthal added, Stalin realized that Mao had succeeded—despite him. Thus, a feeling of mutual suspicion was built into the alliance from its inception.

And by 1956 Peking began to think in more independent terms. China could not take on the world, but its armies had held their own against the United States for more than two years during the Korean War. Moreover, Stalin's death in 1953 left Mao the only authentically "creative" thinker in the self-conscious world of Marxism-Leninism; and, in international politics, even Washington was beginning to understand that China had made a powerful impression at Geneva in 1954, at Bandung in 1955, and at Moscow in 1956, and that China had to be taken into consideration in any major international situation.

Thus, Lowenthal asserted, Peking was enjoying a silent measure of spirited cockiness toward Russia in late 1956. The great Soviet Union was in trouble, and China was leaping to its rescue.

This sense of Chinese self-esteem crept into Lowenthal's answer to another of my questions: Why did the Chinese proclaim the communes as the "quickest" road to Communism? Undoubtedly, Lowenthal commented, they sincerely believed in the economic potentialities of the communes, but the flavor of the original proclamation also reflected the brashness of ideological adolescence. With a deeply expressive gesture, Lowenthal said that there is no more dedicated, selfless Communist in the world than the Chinese Communist, whose life is labor and whose "faith is in the economic hereafter."

Yet even the Chinese Communist—"because he is Chinese," Lowenthal said—is a realist; and in the fall of 1958 he realized that Moscow was deeply distressed by China's historical leapfrogging, and he backed down. In his December, 1958, resolution, he retreated from many of his former assertions.

"Isn't it possible that the Chinese didn't really back down at all? The December resolution did not call for an abandonment of the communes—only for a retrenchment of the entire program," I observed.

"No," Dr. Klatt countered.

"No," Griffith echoed.

"No, no," Lowenthal repeated. "The December resolution was clear proof of a Chinese withdrawal."

"Whenever the Chinese have come face to face with Russian displeasure," Dr. Klatt stated emphatically, "they have backed down. The December resolution is just another example of backing down."

I wanted to check this idea with the British Foreign Office—more specifically, with the Russia- and China-desk specialists of the Foreign Office, people with long diplomatic service in Moscow and Peking. With only one exception, they all believed that the

December resolution could *not* be interpreted as a Chinese retreat.

One Russian expert said: "It was the same kind of resolution as Stalin's famous 'dizzy with success' speech of 1930, when he temporarily called off the excesses of collectivization only to push ahead later on a more rational basis. In fact, I might say, the phrase 'dizzy with success' was used in the December resolution. All it means is that they know they have to slow down on the commune drive, but there is really no indication at all that the Chinese mean to give up or downgrade the communes as the fundamental transition vehicle to Communism."

A young British diplomat, who had just come back from Peking, pointed out that the language of the resolution was "vigorous" and "uncompromising" in substance. "A new form of economic organization has risen over the East"—that, he said, was the way the December resolution began. "Hardly what one might call 'backing down,' what?" he added, a twinkle in his eye. "No, the Chinese seemed to me to be more self-confident than ever before—certainly in their relations with the Russians."

On still another critical question there seemed to be a clear difference of opinion between the journalists and the diplomats. When I asked the journalists how they assessed Khrushchev's summit reversal of August, 1958, they answered that Mao's influence had been paramount in calling off the summit meeting, while the diplomats answered that Khrushchev had changed his mind about a summit conference even before he went to Peking.

The journalists, including such outstanding specialists as Victor Zorza of the *Manchester Guardian,* felt that Mao did not want Khrushchev to discuss world problems in the United Nations with a representative of Chiang Kai-shek. This might have been interpreted as an affront to Peking, since, many of them believed, China's influence in the bloc had risen so considerably that Khrushchev could not speak for Mao.

The diplomats, who had better sources, were not convinced. They said that Khrushchev's attitude toward a summit conference underwent a definite change two weeks before he talked to Mao. Khrushchev realized that he had been momentarily outmaneuvered by the West into agreeing to a meeting in the Security Council, where he would have to talk with Chiang's representative. Originally, he had thought he would be discussing world problems only with Britain, France, and the United States. When he understood that he had miscalculated, he called off the conference.

Khrushchev's unexpected journey to Peking, they continued, was more closely associated with Formosa. Mao needed a scapegoat for domestic reasons, and nothing is so handy as Formosa. When it became clear that Mao was going to open a major bombardment of the offshore islands, Khrushchev had to go to Peking to outline the furthest limits of Soviet support. He wanted Peking to know exactly how far it could go in this latest example of Chinese brinksmanship.

These diplomatic experts believed that China was prepared to go to the very brink of war to recapture Formosa. None of them seriously felt that China would have stepped over the brink—not at a time when all its energies were bent on launching the commune drive; but they were all convinced that the Mao-Khrushchev talks provided an excellent yardstick for measuring China's undeniably growing stature in the alliance. Mao's regime, they believed, had attained the unique position in the bloc where it regarded itself as Moscow's equal in every sphere except the military.

Evidence was sparse, but the diplomats did weave a plausible explanation with scattered threads of information. First, they said, the communiqué growing out of these talks no longer spoke of the "leading" role of the Soviet Union. Instead, "mutual co-operation" was stressed. Second, China was mentioned ahead of the Soviet Union nine out of ten times; and in an atmosphere where major political decisions are reflected in a word or in name order this was a change of considerable importance. Third, two weeks after the meeting the Chinese began herding hundreds of millions of peasants into communes. The ideological implication of their awesome drive was that China had come upon the magic key to Communism and that Russia was still floundering in the error of collective farming. Finally, Khrushchev's dictum to the twenty-first Party Congress that all socialist nations would "more or less simultaneously" reach Communism was interpreted in Peking as an ideological retreat by the Russians.

One British diplomat, fresh from Moscow, provided what he considered to be "proof" of this Russian ideological retreat. A few months before Khrushchev pronounced his new dictum on Communism, he said, a top Soviet philosopher attempted to set the record straight on which nations would reach Communism first. In an important journal, he wrote that the Eurasian bloc was divided into two parts—the advanced, industrial nations of the West and the predominantly agrarian countries of the East; and, he went on, the advanced nations would reach Communism first. This had been prophesied by Marx, and it would be borne out by experience. In the light of this contention, which is consistent with pure Marxism, Khrushchev's dictum had to be read as a Russian retreat.

Other diplomats tended to agree. One of England's "old China hands" said: "The Russian press rarely mentioned the communes, and this silence was intended as a warning to the Chinese to stop. The December resolution partially calmed the Russians, but it still contained enough ideological heresy to force Khrushchev to put forth his compromise in February, 1959—that all countries would reach Communism 'more or less' at the same time."

The Russians paid for this compromise in hard currency. In the opinion of the economic section of the Foreign Office, the Soviet promise to provide Peking with 5,000,000,000 rubles in technical assistance over a nine-year period was extracted after lengthy, frustrating sessions during which the Chinese must have repeatedly shown their displeasure with Moscow's obvious procrastination. This promise, as we know, was made in February, 1959. The last previously announced Russian loan was made in April, 1956. In the intervening time the Chinese saw the Russians grant the Poles and Hungarians huge sums in economic aid, while they received nothing. One Foreign Office expert speculated that the Chinese felt they had saved Poland and Hungary for the bloc in 1956 but that their only payment was Russian suspicion.

The fact is that Russian assistance to China over the past seven years equals only a fraction more than Soviet aid to eastern Europe in the nineteen months following the 1956 revolts. And the new loan would mean an annual Russian-aid commitment of about

$150,000,000 a year to China, which, though not insignificant, is certainly not an impressive sum.

In fact, it has been further estimated by Foreign Office experts that the Chinese have maintained a favorable balance of trade with the Russians since 1956 and that they may already have paid Moscow back fully for all nonmilitary aid since 1950. One expert even mentioned that the February, 1959, loan may have been contingent upon a balanced book on Chinese trade with the Soviet Union.

Obviously, the Russians have been exceedingly cautious about helping the Chinese industrialize their huge but backward nation. I asked all the experts for a possible explanation. Though all prefaced their comments with the necessary "ifs," "buts," and "althoughs," all of them seemed to be in general agreement on the following points:

First, China occupies a special position within the bloc. The Chinese rode to power on their own steam—a fact that immediately placed them in a somewhat independent role. They have always exercised the dominant influence over the direction of their domestic policy, and for this very reason the Russians have been less than enthusiastic about leaping to China's economic assistance. Indeed, the Russians might feel that there is really no limit to China's needs, considering its extraordinary population.

At the same time, China's size has granted Russia, or Communism, a tremendous strategic and propaganda advantage, which the Kremlin realizes. The bloc was born, in effect, when China fell to Maoism.

Second, the Russians have begun to show concern over China's economic potential. All the experts agree that Russia need not fear China's economic progress for another ten or fifteen years. It is even possible that Russia's economic might during the 1960's will grow even faster than China's. But what will happen during the 1970's? Will China's economic challenge rival Russia's in Asia and Africa? Will China develop so rapidly that it may become the economic equal of Russia, and—motivated by a traditional feeling of superiority and a ferocious dedication to Communism—slowly begin to overwhelm the Russians? The British feel that Russia has already begun to think about these questions in deadly earnest.

Third, there is a section of the Foreign Office that shares *this* belief with many of the British journalists—that the Kremlin is so concerned about its own economic progress and political instability that it has been negligent about assessing the degree of Chinese dissatisfaction with Russia's niggardly aid; and that the Khrushchevs of today—all of whom are thoroughgoing pragmatists—will not be around in twenty years to concern themselves about China, so why worry today? As one expert put it: "China is not Khrushchev's problem; it is his successors'."

Finally, they all believe that, these problems notwithstanding, the alliance represents a dynamic and dangerous challenge that the West simply does not understand. Through a policy of negligence, stupidity and diplomatic nearsightedness, the West has lulled itself into a fitful slumber of complacency that may eventually induce its own destruction. One British diplomat said: "Never before has our civilization been so threatened, and never before has there been such complacency." Then, he added, "I am forced to say that in America I was shocked at how self-defeating your China policy is."

He recommended unofficially that Washington extend diplomatic recognition to Peking "in as short a time as possible." "If you do," he continued, "the Chinese will not be forced into Moscow's arms; they will have an important economic and political alternative. Your attitude toward Africa, if I may say so, is far more sensible. There we believe you are responding with considerable intelligence to the emerging power of African nationalism, but in Asia you seem to ignore these very forces."

I was curious about how the Africans viewed the United States, and fortunately I had a chance to talk to some young African students and revolutionaries who made London their university and headquarters. My wife had just finished a Russian Institute thesis, at Columbia University, about the Soviet view of South Africa, and naturally she was keenly interested in checking her library impressions of African nationalism against personal encounters with African nationalists. While I was discussing the Russian-Chinese alliance in the Foreign Office, she was discussing Africa with representatives of the Committee of African Organizations. At first I was unaware of the connection between our topics, but as soon as I began to talk politics with Africans I realized the close tie.

The committee's headquarters is at 200 Gower Street, and Gower Street, 1959, looks much the same as Gower Street, 1837, when a fiery idealist named Mazzini plotted the reunification of Italy just down the block. The narrow street seems to run out of the back of the British Museum, where another exile named Marx wrote *Das Kapital,* and stunned the world. Drab three-story buildings that now serve as fleabag hotels and pubs give the street a peculiarly unkempt appearance, but, oddly, its atmosphere conveys a sense of dedication and intellectual probing; and the street looks more like a dusty library shelf than like the site of fervent nationalistic talk about Africa and its destiny.

More than two hundred million people in Africa are trying to jump from feudalism to modernity. Many of their leaders, I soon discovered, are Marxist by orientation, anticolonial by background, and anti-Caucasian by prejudice. The Russians, who have been making the grand gesture toward African nationalism, are Marxist and anticolonial—at least, so they claim for the record—but they are Caucasian. The Chinese are not, and many African nationalists, who are very sensitive about color, have begun to look toward China with keen fascination.

The counter-tug to China is the eighteenth century image of the United States—also anti-imperialist, vigorous, young, and revolutionary. The twentieth century image has been thrown out of focus by the emergence of the United States as the leader of the Western world—a world that the African sees as a reactionary, oppressive coalition of white nations. Young Africans tend to view America through a prism of racial bitterness and economic backwardness. Nevertheless, they do see some good in the United States. They like the idea of a government controlled by checks and balances, and they thirst for the implementation of an African Bill of Rights. Possibly, the story of Ade Omojola or Tennyson Makiwane is the story of Africa today.

Ade, a twenty-one-year-old student from Nigeria, was a freshman at the London School of Economics in June, 1959, when I met him. During the day he attended classes; in the evening he worked for the committee. When Ade discussed Africa's future, his shining black eyes burned with a fierce intensity. He smiled easily, and his manner was engagingly shy. Short and thin, Ade was a wiry bundle of nerves that wanted to see Africa smile.

Ade was a Nigerian nationalist, but I had the feeling that his vision of the future was not restricted by the boundaries of Nigeria. Frequently, he talked more about Africa than about his country. He wanted to attend the Communist-sponsored World Youth Festival that was scheduled to open in Vienna in July, because "Africa's leaders must meet and talk with the leaders of both East and West." When I suggested that the festival might be the wrong atmosphere for such a meeting, Ade disagreed.

"But you know that the Communists will only use it as a forum for an attack against so-called 'Western imperialism,' " I objected.

"There's nothing 'so-called' about Western imperialism. It exists," Ade answered. Ade has a fundamentally Marxist view of the world. The reason is to be found in his life.

"I was born a member of a subject race," he began. His voice cracked, and his eyes suddenly looked so sad that I felt the guilt of an entire race and generation burn through my soul. "Ever since I was old enough to think," Ade continued, lowering his eyes, "I knew I was regarded as inferior by white people. There is a long history to this race prejudice, I know, but it was more than just prejudice that upset me. I remember how I cried when I realized that the real culprit was imperialism, or colonialism. It was the presence in my country of white people who had no right to be there—nor had they any right to hold back our development just for their own profits. I grew more and more angry at Whitehall's absentee rule, and I wanted to have a hand in running my country —not for glory, not for raw materials, but to help the people, to raise their standard of living."

Ade said his father was a printer, who wanted him to follow in his footsteps—to return to Nigeria to run the shop. "But I can't. I don't mean to be disrespectful to him, but I can't. I want to work in industry; I want to work in plastics—and I want to have Nigeria control Nigerian prices, not England or America."

"Do you really think America controls your prices?" I asked.

"Yes," Ade answered. He then said he wanted Nigeria governed according to the principles of John Locke. He wanted a free press and a Supreme Court, and he wanted a President, elected by popular referendum. He also wanted the President to appoint his own Cabinet and the Cabinet to be responsible only to him. "Of course, we shall have to nationalize all basic industry, and we shall have a social welfare state with a social-democratic constitution."

Was he afraid of Communism? "What is there to be afraid of? Communism is not a disease; and besides, we know what we have to do."

What did Africa have to do? "We must raise the standard of living, and achieve rapid industrialization, so we can be economically independent."

Did Ade have any model in mind? "Originally, we thought about the Soviet model for economic development, but maybe the Chinese model is more appropriate. For political development, I would stick with Locke over Marx."

What about religion? "I am not a Christian. I am a humanist. The Bible has had the most lasting effect upon my life, and Christ is undoubtedly the greatest and wisest man who ever lived. He taught me love, humility, and service."

Ade had to rush off to school; he said he had to attend a group discussion about Harold Laski, "who was a great man." He left, and I kept thinking of love, humility, and service.

The following day, I had an opportunity to talk with Tennyson Makiwane, a South African revolutionary who had recently arrived in London. Wiry and handsome, a scraggly beard covering his pointed chin, Makiwane hated his government's policy of apartheid. When he spoke about Afrikaner bigotry, his voice dropped an octave and his eyes glistened with hatred. Only twenty-eight years old, Makiwane was already one of his country's top revolutionaries—one of 156 South Africans arrested for "high treason" against the government. He went into a self-imposed exile, he confessed, to "engage in propaganda. The whole world must know the ugly truth about South Africa's racial policy."

Unlike Ade, Makiwane did not like to talk about his personal beliefs, but he willingly engaged in political debate. He told us one story about the social graces of an American diplomat in South Africa. Stationed in a nation inhabited predominantly by Negroes, representing a nation based theoretically upon the principle of racial equality, this American made it a strict policy never to invite Africans to his home. His cocktail parties were "white" parties. Makiwane said every revolutionary in Africa knows and now associates this practice with "official" American policy.

Makiwane also told us a story about the effect of the Chinese communes on the African revolutionary movement. He said the communes were actively discussed among his friends—an admission that surprised me, since I was not even aware that the communes could be applicable as a social solution to Africa's special needs.

"Let's face it," he explained: "Africa has no industry, no middle class, no political traditions. Communes would give us the framework within which to develop our resources in the quickest possible time. Besides, our tribal society could adjust to the commune much more easily than to any other political or economic form that exists in the world today."

"But what about the sacrifice in human dignity?" I asked.

"Human dignity," he answered sadly, "is for those who can afford it."

Naturally, he continued, no specific proposal on the communes could be officially included in the Charter of the African National Congress, since all proposals have been subordinated to the overriding consideration of independence. "Once independence has been achieved, the communes may very well be applied in our country." Then he added: "I haven't heard a single argument in the West that makes any sense to me. We want rapid industrialization, and we too have a backward peasant mass. I think the communes are *the* solution."

Before we parted, he turned to me, and said: "Tell the American people that Africa is shopping for a political creed. We want to shop at your counter—not the Communists'. But you must permit us to think of your country as a great, libertarian country, full of good principles of democracy. You should not support a government such as South Africa's—not now when so much is at stake."

I was anxious to meet a few British scholars who specialize on Russia and China. I wanted to get their view of the alliance, and I was curious about whether any of them had heard how deeply the communes had affected Africa's revolutionary thinking. Unfortunately, I could not get through to them. Professor G. F. Hudson, one of the world's most accomplished specialists on China, was lecturing in Tokyo for the summer; Peter Wiles, whose economic theories invariably whip up a storm of controversy, was out of town; and Guy Wint, who has been on a first-name basis with Asia for years, could not be reached.

Although we were unable to meet these three British specialists, I was pleased to learn that the Ford Foundation—bless its bountiful heart—had decided to finance an Institute of Asian Studies at Oxford's St. Anthony's College—an institute that would draw upon the knowledge and experience of the Hudsons and the Wints for an intensive examination of modern China and its impact on the rest of Asia and the world. Thus, St. Anthony's would soon become the foremost British college delving into Chinese affairs, attracting a group of dedicated scholars who would begin to penetrate the Chinese enigma—in effect, to convert the enigma into simple data.

I called Sir Isaiah Berlin at Oxford—not because he is a specialist on China but because he is one of the West's outstanding intellects, and I wanted to hear his views on the alliance. But Sir Isaiah was leaving for Paris.

"Could we meet there?" he asked.

"Yes," I answered.

CHAPTER THREE Paris

PROUD AND DEVASTATINGLY BEAUTIFUL IN JUNE, PARIS WAS NO place to study the alliance. The food was too good, and the wine had a way of diverting my attention from the mystery of the Kremlin to the glory of the Arc de Triomphe.

The diplomats did not talk about China; neither did the journalists. Their interest was riveted on Algeria. True, Pierre Mendès-France, a former Prime Minister, had recently returned from a trip to China, and so had Edgar Faure, another former Prime Minister; but neither politician was available for an interview. True, too, President Charles de Gaulle took time out of a 1959 news conference to offer his flowery assessment of the alliance:

"No doubt, Soviet Russia," he said, "in spite of having aided Communism to take roots in China, recognizes that nothing can change the fact that she is Russia, a white nation of Europe which has conquered part of Asia and is in sum richly endowed with land, mines, factories and wealth, face to face with the yellow masses of China, numberless and impoverished, indestructible and ambitious, building through trial and error a power which cannot be measured and casting her eyes about her on the open spaces over which she must one day spread."

De Gaulle's reference to Russia as "white" and China as "yellow" again raised the question of race. The Africans had also mentioned race. I felt I would come across this problem more frequently as we cut through Russia toward Asia.

But, despite a passing journey or reference to China, France was preoccupied with Algeria. Since her ungraceful departure from Asia in 1954, France has devoted all of her energies toward salvaging this last part of her African Empire, to which Algeria is the key.

For this reason, I was surprised that Paris was not bursting with talk about Peking's alleged intrusion into Algerian affairs. I had heard that China was shipping arms to Algerian rebels, and I had also heard that the Russians had actually prevented one shipment from crossing their territory. As Khrushchev courted De Gaulle, he obviously did not want Mao to incite the rebels. Still, there was painfully little conversation, or speculation, about this situation.

One beautiful afternoon, I met Sir Isaiah for a drink at the Café de la Paix, which he described as "so very bourgeois but so very convenient." Sir Isaiah, who speaks very rapidly, with a strong Oxford accent, was also surprised that Paris was not discussing this report of Chinese weapons in Algeria, but he added, with a quick gesture of his right hand, "Who really knows anything about China?"

I told him that I was anxious to learn about the Russian-Chinese alliance because I felt that our entire civilization was being threatened by a powerful, but mysterious, coalition of forces.

Sir Isaiah agreed. "Certainly the threat is mysterious and powerful, but I think that the mystery is very largely China. Russia's actions can be determined, but China's are complicated by historical and psychological factors. Moreover, we are severely restricted in Peking. Our diplomats have difficulty getting about, and we obtain few firsthand impressions, and no source material.

"It is difficult for us," Sir Isaiah continued, "and, I might add, it is even difficult for the Russians, to understand the Chinese. Recently, I had a chat with Sholokhov about the Soviet Writers' Conference that was held in Moscow in May. He told me that a delegation of Chinese writers attended the conference. After long debates about 'socialist realism,' the Russians threw a truly lavish party—with lots of vodka, caviar, and *blini*. Everyone, Sholokhov said, had a glorious time—except the Chinese. They stuck together, drinking tea and talking 'socialist realism.' One of the Russians, a bit tipsy, urged the Chinese writers to try some caviar and vodka and possibly a few *blini*. Somberly, the Chinese told him: 'We do not have these luxuries in China *yet,* and we will not have them in Russia either.' "

Sir Isaiah said the Russians were dumfounded and annoyed—dumfounded at the incorruptibly austere habits of the Chinese Communists, and annoyed at the haughty implication that the Russians were getting "soft" and "bourgeois."

CHAPTER FOUR Munich

FOR INFORMATION ABOUT THE RUSSIAN-CHINESE ALLIANCE, WE had been told in London, all roads lead to Ritvo.

Ritvo is Herbert Ritvo, an informal, charming American with twinkling blue eyes who was until the end of 1959 Chief Political Adviser to Radio Free Europe in Munich. RFE is supported by American funds, and it broadcasts news to the East European satellites. It should not be confused with Radio Liberty, also in Munich, which broadcasts only to the Soviet Union.

Ritvo was with RFE for six years, and his job was to interpret events "behind the Curtain." He apparently did this so brilliantly that he became a kind of pivot for all specialists on Russia, eastern Europe, and China.

Like Lowenthal and Klatt, Ritvo studies the labyrinth of Moscow-Peking convolutions with just the right balance of imaginative intuition and intelligent skepticism. He conjectured infrequently, and he felt the West must not indulge in the luxury of scholastic alchemy—that is, in assuming that rumor is fact just because facts are hard to uncover.

I asked Ritvo a few of my favorite questions: Did Chou seize the initiative in 1956? Did Khrushchev ask for Chou's help? Ritvo said he did not know, but he felt certain that the Chinese did not want to take advantage of Moscow's difficulties to assert Peking's importance. Wherever Chou barnstormed in eastern Europe in January, 1957, he always hailed "Soviet leadership" of the bloc. Never once, Ritvo maintained, did Chou give the impression that the Chinese wanted to embarrass the Russians; instead, Chou consistently heralded Moscow's unquestioned guidance in domestic and foreign policy. Chou's role in the drama of East European diplomacy was to enhance the Kremlin's prestige, and, according to Ritvo, Chou played that role very well.

Ritvo felt strongly that the Chinese did not encourage the Poles in 1956. That theory, Ritvo said, was propagated by Polish sources and advertised by American reporters. "The Poles would desperately have wanted Chinese support, but I don't think they got it." Ritvo believes that it was never in China's interests to reduce Russia's hold over eastern Europe. Mao's pronouncement on "great-power chauvinism" was aimed at an Asian audience. "Mao did not want nations such as Cambodia and Burma to believe that China would resort to brute force as Russia had in Hungary." Mao also spoke against the "dangers" of "chauvinism" to calm the fears of minorities living in China. But, Ritvo continued, "Mao never had any intention of breaking Moscow's grip over eastern Europe, even though he realized that there was dissatisfaction in Warsaw and Budapest with Russia's tactless elbowing into domestic affairs." Moreover, Ritvo said, there was no tangible evidence to support the Polish story about Chinese encouragement—except Polish sources which are traditionally emotional and persistently unreliable.

Ritvo then proceeded to demolish "another Polish pipedream." The Chinese, it had been claimed, changed their entire attitude toward Poland and Hungary after the 1956 revolts. First they were encouraging; then they were critical. Ritvo said that there has never been any good reason for thinking that the Chinese attitude toward Warsaw and Budapest underwent a fundamental alteration after 1956. "China did not turn Stalinist after the revolts," he asserted. Ritvo agreed that the Chinese have been in the forefront of the ideological attack against Yugoslavia since early 1957; but, he said, the Chinese were merely reflecting the Kremlin's aroused displeasure with Marshal Tito.

China wanted stability in the Communist world before and after the revolts. Instability in eastern Europe, Ritvo went on, would not have pleased Peking, because it would undoubtedly have interfered with China's drive toward industrialization. This, Ritvo stressed, was a luxury Mao could not afford.

Did this mean that China never talked back to Moscow? "Not

at all," Ritvo answered. "When China's personal interests are adversely affected by any Kremlin decision, you can be sure that Mao tells Khrushchev all about it." Ritvo had a ready example.

Peking, he said, has been visibly disturbed "on two or three occasions" by Russia's obvious reluctance to furnish China with more economic help. Time after time, Chinese economic delegations have had to sit tight in Moscow, waiting for the Russians to make up their minds about whether they were going to give Peking more economic aid. The Kremlin even kept Liu Shao-chi waiting in Moscow for three months in 1952 while deciding whether to increase its aid to China. In early 1953, Liu went home—without a kopeck.

These incidents have burned deep impressions into the sensitive Chinese psyche. Diplomatic observers in eastern Europe have heard the Chinese grumble about Russian parsimoniousness, and they are convinced that a major reason for the "great leap forward" was the Chinese belief that Peking would have to pay for rapid industrialization with drastic domestic sacrifice. The Russians, they feel, will not pay for Chinese industrialization—certainly not at the pace the Chinese desire—and Peking will have to foot the bill.

I asked Ritvo whether he felt the Mao-Khrushchev meeting in August, 1958, might have taken place because of a desire to discuss the institution of communes. "I'm not sure," Ritvo answered, but he said there were very "good reasons" for believing the two titans of Communism did talk about the communes.

In October, 1954, Khrushchev and Mao had agreed to discuss "questions of mutual interest"; the communes, Ritvo said, were undoubtedly of "mutual interest." Moreover, Khrushchev was accompanied by one of the Kremlin's top ideologists, Boris Ponomarev, editor of the new *History of the Communist Party of the USSR*. It was Ponomarev's job to discuss with Mao the permissible limits to which the communes, as a solution for social ills, could be pushed. And, Ritvo adds, it was no accident that the commune drive was launched exactly two weeks after the talks ended.

As Ritvo sketched in the details of this analysis, I was reminded that it was very similar to the ideologically inclined hypotheses of Wolfgang Leonhard, the German journalist who wrote *The Revolution Betrays Its Children.* Yet there was a major difference. Leonhard believed in ideology; Ritvo believed in facts. If ideology were a factor in Ritvo's analysis, which it was, it was only one factor. The other factors, which Ritvo considered more significant, were the Midle East and Quemoy. Both were of paramount importance, since both involved the threat of war.

First, Quemoy. To communize a nation—even so technically backward a nation as China—involved a sacrifice so great that Peking needed a scapegoat. That scapegoat was the United States and our "puppet," Chiang Kai-shek—both communing about righteousness on Formosa, an island the Communists say belongs to them. August, 1958, was deemed a convenient time to reassert Peking's historic claim to Formosa. The reassertion came dramatically as the Communists opened a heavy bombardment of the offshore islands. The bombardment created a war scare that frightened Washington and Moscow. An ailing Secretary of State Dulles flew halfway around the world to calm Chiang's anxiety that the United States would be pressured into withdrawing the Seventh Fleet from the Formosa Straits. At the same time, Dulles managed to extract a promise from Chiang that he would not attempt to overthrow the Peking regime by armed invasion. In retrospect, the promise had a hollow ring, since Chiang probably could not launch a full-scale invasion of the mainland without American help.

Khrushchev went to Peking, Ritvo said, to warn the Chinese that they were playing with fire, that the United States was not a "paper tiger," and that Russia would offer China moral support—possibly even a few planes—but that was all. Apparently Khrushchev was persuasive, because the Chinese abandoned the attempt to seize Formosa—at least at that time—and saved face by bombarding the offshore islands on alternate days.

On the mainland, the Formosan crisis produced not only a war scare but also a strong motivation for communization. While confronted by a "barbaric" United States, the Communists seemed to be saying, every "loyal Chinese worker" must make major sacrifices to "strengthen the Motherland." The crisis thus served to justify the initial economic and psychological agony of herding 500,000,-000 peasants into communes.

Second, the Middle East. Ritvo believed that Russia had not been outmaneuvered by clever Western diplomacy. On the contrary, once the United States landed troops in Lebanon the Russians were handed a propaganda victory. Moscow Radio and *Pravda* made it crystal clear to the Middle East that the United States acted no differently in 1958 from the way France or England had in 1956 when they joined Israel in attacking Egypt. The Kremlin pounded one point home—*all* Western nations are imperialistic, and all will use force to support their imperialism.

As soon as Khrushchev realized that the United States would not restore the old monarchy to the Iraqi throne, he could see no reason for a summit conference at that time. So, he began to hedge. When he went to see Mao, he had already made up his mind not to attend a summit meeting. The talks then got down to the real issues—the communes and Formosa.

Obviously, Ritvo believed, the talks were not conducted in a "friendly" or "harmonious" fashion. The joint communiqué of August 3rd shattered precedent by mentioning China ahead of Russia nine out of ten times, and the Russian translation of the original Chinese communiqué mentioned Russia ahead of China ten out of ten times. Moreover, Ritvo continued, when the Chinese finally announced their commune drive, the Russian press ignored it. This implied the strongest kind of disapproval.

The Kremlin was furious at the Chinese implication that communes represented a "higher form" of social development. This was a direct affront to Moscow, and Khrushchev was angry. Actually, Khrushchev did not care how the Chinese peasants lived—whether in communes or in mud huts—so long as Peking did not deify the commune as a Marxist formula for global application. But Peking did deify the commune, and, Ritvo conjectured, this deification forced Khrushchev to convene the twenty-first Congress of the Soviet Communist Party.

There was no other good reason for the congress in February, 1959. Not economics, not foreign policy—only the necessity to spell out a new Kremlin dictum: that was the reason for the twenty-first Congress. The decision was apparently reached in late September, 1958, when Chinese boasts about "quick roads" to Communism began to pick up echoes in eastern Europe and in Africa.

Between September, 1958, and January, 1959, the Russians told the Chinese in the special language of the dialectic that they would have to back down from their original decree on the communes. In December, Ritvo feels, they did. When I mentioned that the Foreign Office did not think the Chinese backed down at all, he merely shrugged his shoulders, and smiled. "A clear backing down," he repeated softly.

Khrushchev's new theory about the "simultaneous" admission of all socialist countries to the "paradise" of Communism was no compromise. Again, it was a Khrushchev coup, because its deliberate vagueness did not bind Russia to reach Communism at any special time, and freed Moscow to roam indefinitely in the hazy world of the "transition from socialism to Communism."

I distinctly got the feeling that Ritvo did not think China was any major threat to Russia, and I mentioned this to him. "That's right," he answered. "China will become Russia's problem in ten, maybe twenty years, but it is not now."

He also discounted all speculation that China's booming population would force Peking to expand into Russia's soft Siberian underbelly. "That is one theory which we really should not take too seriously at all. China still has vast areas for cultivation and irrigation—especially in Sinkiang. No, Peking is not going to attack Siberia, and Khrushchev is not settling Siberia because of an imminent Chinese thrust."

Well, how about recognition? Did Ritvo think the United States should recognize Communist China? I told him the Foreign Office had answered this question with an emphatic Yes. Ritvo snapped, "Add an equally emphatic 'Yes' for me." He then explained his position, making it clear that he spoke for Ritvo, not for Radio Free Europe. "Nonrecognition is a negative gesture that means nothing but embarrassment for our government. Besides, it forces the Chinese to reconcile their differences with the Russians, because they can not turn to any other nation. In this way, the Chinese do not have any alternatives. It's Moscow or nothing."

Ritvo concluded that he felt all "sensible" diplomats in Europe believed the United States should recognize Peking. But recognition must not be announced with the casualness of a weather report; it must have punch, and it must serve a specific diplomatic end that benefits America. Only in this way will recognition take advantage of the "frictions" that surely exist in the alliance.

CHAPTER FIVE Vienna

IT USED TO BE THAT VIENNA WAS DESCRIBED AS THE CITY OF romance and gaiety—the Central European capital that danced in three-quarter time to the waltzes of Johann Strauss and sang tunes from the operettas of Franz Lehár. But in Central Europe the currents of history are as swift as the Danube's—the brown, not the blue, Danube—and somehow Vienna did not live up to its reputation.

The Viennese may be the happiest people in Central Europe. Certainly they look robust, eating delicious pastry and drinking Grinzing's wine; but they seem to have lost their spirit. An Austrian newspaper vendor suggested this explanation: "We have a large capital with no country around it." Perhaps he was right. Pear-shaped little Austria, squeezed between the Communist bloc on the east, Germany on the north, and an occasionally irritating Italy on the south, may have become too insignificant these days for its capital. Perhaps, too, the partial Soviet occupation of Austria, lifted only four years ago, in 1955, when Vienna signed a peace treaty with Moscow, has left a grayness over the city.

Whatever the reason, Vienna looks tired. The towering Gothic Cathedral of St. Stephen; the imposing Hofburg, Imperial Palace of the Hapsburgs since the sixteenth century; Schönbrunn Palace, a more elaborate version of Versailles; and the impressive Opera House and government buildings around the Ring, built in the last century—all of these are but the lingering memories of a former greatness, of the days of Maria Theresa, Metternich, and Franz Joseph, when Vienna ruled an empire that rubbed shoulders with the czarist and Ottoman empires.

And yet Austria still imagines that it has a great role to play in world politics. Viennese diplomats say, quite seriously, that their country, an imperial vestige, has a unique destiny—to serve as mediator between East and West. They believe that their history has endowed them with a special genius for understanding the East. "We are Westerners," an Austrian writer said, "but we know how to deal with the Russians. Don't worry!"

By early July, 1959, when we arrived in Vienna, Austria was being given an opportunity to demonstrate its talent for mediation. The seventh World Youth Festival—a Communist-sponsored and Communist-supported propaganda show—was about to begin. Colorful abstract posters, applauding "peace" and "friendship," had been pasted to every bulletin board.

It was the first time that the festival was to be held in a non-Communist capital, and Vienna could not make up its mind whether this was a good idea. Chancellor Julius Raab, who thought of himself as the honest broker dealing in neutral securities, liked the idea of Vienna being an international capital again, and enjoyed the glamour of foreign reporters meeting deadlines there. But, more important, he sincerely believed that democracy should not be afraid of locking ideological horns with Communism.

Many Austrian officials disagreed. They felt that Raab had granted the Communists a golden platform for propaganda, that he had forgotten the Soviet suppression of Hungary, and that he had chosen to ignore the Russian occupation of his own country. Raab argued that Austria was again a sovereign state—thanks to the 1955 peace treaty with Russia—and that Austria must maintain its neutrality with deeds, not slogans. Thus, despite strong opposition, Raab had given the Communists permission to hold their festival in Vienna.

The festival opened triumphantly in Vienna Stadium on July 26th. Sixty thousand Austrians, prompted by sympathy or curiosity, filled two-thirds of the stadium. They cheered and applauded the young delegates who marched around the oval track singing the folk songs of their countries. "Peace and friendship, peace and friendship," they sang. Thousands of starlings floated gracefully over the stadium. The Chinese Communist delegates, neat and punctilious, serious and impressive, clashed Oriental cymbals and chanted

Marxist slogans. The rhythmic songs of the smiling Russian delegates won warm approval—especially from Africa's and Asia's dark-skinned delegates, many of whom were their guests. Indian girls in bright saris twirled in exotic dances, and Burmese and Indonesian men wore their traditional white and black hats. Everyone sang, cheered, applauded, and danced, as the stadium roared with one of Communism's biggest propaganda shows.

For the Communists, a youth festival is serious business. *Trybuna Ludu,* Poland's *Pravda,* cautioned the organizers: "It must be realized that the Festival is not only for song and amusement; it is above all a political event on a major scale. We must help the youth to understand the lasting link between their work and the struggle waged by their revolutionary fellows throughout the world. Young people from capitalist and colonial countries must leave the Festival with a still stronger faith in the invincibility of the peace camp, and in the correctness of the struggle. It is necessary to teach the youth who the main enemy is . . . to teach the youth how to hate him and to teach the youth how to fight against him."

Russian youth received this word of warning from *Komsomol Pravda:* "Komsomol organizations, while preparing for the Festival must insure the further improvement of ideological, educational, mass educational and sports work among youth, and still more actively educate young men and women in the spirit of a Communist attitude toward labor, Soviet patriotism, friendship between peoples and proletarian internationalism."

Nothing is left to chance. The Kremlin realizes that "with each new Festival, fresh millions of young men and women from all the continents of the globe flow into the ranks of the World Federation of Democratic Youth and the International Union of Students." Like the International Preparatory Committee, the WFDY and IUS are Communist organizations, who want to make friends for Communism.

Official statistics say there were 3,090 delegates at the festival from "underdeveloped Asia, Africa and Latin America." (It is interesting that the Kremlin began lumping Latin America with Asia and Africa at this time as its prime propaganda targets.) From the "socialist" countries, among which they include Yugoslavia, 7,306 delegates attended the festival; and from the "capitalist" countries—6,375 delegates.

For young Africans, such as Ade Omojola and Tennyson Makiwane, whom we had met in London, and who were convinced that the Russians and the Chinese would never be "so foolish" as to use the festival for propaganda purposes, the festival was an opportunity to meet the "future leaders of the world." They could enjoy the two faces of the festival. The gay face of dancing and singing could appeal to everyone. The serious face of political discussion was turned to the Ades of all underdeveloped countries, and they were flattered. Russian youth discussed *their* problems, and they seemed to understand *their* dilemma. And they could not have failed to be impressed by the dedication and fanaticism of the young Chinese Communists, who, in the final analysis, had one great advantage over the Russians. Like the Africans, the Chinese are colored; they too have been the victims of a "white" colonialism, and no one mentions aloud that one of the white nations was Russia.

Was the festival a success? Yes.

The Communists wanted to show that they could stage a youth festival outside the Iron Curtain; they did. The Communists wanted to impress the delegates from the backward, underdeveloped nations; they did. The Communists wanted to show that they could bring over 7,000 delegates to Vienna without any serious political defection problems; they did. They knew they would meet a tougher, firmer group of anti-Communist youth than they had met in Moscow in 1957. They knew that they would lose a few of the debates. But they also knew that their main aim was to make friends for the Communist view of "peace and friendship," and in this aim they succeeded.

The Russians and the Chinese exchanged ideas and propagated viewpoints in an open society, and they still made friends. Together, the Russians and the Chinese made a rough team to beat. The Russians had the economic power and the military might; the Chinese had the manpower resources and the ideological zeal. The big question, I felt, was whether the close co-operation that had made the festival a success was typical of the Russian-Chinese relationship, or whether it was an unusually harmonious joint effort by two powers with a number of outstanding differences.

I canvassed Vienna's opinion. Diplomats and journalists seemed to emphasize the differences, and pointed out several areas of potential friction.

First, they all agreed that China was beginning to have a great impact on East European developments and that East European Communists were genuinely upset when the Chinese launched their commune drive in August, 1958—a year before. They thought that the commune would become the ideological example for the entire Communist bloc. As one Hungarian diplomat, who wishes to remain anonymous, said: "A general nervousness swept through this part of the world. We weren't sure of what the Russians were going to do, because they didn't say anything."

He felt the communes were regarded as merely a "militant phase" of Communist development; however, he added, if they were regarded as a "higher form of Communism to which we must aspire," then they became "thoroughly disquieting and objectionable." This Hungarian spoke in an unmistakably condescending tone about the communes. His argument seemed to be that they were "acceptable" for backward nations, such as China, but that they were "unacceptable" for advanced nations, such as Hungary. Certainly, he implied, they were not to be exported to eastern Europe, which was having enough trouble setting up collective farms.

Second, these diplomats felt that Russia and eastern Europe were growing more concerned about China's bursting population. The West German Embassy, which is reported to have the finest staff of intelligence analysts in Vienna, was especially fond of telling the Oscar Lange story about Russia's new role in Eurasian politics. "Thank God," the Polish economist was said to have commented, "thank God, we have Russia as a buffer state between us and the Chinese." This story may be apocryphal, but the concept has already become a permissible cliché in satellite capitals.

Officially, of course, the Russians deny any anxiety about China's mushrooming numbers, but, unofficially, the Soviet ambassador in

Vienna, a tough politician who hates small talk, called a British journalist aside recently at a cocktail party and murmured, "Can you imagine, there are going to be one milliard Chinese in twenty years!" The journalist told the diplomat he thought the Russians didn't believe in Malthusian gossip. "Come now," the Russian answered. "We've got to feed our population, too; but how is China going to feed a milliard people?"

Third, none of Vienna's talkative diplomats was willing to push Points One and Two too far, but they were all certain that in at least one respect the Chinese have been leapfrogging the Russian buffer ever since the beginning of 1957—that is, in Peking's trade with eastern Europe. The statistics were extremely revealing, for they seemed to prove that Chinese trade with eastern Europe has skyrocketed in the past two or three years and that Russia apparently has done nothing to brake its momentum.

For example, on April 12, 1959, the Chinese Communists signed their first long-term trade agreement with Czechoslovakia. The terms of the agreement specified that China would send Prague raw materials and that Czechoslovakia would send Peking industrial equipment, such as locomotives, tractors, and power stations. Chinese raw materials would include molybdenite concentrates, iron ore, tin, hemp, jute, wool, cotton, and silk. The agreement also contains this ironic provision—that China, which periodically is plagued by famine, would supply one-third of Prague's total food imports for 1959 and 1960. In other words, China has become Czechoslovakia's breadbasket, exporting thirteen times as much wheat to Prague in 1958 as she did in 1955.

China's trade pattern with Bulgaria is similar. There had been a trickle of trade between Peking and Sofia ever since 1952, when they signed their first trade agreement; but it picked up considerably in 1957. Again, China exported raw materials and foodstuffs, and imported industrial equipment.

With Hungary, it is the same story. The major trade agreement between Budapest and Peking was signed on April 22, 1958. It too was long-term, expiring in 1962. According to its provisions, China would send Hungary molybdenum ore, mercury, lead, and tungsten—all of which China appears to have in great abundance.

Hungary would send China electric-power-station machinery and engineering equipment.

There have been no significant variations in Peking's trade with Poland and Albania since 1957. China wants to trade with industrialized Europe because she needs industrial equipment. Peking even trades with West Germany—Russia's major propaganda enemy in Europe. Peking-Bonn statistics show that West Germany has a more flourishing, profitable trade with China than with Russia. By June, 1959, it was clear that Bonn's trade with Peking in the first quarter of the year had already doubled in comparison with the same period of the previous year.

Why did China's trade with eastern Europe suddenly skyrocket at the beginning of 1957? An important clue is contained in a press conference with Josef Bognár, Hungarian Minister of Foreign Trade, that was reported in Budapest newspapers on October 20, 1956.

According to these Communist news reports, Bognár asked the Chinese if he could visit Peking in September, 1956. He was granted permission.

"I am the first Hungarian Minister of Foreign Trade to visit China," he told newsmen, "although an improving of relations between our two countries is of the greatest importance. . . . I held no formal trade discussions with any Chinese officials. . . . There were only some informal exchanges of opinions about the possibilities of trade in 1957. . . . The Chinese complained about the poor quality of the goods that they have been receiving from us in the past. . . . There were many political and economic mistakes that have been made and that have to be corrected."

In these unusually frank admissions, there is evidence that in early October, 1956, the Chinese were decidedly reluctant to do business with Hungary. Not long after Bognár's press conference was reported in Budapest newspapers, the Hungarian Revolution erupted. Obviously, there was no connection. A week later, the Red Army crushed the revolution, leaving Budapest a bloody memory of David against Goliath. Two months later, Chou En-lai arrived in Budapest, appealing for bloc solidarity. After Chou returned to Peking, trade suddenly began to blossom between China and Budapest—indeed, between China and all of eastern Europe.

Part of the explanation for this apparent about-face is economic. The shattered economies of Hungary and Poland needed help. Russia contributed bountifully toward their economic recovery, and Khrushchev apparently encouraged Mao's contributions. So, in January, 1957, China increased her trade with Budapest, and, in April, even "lent" Hungary the equivalent of 100,000,000 rubles in convertible currency.

But economics was plainly peripheral, for China also began to flood Bucharest and Sofia with "cultural" and "ideological" delegations. For the first time, Chinese Communists began to appear in eastern Europe in great numbers. In some obscure way, China's new interest in eastern Europe had to be connected with Peking's mysterious role in the Polish and Hungarian uprisings of 1956. I had heard a lot of speculation about China's importance in triggering Polish Communist leader Wladyslaw Gomulka's return to power. I had even heard that China saved Khrushchev's political neck. I had to check these stories.

"Where?" I asked Vienna's experts.

"Warsaw," they answered. "Warsaw is the key."

CHAPTER SIX Warsaw

THE STORY OF POLAND IS THE STORY OF A MAP. IT IS POLAND'S unique and terrible curse to live between an aggressive Russia and a sneering Germany.

On August 5, 1772, Austria joined Prussia (Germany had yet to be united) and Russia in the annexation of 201,000 square kilometers of Polish territory. They had no legal right to it, but they claimed that Poland had sunk into anarchy. In a sense it had. Poland's villages had been plundered during a costly and exhausting civil war; public order had vanished; and Polish aristocrats, who loved their comfort, had fled to the plush confines of Paris. Moral courage had disintegrated into shameful cowardice. Poland's Parliament ratified the annexation.

For the next twenty years Poland was a pitiful pawn on Catherine the Great's diplomatic chessboard. Helpless and alone, Poland could not encourage the occasional sparks of political initiative that were ignited in her Parliament; nor could she delight in the revolutionary breezes from Paris. Trapped in a Russian-Prussian-Austrian vise, Poland was pathetically weak. On June 17, 1793, she was forced to submit to another annexation. This time, Poland was left with only 146,000 square kilometers of land—in effect, a small principality of 4,000,000 Catholic peasants and aristocrats surrounding the capital of Warsaw.

On March 24, 1794, one of these aristocrats raised Poland's national flag over the market place of Cracow, enlisting soldier volunteers, creating a National Council, and freeing the serfs. His name was Thaddeus Kosciusko, a young, magnetic, brilliant Pole who had fought with Washington and Lafayette for American independence. On April 4th his troops defeated a detachment of five thousand Russians at Raclawica. The news of his victory stunned Catherine of Russia and Frederick William II of Prussia. "The Jacobins of the East," Catherine stormed, the frightening image of a Polish Robespierre rising on her flank, "must be destroyed." Frederick William II struck Kosciusko from the west, but he could not dislodge the Polish patriot from Warsaw. From the east, Catherine hurled three Russian armies at Kosciusko. At Praga, Warsaw's eastern fortress, Polish and Russian troops clashed; and the young Polish peasants, fighting heroically for land and faith, were simply overwhelmed by Russia's superior manpower.

Kosciusko's insurrection was suppressed by a Russian army—a pattern that was to be repeated with terrible regularity.

On October 24, 1795, Poland disappeared from the European map. Russia received Kurland and Polish Lithuania; Austria picked up Cracow and Lublin; and Prussia took Warsaw.

Under Czar Alexander I, there was a chance—for a time, a good chance—that Poland might take a large step toward national autonomy. One of Alexander's closest friends, a young Pole named Czartoryski, urged the Russian monarch to use his prestige at the Congress of Vienna to restore Poland as an independent nation. Alexander, the grandson of Catherine the Great, could not imagine an independent Poland, though he was perfectly willing to chase Austria and Prussia out of Poland. He was even willing to grant Poland full autonomy over her domestic affairs if Russia could control her foreign relations.

He brought this plan to the Congress of Vienna, where Metternich, Castlereagh, and Talleyrand were drawing the map of a de-Napoleonized Europe. They had not envisaged an autonomous Poland under Russian suzerainty, but they conceded that Russia should be well paid for its major contribution toward the defeat of Napoleon. Russia's payment was the Grand Duchy of Warsaw.

Alexander's successor, Nicholas I, who ruled Russia from 1825 to 1855, was alarmed by a revolt of liberal Russian aristocrats in December, 1825, and for thirty years he fanatically opposed any manifestation of liberalism. He crushed one Polish uprising in 1830; and, in 1848, when most of Europe seethed with revolution, he sent an army into Warsaw once again to crush a Polish revolt, and another army into Budapest to suppress a Hungarian uprising against the Austrian Crown. Nicholas did make several meaningless gestures toward Polish nationalism, but Poland was really a Russian province—restive, unhappy, bitter, but still a province.

Even Alexander II, the so-called Czar Emancipator, refused to grant Poland independence. In 1863 Polish intellectuals sparked an insurrection against Moscow's control. Russian writers, such as Herzen and Turgenev, pleaded with Alexander to liberate Poland just as he had liberated the serfs. But Alexander believed he was protecting Russia's western borders. Poland was Russia's buffer state against any possible Austrian or German incursion.

Only after the chaos of World War I, when the czar, the kaiser, and the emperor were swept into the dustbin of history by revolution, defeat, and nationalism, did Poland again emerge as a European nation.

But Poland had been a memory for so long that history had forgotten her boundaries. On the west, the Allies could etch a clear, if controversial, German-Polish boundary; but on the east the line shifted with the conflicts between the Russian and Polish armies, which for more than three years swept back and forth across the uncertain borderlands from Warsaw to Kiev.

By 1921 Bolshevik power was firmly established—but Russia was so weakened by years of war and economic dislocation that she wanted, and needed, a rest. In March, Lenin signed the Treaty of Riga, in which he grudgingly conceded a thick slice of the Ukraine and Byelorussia to Poland. So Poland, a hazy national entity for over 150 years, was finally restored to her prepartition status.

This national glory did not last for a long time, for independent Poland, under dictator Pilsudski, still had to live with her terrible curse. Germany, on the west, grew maniacally compulsive, and Russia, on the east, began to flex its collectivized and industrialized muscles. By 1938 Hitler told the world that he was going to war, and he glanced menacingly across Poland at Russia's *Untermenschen,* who "unfairly" inhabited the rich Ukrainian breadbasket. Moscow, leader of world Communism, had attacked Hitler's fascism—so had Moscow's puppets. That was why the world was startled, on August 22, 1939, when Stalin signed a pact with Hitler—a pact that must have struck the Poles as a combination of perfidious treachery and old history. Germany and Russia were playing a curious cat-and-mouse game. The stakes were enormous, and little Poland—herself dictatorial, bigoted, and undisciplined—was again a pawn.

By September 17th, Russian troops marched into Poland as far as the Bug River, an ancient dividing line between Moscow and Warsaw. The Germans, by this time, had already occupied the rest of Poland. World War II had begun.

During the war, a Polish government-in-exile set up headquarters in London—first under the premiership of General Sikorski, later under the peasant leader Mikolajczyk. Stalin agreed to discuss the future of Poland with Mikolajczyk, who went to Moscow in the summer of 1944, as Soviet troops chased the retreating Nazis into Poland. Stalin and Mikolajczyk came to a vague understanding, but it was rejected by the Polish Government in London. The Polish underground, commanded by General Bor, apparently received orders at this moment to stage an uprising against the Nazis in Warsaw. The Poles fought gallantly, and they might have won, *if* the Red Army had helped.

But Marshals Rokossovski, Konev, and Zhukov called the rampaging Red Army to a strange and sudden halt on the eastern bank of the Vistula. With their binoculars, they watched the Germans systematically level Warsaw and massacre the Polish underground. Then, two months later, as the Germans began to retreat, the Russian Army occupied the devastated city. There were not many Poles on the streets of Warsaw to greet the Russians.

A few months later, the National Committee of Liberation, a group of Polish Communists supported by the Kremlin, set up a People's Republic of Poland in Lublin.

After the war was over, Poland was a problem only to the conscience of the West. To Stalin, Poland was no problem. The Red Army had occupied all of eastern Europe; a socialist government ruled in Warsaw. Now Stalin proposed that Poland's western boundaries be pushed one hundred miles westward—as far as the Oder-Neisse line—cutting into what was once Germany, and that her eastern boundary remain the Bug River. Poland should also "receive" the port cities of Stettin and Danzig. Stalin's terms sounded vaguely familiar—almost as though they were dictated by Catherine the Great. But now Russia was one of the world's most powerful nations, and the West, outraged and incensed, did nothing.

Under the new Communist government in Warsaw, "socialism" became Poland's freshest import. The Poles were not impressed. They knew that their country was once again a Russian satellite; they knew that their Catholicism could not abide Marxist atheism; and they knew that their peasants would refuse to enter collective farms. In 1947 Wladyslaw Gomulka, a Poland-firster, became Secretary-General of the United Workers Polish (Communist) Party. Under his leadership, Poland seemed to yield to her national taste—a little. Instinctively, Stalin distrusted Gomulka, who had not sat out the war in Moscow, as Boleslaw Bierut and Jakub Berman had, but instead had fought in the Polish underground. A tough, energetic Communist, Gomulka was expelled from the Party in 1949; two years later he was arrested during the darkest period of Stalin's reign. He lived under house guard in Miedzeszyn, a Warsaw suburb, until 1954. Under Bierut's command, Poland's spirit was crushed. Only the spirit of vodka reigned.

* * *

In March, 1953, Joseph Stalin died, and, as Flora Lewis has observed, "Stalin's death cracked the psychological ice jam which had frozen his colossal empire into a kind of frenzied inertia." Under Nikita Khrushchev's dynamic leadership, a malevolent dictatorship was gradually transformed into a benevolent despotism. Slowly, painfully slowly, unorthodox ideas began to fuse with Marxist dogma, and Warsaw's coffeehouses became forums for political debate. Polish youth, who have always had a little more style than Soviet youth, started to listen to American jazz and to adopt a French coiffure.

The Palace of Culture, a Soviet architectural monstrosity that towers over Warsaw's gutted Marshalkowska, became one of Poland's best punch lines. "You know," one Pole would say to another, "where you can get the best view of Warsaw?" "Where?"

the other Pole would ask, straight-faced. "From the Palace of Culture, of course, because then you can't see the Palace of Culture." By now, this is an old joke, but in 1954 and in 1955 it was still gutty humor.

In August, 1955, Antoni Slonimski, Poland's proudest poet, penned his revolutionary "Manifesto":

> "Down with those trashy icons,
> Whose only value was their power
> To conceal the even trashier architecture
> On which they were displayed.
>
> "We want the right to gripe,
> To joke,
> To hold some high-placed dignitaries
> up to ridicule. . . ."

Soon, Poland began to take the right, and, by October, 1956, proletarian dissatisfaction and intellectual frustration had swelled to such proportions that Poland's Moscow-firsters were forced to yield power to Poland's Poland-firsters, among whom was Wladyslaw Gomulka, a devoted Marxist who happens to feel Poland can find its own way to Communism without too much Russian guidance. The torch of revolution burned ominously in Warsaw, and Moscow got jumpy. On the night of October 19, 1956, an angry delegation of Soviet leaders arrived in Warsaw. The delegation included Khrushchev, a pudgy package of fury, and Molotov, Mikoyan, Kaganovitch, and Zhukov. A contingent of Polish leaders sped to the airport to greet them. The contingent included the Big Three of Polish Communism—Ochab, Cyrankiewicz, and Gomulka.

"We have come to stop you," Khrushchev shouted, "from handing your country over to the Americans and Zionists. Our Red Army has shed its blood for your country." Then Khrushchev spotted Gomulka. "What is that traitor doing here?" he roared.

Quietly, but boldly, Ochab told Khrushchev that many Poles had also died defending their homeland. Then, pointing at Gomulka, Ochab said that Khrushchev ought to respect the new member of the Polish Politburo who was soon to be elected Secretary-General of the Party.

Later that night, when both delegations resumed their undiplomatic discussions in Warsaw's Belvedere Palace, Khrushchev continued his tirade against the "bourgeois Zionists" who were trying to sell Poland to the Americans. The Poles did not yield. Finally, Mikoyan interrupted his incensed leader. In a low voice, the Armenian trade expert suggested that Khrushchev join him in a far corner of the room for a private chat. When the two Soviet leaders rejoined the others, Khrushchev was smiling. The discussions resumed.

"That night, nobody slept in Warsaw"—begins Juliusz Zulawski's memorable poem describing the uncertain, rebellious mood of Warsaw on the night of October 19, 1956. Until six o'clock the following morning, the Soviet and Polish leaders argued. Then, as abruptly as they had arrived, Khrushchev and his delegation returned to Moscow. The Poles and the Russians had apparently agreed on three major points: first, that Soviet Marshal Konstanty Rokossovski, who held the portfolio of Polish Defense Minister, be relieved of his responsibilities; second, that Poland's new Communist leadership brake the momentum of popular anti-Soviet sentiment; and finally, that Gomulka promise to keep Poland within the bloc.

These agreements had no immediate effect upon Poland's restive masses, who continued their anti-Russian roars and their anti-Communist demonstrations; but they did set the mood for China's grand debut in European politics. Peking's suave politician-diplomat, Chou En-lai, entered Moscow, Warsaw, and Budapest in January, 1957, with the gentle wisdom of a Confucian scholar. His role in the East European revolutionary drama of 1956–1957 is the key to an understanding of China's historic intrusion into European affairs and of Peking's singular stature in bloc politics ever since. That was the story I wanted to check in Warsaw.

* * *

When we arrived in the Polish capital in mid-July, 1959, red-and-white bunting hung from every government building and lamppost. Bright flowers peeked over the uneven tops of flowerpots, and small armies of women scrubbed the streets. Impressionistic posters, in honor of July 22nd, Poland's Independence Day, were pasted on battered, grotesque shells of buildings—searing memories of wartime devastation. Gigantic posters of Polish Communists—many of whom were murdered by the Russians during the great purges of the 1930's—were suspended from the twisted hulls of prewar apartment houses along the broad, blasted Marshalkowska, where small shops with unusually pretty displays sell consumer goods according to the "outdated" principle of supply-and-demand.

Weary Warsaw tried to look reasonably attractive, for she was expecting an important guest who would help Poland celebrate Independence Day. The guest was Nikita Khrushchev; his host was Wladyslaw Gomulka. "Tomorrow," a hotel concierge mumbled unenthusiastically, "tomorrow our liberator arrives."

Khrushchev the liberator arrived in Warsaw on July 12, 1959. His turboprop plane landed fifty-five minutes late. At Okecie Airfield, thousands of neatly dressed children, carrying flowers, waited restlessly. Before them, shifting nervously, was the Polish Politburo, led by bespectacled, balding Gomulka and beady-eyed, bald Cyrankiewicz. Polish guards stood in sloppy formation. An air of informality reigned over the airfield. Warsaw was indeed a refreshing contrast to Moscow.

Soon, Khrushchev's plane landed, and the Russian leader, dressed in a white linen suit, stepped out of it. Gomulka applauded. The Politburo applauded. The people applauded. The children held up their flowers. Khrushchev touched Polish soil and embraced Gomulka. "Welcome," the Polish leader said, and if at that moment he did not remember Khrushchev's crashing arrival three years before, he must have been a man of steel. Certainly the memory of October 19, 1956, was fresh in everyone else's mind.

Khrushchev had come to Poland on a reconciliation visit. He wanted to tour the Polish countryside and to talk politics with Polish leaders. He was anxious to forget the past and to make the best of the present. In steel mills, he congratulated the workers on their production, and on Poland's uncollectivized farms he gently encouraged the peasants to "abandon" their private farms and "voluntarily" join collectives. He even lectured the Polish peasants on the "foolishness" of the Chinese communes—a lecture that was to infuriate Peking. In Warsaw, he politely placed a wreath on the tomb of the unknown soldier, and he held his arms over his head in a gesture of affection. Warsaw was neither deliriously delighted with Khrushchev nor terribly distressed.

One night, while Khrushchev was in Stettin, postponing a scheduled trip to Scandinavia while preparing for an unscheduled trip to the United States, I had a talk with a middle-aged Pole in the small park near the Bristol Hotel. Because he did not speak English, we spoke in Russian. I asked him whether he was pleased to see Khrushchev. He spat. I asked him whether he was making a living. He was tight, and his breath smelled of vodka. "You must make ends meet," he whispered, raising his hands in a helpless gesture. "Gomulka tells us we must make ends meet. So we steal a little here and we steal a little there—you know, the way the Russians do—and we make ends meet."

"You don't sound very happy."

"I am not," he answered, and his voice was so sad that it brought a lump to my throat. "Here we can't live; here we can't even die." He looked at me. "My American friend, we all remember your aid to us, but the Russians took it. Listen, I have read all those Communist books, too. Lenin, you know, spoke about the evils of white imperialism. To me, there is nothing worse than red imperialism."

I talked with Poland's people during the night; I talked with her leaders during the day. Many of them were with Khrushchev, but there were a few influential, fairly reliable Poles in Warsaw who were willing to talk about China's role in "the October days," as the 1956 Revolution is called. I cannot mention their names. Poland may be less rigid than Russia, but she is still a Communist dictatorship; and, as A. M. Rosenthal has observed, "there may be freedom of conversation in Poland, but there is not freedom of speech." I say "fairly reliable" because Poles have a way of exaggerating their importance in the world; and they may have given more weight to certain key issues than the issues deserve. In any case, this is their story.

In 1956 the Poles said that the Chinese definitely supported their drive toward liberalization. Mao was believed to have given his blessings to Gomulka; it was even assumed that Mao cabled his support to Ochab during those historic October days. Ochab was supposed to have had excellent relations with the Chinese Communists, especially with Mao Tse-tung. The Polish leader was in Peking in September, 1956, to attend a meeting of the Chinese Communist Party. Anastas Mikoyan represented the Soviet Union. One evening, Mao joined Mikoyan and Ochab in a disturbing discussion about the Poznań uprising. He questioned Ochab closely about Poznań. Ochab, representing the anti-Stalinist wing of the Polish Party, pointed to a failing economy and excessive Russian control as the major reasons for the outbreak. Mikoyan grew angry. That is not true, he cried; the real reason is the presence in Poland of anti-Communist "elements."

Ochab disagreed: "Our people will no longer tolerate taking orders from abroad."

Mikoyan countered with an insulting blast against Ochab. "People who voice such anti-Soviet ideas can only be regarded as enemies, and treated accordingly. The same goes for those who listen to them." Ochab shook hands with Mao, who had "listened" to Ochab, and silently left the room. Mao followed. Miffed, Mikoyan returned to Moscow, although the congress had not yet concluded its work.

Ochab brought this story back to Warsaw, and it spread like wildfire. The Poles believed it, and they used it as a weapon against the Russians. For, if the Chinese supported the Polish view of Poznań, then Soviet opposition had to be interpreted as opposition to both Poland and China. Indeed, in the heady atmosphere of October revolt, the Poles even believed in the possibility of a Peking-Warsaw-Belgrade axis against Moscow. And, when Chou En-lai arrived in Warsaw in January, 1957, they were convinced even then, after the Hungarian Revolution, that the Chinese still supported their movement toward internal liberalization.

These days, the Poles tell a different story. The Polish Communists, under Gomulka, have systematically retreated from their

1956 liberalism. In certain ways, they have reinstituted "Stalinist" controls, and they have brought many Moscow-firsters back to power. Now the keynote of Warsaw's tune is: Don't rock the boat. The Poles still maintain that the Chinese supported them; and they insist that Chinese support was fully consistent with Mao's new theory of "one hundred flowers" blooming and "one hundred schools of thought" contending. But they have their doubts that Mao ever sent Ochab a telegram expressing Chinese support, and they are not sure that Mao really contemplated joining an anti-Moscow coalition of socialist countries.

* * *

One Polish source, of a decidedly scholarly inclination, suggested that if I ever hoped to bring a sense of perspective to a story in which Poles play an important role, I would have to go back to the original sources. That meant—among other things—going back to the Russian, Chinese, and Polish press for 1956, for, in each country, 1956 was a big year.

For Russia it was the year of the thaw. In February, 1956, Khrushchev stunned Mao, Moscow, and Marxism with a sharp attack against the legend of Joseph Stalin. He called the late dictator a "tyrant" who did not listen to sound military advice in 1941 and almost ruined Russia. He accused Stalin of having encouraged a "personality cult" and of having destroyed the principle of "collective leadership." Only in his early years was Stalin a good Communist, Khrushchev charged, for, afterward, he began to place the interest of Stalin ahead of those of Russia.

The attack against Stalin had important consequences. The legend of infallibility was demolished. Stalinist restrictions were eased. Students openly began to criticize the Kremlin, and Khrushchev stepped up the move toward a more consumer-oriented economy. Finally, in foreign affairs, Khrushchev entered the arena of suitcase diplomacy by visiting England and by inviting the renegade Tito to Moscow. In fact, the Tito visit was properly interpreted as a concession to the national-road-to-socialism school of Communism. If Tito was the headmaster of the school, Mao was a prize pupil; and Gomulka was trying to gain admission. By asking Tito to visit Russia, Khrushchev was admiring the school and patting its headmaster on the back.

For China, 1956 was a year of increasing ideological maturity and economic frustration. As usual, the Chinese were having trouble feeding their exploding population. They were having so much trouble that they launched a gigantic birth-control program that embarrassed many foreigners by its graphic frankness. Nevertheless, peasants were hungry, and Mao realized that economic discontent was widespread. The first five-year plan may have been laying the foundation of an industrial China, but no one seemed very happy with the pace.

Possibly as a form of compensation, possibly as a sign of ideological maturity, the Chinese began to act as though they had invented Communism. First, the mayor of Peking, Peng Chen, announced triumphantly one day in early January that the city of Peking had already entered the stage of "socialist" development. The Russians had thought that the Chinese were still struggling through their "new democracy" phase; now, suddenly, inexplicably, one Chinese city had leaped over the hurdle of social and economic transition into the bliss of socialism. Second, the Chinese said that they did not have to offer any excuse to the Kremlin for launching a program of birth control. If the program smacked too much of Malthusian doctrine, then, in effect, that was too bad. Third, the Chinese openly disputed Khrushchev's assessment of Stalin. In an article, entitled *On the Historical Experience of the Proletariat,* Mao disagreed that Stalin was a bad Communist. "Some people say Stalin was wrong in everything," he wrote. "This is a grave misunderstanding, for Stalin was a great Marxist-Leninist."

In the same article Mao also introduced the core of a new doctrine on "contradictions" that the Poles took very much to heart. Mao said that "contradictions" between rulers and ruled could exist in a socialist society. Khrushchev did not agree with Mao, and he said so.

Finally, on May 5, 1956, Lu Ting-yi, China's propaganda chief, indicated that Mao had still another ideological innovation in mind—one that was to become formal a year later. "To the artists and the writers, we say: 'Let a hundred flowers bloom.' To the savants, we say: 'Let a hundred schools of thought contend.' " Mao had recognized the extent of discontent in China, and he wished to give Chinese intellectuals a chance to let off steam. The Russians did not approve—although the Poles did. For the liberal Communists of Warsaw, China began to loom as a man-sized friend who was not afraid of the Russians.

For Poland, 1956 was a year of history. In 1794 the Poles rebelled against the Russians, and lost. In 1830 they rebelled, and lost. Again—in 1848. In 1863 the same story. Now it was 1956, and it was time for another rebellion. Unfortunately, it was also time for another defeat.

The Poles listened carefully to Mao's new pronouncements, as they had listened carefully when Khrushchev strongly implied that national roads to socialism were "acceptable." They also listened to the rising tempo of proletarian anger and intellectual frustration. Poets, such as Slonimski, wrote anti-Soviet stanzas, and youth refused to attend Marxist lectures in the universities. Suddenly their Stalinist leader, Bierut, died while attending a meeting in Moscow. Hopes were raised, as Edward Ochab became the leader of the Polish Communists.

On June 28, 1956, the workers of Poznań staged a massive demonstration against their Marxist rulers. They wanted more bread and more money. The demonstration was quickly brought under control, but Poznań became a symbol of freedom. Some Poles demanded a much larger measure of domestic autonomy; others even threatened to break away from Russia. Polish Communists interpreted Poznań as a warning to improve economic conditions and to reduce Russian influence. Bulganin, who was then Premier of the Soviet Union, attacked the Poles who were attacking Russia. "It would be erroneous not to note," he warned, "that in connection with the struggle against the personality cult, not only have hostile and opportunistic elements become more active, but unstable and vacillating people in our own ranks have also come out into the open. These people, misled by hostile propaganda, at times incorrectly interpret individual propositions connected with the personality cult, and this has found its reflection in some press organs of the socialist countries, Poland included."

On October 5, 1956, after Ochab had returned from Peking with his story of Chinese support, Wladyslaw Gomulka joined the liberal faction of the Polish Communist Party, cutting loose a train of events that were to entwine Poland, Russia, and China in an extraordinary diplomatic and political tangle. Cyrankiewicz told a divided Party that only Gomulka could unite discontented Poland behind Communism. The Stalinist faction of the Party violently disagreed, but in the face of a sharply deteriorating economy they were helpless. A Party congress was scheduled for early November, to which Gomulka was reluctantly invited.

The Polish Revolution had begun.

At this point the events move with mercurial speed.

October 9—The economy continues to disintegrate, and the people grow more restive. Violence erupts, and strikes abound. The Party reinstates Gomulka to full membership.

October 16—China bursts into European politics—possibly for the first time in history; certainly for the first time since the Mongol hordes swirled out of Asia seven hundred years ago to terrorize Russia and to breathe fire on Vienna. Ochab tells a closed meeting of the Party that Mao supports Polish liberalism. This story is then relayed to Western reporters, who spread the word around the world. It lands in the Kremlin with explosive significance.

October 19th—Khrushchev, Mikoyan, Molotov, Kaganovitch, and Zhukov arrive in Warsaw angry and intolerant; they issue their demands.

October 20th—The Russians return to Moscow, as the Red Army begins threatening "maneuvers" around Warsaw.

October 21st—The Poles grow more belligerent. Gomulka, whom Khrushchev called a traitor, is elected Secretary-General, or First Secretary, of the Polish Communist Party, and Marshal Rokossovski is dismissed as Defense Minister. His place is taken by General Marian Spychalski, who, like Gomulka, had been arrested during Poland's Stalinist period.

October 30th—*Pravda,* reflecting Moscow's mood of conciliation, promises a Commonwealth of Socialist Nations, in which mutual trust is highlighted. Discussion and negotiation are stressed.

November 1st—*People's Daily,* Peking's *Pravda,* echoing Moscow's conciliatory proposal on a Socialist Commonwealth, says that the "demands of the people of Hungary and Poland are completely proper." It is beginning to look as though Moscow and Peking have been forced by the pace of East European events to agree to a looser federation of socialist states, in which Moscow's role would be drastically reduced.

November 2nd—Imre Nagy, Premier of Hungary, where angry mobs of proletarian workers have been storming Communist Party headquarters, asks the United Nations for help against Russia. Nagy also asks that Hungary be permitted to leave the Warsaw Pact.

November 3rd—The Chinese are first to react. Now it has become a question of real estate, and the Communists are tight landlords. *People's Daily* says: "It is very painful for the Chinese people to see a handful of counterrevolutionary conspirators attempting to use Hungary to breach the unity of the socialist countries and to sabotage the Warsaw Pact."

November 4th—*Pravda* declares war on Hungary, agreeing fully with Peking. Soviet tanks start to move into Budapest, and the slaughter begins: man against machine.

November 10th—Flora Lewis reports from Warsaw that the Poles now feel the Chinese have withdrawn their support and that Warsaw feels alone against the entire bloc. In this nervous atmosphere, the Poles begin to look for straws in the wind. A story sprouts in the Polish imagination; its source is uncertain. It is that Mao called in Poland's ambassador in Peking to assure him of China's continued support. So long as the Poles do not emulate the Hungarians—and ask for a return to capitalism—China will continue to maintain the most cordial relations with Warsaw. If the story is true, China has begun to mediate Russia's dispute with eastern Europe. If the story is not true, the Chinese have never denied it.

November 22nd—*People's Daily* promises that Russia will turn over a new leaf in its relations with eastern Europe—an unusual promise, coming from the Chinese! Peking says that both small and large nations have made "mistakes" and that the "mistakes" will be corrected.

November 27th—Chou En-lai begins a good-will trip through Southeast Asia. In Pnompenh, Cambodia, Bernard Kalb, *New York Times* correspondent in Asia, reports that Chou launches a blistering attack against "great-power chauvinism." He explains that China will never make the "mistake" of misusing its power. "It is very easy," Chou pontificates, "for a big power to injure the dignity and affront the independence of smaller nations." These remarks, Kalb reports, are made for an Asian audience that fears China may one day ape Russia's tactics in Hungary. Implicitly, they are also Mao's way of telling Russia that its relations with eastern Europe should have undergone a fundamental change much earlier.

December 29th—*People's Daily* carries long articles, entitled *More on the Historical Experience of the Dictatorship of the Proletariat,* in which China makes three major points: first, that Peking now supports Russia's military action in Hungary; second, that Peking feels Titoism is a threat to bloc solidarity; and finally, that Stalin is a "great Marxist-Leninist" who has been misunderstood. "In our opinion," *People's Daily* remarks, "Stalin's mistakes took second place to his achievements." This last-mentioned point actually signals a reappraisal of Stalinism for the entire bloc.

December 30th—*Pravda* reprints the *People's Daily* article. The fact that the article appears in *Pravda* the morning after it appears in *People's Daily* seems to indicate a measure of prior planning.

January 1st—The Poles, still defiant, sign a communiqué with the Yugoslavs—an act that astonishes observers, since it follows by only two days a major attack against Tito by China and Russia, and it again underscores the importance of "national roads to socialism." On that same day Chou abruptly leaves New Delhi and returns to Peking.

January 7th—Chou arrives in Moscow, where he is received like a conquering hero. A gala banquet is held in his honor in the Kremlin. Bulganin raises a toast to Chou: "The Soviet Union values highly the position you took in connection with the counterrevolutionary uprising in Hungary." Chou smiles.

January 10th—The liberal Poles, who surround Gomulka, attribute their success to Chinese support, but now they are somewhat anxious about Chou's expected arrival the following day. They feel he will urge them to slow down their liberalization drive and modify their differences with the Russians.

January 11th—They are right. Chou arrives in Warsaw, where he is received triumphantly. Instantly, he hails the "leading role" of the Soviet Union in the Communist world. Quietly, Gomulka responds, hailing "equality and mutual respect." That night, at a ball, Chou's diplomatic smoothness is displayed. He says all nations make mistakes, including Russia, China, and Poland; these mistakes, he promises, will be corrected. Again, Chou acts as Russia's mediator. Then he applauds Russia's "leading role," but adds: "Your achievements are our achievements and your difficulties are our difficulties. We are comrades in arms in the task of constructing socialism. The Polish nation may always count on the support of the Chinese nation." Like a skillful juggler, Chou is playing Russia's "leading role" off against Poland's "liberal achievements," and both Gomulka and Khrushchev are satisfied.

January 15th—Chou plays a similar game in Budapest.

January 16th—Chou returns to Moscow, where he is again cheered, and then goes back to Peking.

Chou's mediation trip apparently resulted in a bargain. The Poles recognized Russian leadership over the bloc, although for domestic reasons they did not say so publicly, and the Chinese promised to continue supporting Poland's liberalization.

These days, the Poles are less emotional, more realistic, about 1956, which still has a kind of B.C.–A.D. connotation in Poland. They recognize that they might have exaggerated the degree of Chinese support, but they are all convinced that for a time they had that support. Indeed, a chronological review of the main events tends to support the Polish view. Until November 3rd, when the Chinese felt the major issues were ideological, not territorial, they were perfectly willing to support a Polish drive toward liberalization. Khrushchev himself had approved of "national roads to socialism" and of a socialist Commonwealth of Nations. Moreover, Chinese support *was* fully consistent with Mao's latest ideological pronouncements about "one hundred flowers," "great-power chauvinism," and "contradictions."

However, when it became clear that the solidarity of the bloc might have been adversely affected by continued support, China's affection for liberalism cooled. Mao initiated the attack against Tito, and justified Khrushchev's brutality in Hungary. Peking needed Russia's economic support, and not for a moment did Peking want to hurt Moscow. Mao believed that all socialist nations should be as free of Moscow as he was; and to that extent he supported Poland. But no further.

Still, Chinese support—even for a short time—did have tremendous significance. First, in a broad sense China had served notice on the world—not only on the socialist camp—that it was a major power with a big and influential voice. It had leapfrogged Russia to become a giant influence in eastern Europe. This was a historic event that should have shaken every Western capital. It did not.

Second, having helped Russia to reassert its control over eastern Europe, China suddenly realized how critically important it had become in interbloc relations. It was being used in eastern Europe as a counterweight to Moscow. To encourage this belief, the Chinese opened large-scale trade with Russia's European satellites—a development that seems to answer the questions raised in Vienna—and then flooded east European capitals with cultural and political delegations.

Third, China asserted its independence from Moscow far more vigorously than at any other time since Mao came to power in 1949. Indeed, for a time in 1956, China assumed the "leading role" in the bloc at the same time that it said Russia was the first "model" for all socialist countries.

Finally, 1956 was a turning point in the Russian-Chinese alliance. It would never be the same again. Before 1956, China may have felt itself the ideological equal, if not the superior, of Russia; since 1956, China has begun to act the role—much to Russia's dismay.

CHAPTER SEVEN Moscow

FROM EARLY JANUARY, 1956, TO LATE JANUARY, 1957, I WORKED at the United States Embassy in Moscow as a press attaché. In my spare time, I kept a diary, which was published in October, 1958, entitled *Eastern Exposure*. I believe it reflected the journalistic and diplomatic view of an important year in Russian history. On May 27, 1956, I made this entry:

"Forty blue-frocked, enthusiastic, but somewhat bewildered young Chinese Communists had their legs pulled last night at the Metropole Hotel, but they didn't know it. In fact, when they finally got to bed, they must have felt warm and excited in a delightful, naïve intimacy with their Communist dream. At three this morning, they arrived in the lobby of the Metropole, tired, puzzled and more than slightly lost. They had traveled all the way from Peking. Now they were in the socialist paradise, the country associated with Lenin, Stalin, and even the devil Trotsky. A young American happened to be sitting in the lobby, collecting his thoughts after a rough day of sightseeing, the ballet, and a late dinner. His room was too warm, and his mind too active. He was busily cursing the Russian bureaucracy to himself, when he saw this flock of young Chinese, all dressed in blue, like good little schoolboys off to school on assembly days. Nobody from the Metropole staff was there to meet them, and our American friend, unable to hold back a good speech when he feels one coming, burst out in Russian: 'Comrades, on behalf of the socialist paradise, on behalf of the Communist Party and the Soviet government, on behalf of the International Workers' movement, I welcome you to the Kingdom of Marx on earth; I welcome you to Soviet Russia.' The young Chinese were terribly impressed. Our orator, now really beginning to feel his oats, and ascending a table top, continued: 'Our friends from the brotherly Communist Party of China, under the inspired leadership of Mao Tse-tung, pupil and son-in-arms of the great Lenin, who as everybody knows always hated the detestable Stalin, whose cult of the personality was alien to the spirit of Marxism-Leninism, are always welcome to this land where everyone is free, where everyone works for the future, brilliant emergence of Communism, where women have equal rights with men to dig ditches, drive trucks, and use tractors. Thanks to the industrious Soviet people, the Soviet Union is now truly a land of paradise. Therefore, on behalf of the Communist Party and the Soviet government, I welcome you.' The Chinese applauded. The leader, a young man of about twenty, deeply intense, approached the American, who spoke beautiful Russian, and answered, also in Russian, that they were delighted to be there, that this was the culmination of a life's wish. The American then took them to the *dezjurny,* got a key to a large dormitory-like room on the fourth floor of the hotel, and went so far as to tuck them all into bed. The Chinese thanked him profusely. When he left their huge room, he sat down on the floor, and wept."

On November 24, 1956, as student discontent in Russia reached a peak, I heard a story about Russian and Chinese students which I recorded in my diary:

"Within the past two or three weeks, students at Moscow University, who lived in a dormitory near Sokolniki Park in Moscow, went on a kind of hunger strike. They were objecting to the low quality of the food. They wanted to eat and live better. They refused to eat in the dormitory lunchroom. Chinese students, who lived in the same dormitory, continued to eat in this lunchroom. Some of the Russian student strikers strongly suggested that the Chinese stop eating there. They refused. The next day, they stopped. The previous evening, they had been severely beaten by a group of the striking students. Rumor has it that the food has noticeably improved."

Aside from a few scattered references to ideological excitement in Peking, these were the only two stories about the Chinese that I recorded in a Russian journal spanning thirteen months. The reason is clear. In 1956 the Russians did not talk very much about

China—principally because China was not a controversial topic. Peking was recognized as an important ally, and Khrushchev was obviously grateful for Chou En-lai's persuasive diplomacy in eastern Europe after the Polish and Hungarian uprisings.

Everyone assumed that China's "blue-frocked" Communists were loyal allies who were devoted to Moscow and Marx. If a few of them were troublesome, they were beaten up by some Russian bullies. Thus, in 1956, the Chinese may have been occasionally annoying, but, from a Russian viewpoint, they were always manageable.

By July, 1959, when I returned to Russia, China had become a topic of passionate conversation—not only among diplomats and journalists but also among the people. At parties, at theaters, at schools, wherever Russians gathered, they talked about China, and its population, its zeal, its power. These discussions were fascinating blends of admiration and anxiety, and they reflected China's increasing importance in Moscow's life.

The admiration was public. For example, Sergei Obraztsov, Director of Russia's incomparable Puppet Theater, glanced over his shoulder at China's busy millions and told a visiting American: "You are a young country, and you are dreaming of tomorrow. We are younger still—only forty-one years old—and we are dreaming of tomorrow. But China is younger than either of us—they're only ten years old. It is the youngest, most exciting nation in the world—with the youngest dreams of all. I visited China five years ago. It was the most extraordinary experience of my life. People in China have had nothing . . . nothing. Now several hundred million people are dreaming of tomorrow. I cannot describe to you the feeling of excitement there—much, much more than even here in the Soviet Union."

Sometimes, the admiration bordered on awe; and, sometimes, the awe bordered on anxiety. Although the Russians did not like to discuss China in public, it was possible in 1959 to find Russians who were willing to talk about China with an American.

One young Ivy League student had had a chat a week before my arrival with a Russian philologist at Moscow University. He was astonished when the scholarly Slav pointed a trembling finger at a map of China and said: "That's why *we* must be friends. That's why," he added, urgently, "because we Russians are supporting a yellow peril!"

"A yellow peril!" the American exclaimed. "But that's a nineteenth century concept. Surely it makes no sense now!"

"It is only now that it does make sense," the philologist answered sadly. "One hundred years ago, it was a romantic prophecy. Today, it is a deadly reality."

From Leningrad came a report of a similar conversation—this one between a British tourist and Soviet Sinologists. The Sinologists feared that Russia's soft Siberian underbelly would soon be penetrated by "yellow locusts." "Mao himself," one Sinologist is said to have commented, "spoke about the 'yellow wind,' and I am beginning to fear that a yellow peril will again overwhelm Russia." These scholars did not talk about China as a "fraternal democracy"; they talked about China as an aggressive neighbor.

A Russian graduate student in Moscow angrily dismissed my suggestion of a "yellow peril." "It's not the Han race that concerns us," he said. "It is Han ambition; it's tremendous. Why, in Peking, I hear, you can get ten thousand Chinese out in the streets every morning at six o'clock swatting flies—just because you tell them that it is good for China. In Moscow you couldn't get five Russians up at that hour to swat anything."

"Isn't that good—that the Chinese can awaken this drive in their people?" I asked.

"Yes, good for China. Not for us," he answered.

Russian students had always been a little disturbed by Chinese ambition. I recalled that in 1956 students would point to their Chinese colleagues reading thick tomes on science and engineering and then shake their heads in wonder. "All they do is read. They never seem to have any fun. Read, read, read—that's all they do."

To check this earlier impression, I returned to the Lenin Library. Nothing had changed. The main reading room was crowded with students. Portraits of Lenin, Marx, Engels, and Khrushchev adorned the walls (the new apostolic succession). Silence reigned. I spotted about twenty-five Chinese students. For a half-hour, I watched them. Not one raised his head—even once, and I felt myself sympathizing with the Russian students who left for a smoke in the men's room.

After my library visit, I returned to our hotel. Ironically, Intourist had booked us at the Pekin Hotel, Moscow's newest gesture to China's growing stature in the world. The dining room was decorated in pseudo-Chinese style. The menus were in five languages—Russian, English, French, German, and Chinese. Over a lunch of vodka, caviar, and black bread, with a group of veteran foreign correspondents, I heard an extraordinary story of Chinese ideological dedication.

A Chinese university student in Moscow wanted to buy a 35-millimeter camera. He decided to save money from his state stipend of 300 rubles a month. For over six months he went without lunch, and finally he had saved enough money to buy the camera. When his "cell" chairman found out what he was doing, he convoked a "comradely court" to try the student.

"You deprived your body and your brain," the chairman charged, "of the food calories needed to study at your highest capacity. Or, if you are able to work at full capacity on less food, you should have given the extra money back to the state."

The student apologized to the court. He sold the camera, returned the money, and promised to feed his body and brain with enough nourishment to repay the state with great labor.

This is the kind of dedication that awes the Russian, who would much prefer the easy life of vodka, *blini,* and a 35-millimeter camera.

* * *

One of Moscow's headaches is China's population. Before I returned to Russia, an Indian expert on demography had just published a detailed report on the growth of China's population. He was Professor S. Chandrasekhar, Director of the Indian Institute for Population Studies in Madras, and he had toured China for two months at the end of 1958. His report, based on careful observation and meticulous scholarship, reaches four conclusions:

First, mainland China's population in 1956 was 630,000,000;

in twenty years China's population will be 1,000,000,000. That means that one out of every four people in the world will be Chinese; and if the trend toward birth control continues in other parts of the world it is even possible that one out of every three people in the world will be Chinese.

Second, China's population increases by 2.2 per cent every year. That means that approximately 16,000,000 Chinese are added to the nation's over-all population every year and that possibly, within five years, that statistic will have risen to 20,000,000 a year.

Third, China's death rate has dropped substantially. Professor Chandrasekhar attributes this decline to improved medical and sanitation facilities throughout China—especially, he says, in Canton.

Finally, China's population is one of the youngest in the world. Almost 50 per cent of the people are between the ages of fifteen and forty-nine.

Whenever I mentioned these statistics to Russian officials, they got downright annoyed—although one of them admitted that he could not understand why Mao did not institute a birth-control program. Actually, Mao had started a birth-control drive in 1956, but he called it off at the end of 1957—apparently at the same time that he decided to launch his commune program. I had heard in Warsaw that the Poles believed the Chinese would permit their population to reach 800,000,000; then they would make birth control as much of a patriotic duty as swatting flies and killing sparrows.

In the meantime the Chinese maintain that birth control is unnecessary under socialism. In January, 1956, at an international seminar on geography in New Delhi, Professor Sun Ching-chih, China's specialist on demographic prognosis, said that nobody has to worry about overpopulation in Communist China. "The privation and hunger suffered by millions of people are due to the fact that what was produced by the laboring people, instead of being rationally distributed, was seized by a handful of people in the form of rent, taxes, usury, and exchanges on an unfair basis." The world needed a "rational system" to assure an "adequate" food supply for a "growing population." Professor Sun's "system" was not a mystical faith in Communist abundance; it was divided into five parts: land reform, agricultural co-operatives, conservation of water and soil, prevention of floods, and improved technology.

Khrushchev apparently agrees with Professor Sun. A few years ago, Walter Lippmann reported a conversation he had had with the Soviet leader about the increase in China's population. Khrushchev "indicated he had heard that question before, and he dismissed it with some impatience."

In 1959 Khrushchev told a factory full of Russian workers that many "foreign visitors" had posed the question of China's population growth to him. "Here you have an example of typical bourgeois psychology," Khrushchev remarked sarcastically. "Why should the rapid growth of population in brotherly people's China or any other country frighten us? If all peoples will direct their creative efforts, their minds, and their potentialities so as to increase the output of material goods and cultural values, then the needs of the people of the entire world will be satisfied abundantly, and the so-called overpopulation problem on our planet will seem absurd."

Perhaps Khrushchev really does think that China's booming population is no threat to Russia and that China can feed and manipulate 1,000,000,000 people through a "rational system" of economic planning. If he does, he has not convinced one group of Western diplomats who have had long experience in the Soviet Union.

One West German diplomat recalled that in the fall of 1955, when Chancellor Konrad Adenauer visited Moscow, Khrushchev unofficially expressed his alarm over the "implications" of Chinese population growth. He was said to have noted in particular that the Chinese could work very hard on a minimal subsistence level.

A French diplomat believed that Khrushchev accelerated the settlement and industrialization of Siberia in recent years because of his concern over the possibility of Chinese expansion.

A British diplomat told me about a dinner conversation in 1954 among Khrushchev, Molotov, Labor MP Edith Summerskill, and Samuel Watson, a British union leader who had just arrived in Moscow after a swing through China. Miss Summerskill asked

Khrushchev why Soviet women received medals for having large families. "If every woman had ten children instead of five," he answered, "we would have a population twice the size in a very few years." Then, jokingly, Molotov added: "Yes, and if they tried just a bit harder we would soon outnumber the Chinese." This remark must have tickled Khrushchev's funnybone, for the Soviet leader burst into uproarious laughter.

"It might have been just the joke," the diplomat commented, "but I tend to think it was more than that."

Certainly, Khrushchev is aware that the power of a billion people, reaching hungrily toward industrialization and militarization, can be harnessed to accomplish incredible feats. A young Oxford don, visiting Moscow, looked into history for a likely parallel.

"You will undoubtedly recall," he said, puffing on a pipe, "that the pyramids of ancient Egypt were built by human slaves without the benefit of modern technology. The Chinese are numberless slaves who can build any modern pyramid they want—with modern technology. They have an almost unbeatable combination, and I would guess that the Russians know this. They have manpower resources and diabolical leadership, and they are industrializing their country at a phenomenal pace."

Sorrowfully, he added, "I think they can do anything they want to."

The problem is—What do they want to do? Do they want to use their population to drive a wedge into Siberia? Or do they want to absorb the bleak borderlands that divide their country from Russia's Asia?

Sinkiang is a case in point.

* * *

A vast chunk of Central Asia that is now under Chinese control, Sinkiang is an area where Russian and Chinese interests have traditionally collided. Remote and inhospitable, rimmed by giant mountains and scarred by eroded plains, Sinkiang is almost three times as large as France. To its north is Soviet Central Asia; northeast is Mongolia; south is Tibet; east is China. Sinkiang's population of 4,500,000 is composed of Uighurs, a sedentary agricultural people; Kazakhs, a nomadic Moslem people who inhabit the grazing areas of northern Sinkiang; Kirghiz, a nomadic Moslem people who guide their herds through mountainous southwestern Sinkiang; and Chinese who live along the trade routes of this forbidding land.

Sinkiang means "new frontier." One observer said it "continues to combine the color and isolation of a true frontier region with the traditions of a land whose roots go far back into the past. It has preserved a distinctly Central Asian flavor: silks, Khotan carpets, jade, golden Hami melons, deep-blue grapes, and donkeys, spread across a dusty stage with walled gardens, dim bazaars, and turreted mosques, against a backdrop of snow-capped mountains, green oases, and rows of poplar trees."

Westerners call Sinkiang "Chinese Turkestan." They know that for thousands of years Chinese power has surged into Sinkiang whenever China was strong and united. Late in the nineteenth century, Peking's control weakened, and Sinkiang once again came under the influence of local warlords. Thus, it was hardly affected by the Chinese revolution of 1911; and when Chiang Kai-shek established his government at Nanking in 1928 he was too busy unifying the rest of China to worry about Sinkiang.

Stalin was not. In 1931 the Moslems of Sinkiang staged a bloody uprising against the Chinese warlord Mao Chung-ying, which lasted for three years. In 1934 the Soviet Union suppressed the uprising—an intervention that was prompted by two considerations. First, the Russians feared that the Japanese might drive through Chinese Turkestan and invade Soviet Central Asia; and, second, the Russians were worried that Sinkiang's Kazakh and Kirghiz rebels might inspire their cousins in Soviet Central Asia to revolt against the Russians. Although the Kremlin never denied China's sovereignty over Sinkiang, it did control this vast territory for over ten years.

During this time the Russians placed Moscow-oriented officials in key posts. In 1943, for a variety of complicated reasons, the Red Army withdrew. A year later, Chiang sent a nominal force into Sinkiang, but it was unable to establish effective control. Cynically, the Russians took advantage of Kuomintang weakness. They supported one native faction against another. Their aim was to eliminate all Chinese influence from Sinkiang. Their hope was to convert Sinkiang into a Soviet province. In fact, as late as 1949, while Mao's troops were forcing Chiang to seek refuge on Formosa, the Soviet ambassador in Peking was negotiating with the remnants of Kuomintang authority for important economic and territorial concessions in Sinkiang.

Mao's victory signaled a major Chinese Communist drive into Sinkiang. Internal chaos and foreign war prevented the Peking regime from establishing firm control until late in 1954, but, during the famous Mao-Stalin talks of 1949 and 1950, the Chinese leader had already claimed Sinkiang. Apparently, Stalin had agreed, reluctantly, but he did succeed in convincing Mao to set up Sino-Soviet joint-stock companies for the economic exploitation of the area.

For Mao, Sinkiang's joint-stock companies were a sore point, because they represented a form of foreign control over Chinese territory. The Kremlin realized after Stalin's death that these companies would have to be dissolved if Sino-Soviet relations were to be "normalized." This is what Khrushchev did in October, 1954, during his first visit to Peking. At that time, he also agreed to help the Chinese build a railroad from Lanchow in central China to Alma-Ata in Kazakhstan. This railroad would run through Sinkiang. On January 1, 1960, rail service had been established as far as Hami in eastern Sinkiang.

The Chinese have high hopes for the railroad. They believe it will quicken the pace of Sinkiang's industrialization, and they hope it will help Sinkiang to absorb some of China's bursting population.

In the last few years, Peking has sent detachments of engineers to survey Sinkiang's economic potential. Their reports have been optimistic, and Chinese economists have begun to rhapsodize about converting deserts into gardens.

Since 1956, Peking has moved several million settlers into Sinkiang, and the railroad is sure to step up the mass migration of Chinese. This is bad news for the Uighurs, who used to constitute about 80 per cent of Sinkiang's total population. Already there have been reports of at least two Uighur uprisings against the

Chinese—in late 1959 and early 1960—and it seems likely that the railroad will only intensify the friction between Uighur nationalism and Chinese expansionism.

During the late 1920's and early 1930's, many Kazakh nomads fled to Sinkiang to escape Soviet collectivization. It can be assumed that during the Russian occupation of Sinkiang in the 1930's the Red Army tried to corral these renegades. In the vast bleakness of Sinkiang, it is unlikely that the Red Army succeeded. So, possibly, there remains in Sinkiang a bitter residue of anti-Soviet feeling among Kazakh leaders which the Chinese might one day choose to exploit. It is known, for example, that Chinese maps of Sinkiang have deliberately fuzzy borders with the Soviet Union near outer Mongolia. The Chinese have not made any move toward these pockets of land, but, on the other hand, they have not changed the maps. Thus, in the shifting sands of Sinkiang, the seeds of future nationalist rivalry may have been planted.

For these reasons, I did not agree with Moscow reports that Khrushchev was still helping the Chinese develop Sinkiang. On the contrary, I felt that he was fulfilling certain economic obligations he had undertaken between October, 1954, and April, 1956—the most cordial period of Sino-Soviet relations—and that Khrushchev would not be anxious to contribute further to Mao's ambitious schemes for Sinkiang.

* * *

With Harrison Salisbury of the *New York Times* I discussed the question of Outer Mongolia, another remote, landlocked Asian country, over which Russians and Chinese have been feuding for centuries. Salisbury, who was on temporary assignment in Moscow, had just returned from a trip to Ulan Bator, capital of Outer Mongolia. On this trip he had occasion to witness "a real competition between Russia and China." The roots of this competition, he said, are imbedded in the history of this distant land that, like Poland, lives between two aggressive powers.

In 1227 a Mongol general named Genghis Khan died in Kansu, northwest China. Under his successors, the Mongols terrorized the world. China fell before their raging onslaught. Central Asia fell. Persia fell. Russia fell. The Mongols even menaced Europe. Their victories awoke a feeling of national unity among a nomadic people who tended their flocks on the grasslands between Lake Baikal and the Gobi Desert.

Seven centuries later, the memory of Genghis Khan still burned brightly in that ancient land. In 1955 the Chinese Communists built an impressive blue-and-yellow mausoleum in Ezen Horoo, a town in Inner Mongolia where, it is believed, Genghis Khan was originally buried. Apparently, Peking realized that it now possessed a historic monument of value to all Mongolians, whether they lived in the Buryat Autonomous Republic, Outer Mongolia, or Inner Mongolia.

The Buryat Autonomous Republic used to be called the Buryat-Mongol Autonomous Republic, until, without explanation, in July, 1958, the Soviet Union changed its name. The BAR, part of the Soviet Union, is located just east of Lake Baikal. Half of its 671,000 inhabitants are Mongols.

Outer Mongolia theoretically is independent. Actually, it has been a Soviet satellite since 1924. It has a population of about 1,000,000, most of whom are Mongols.

Inner Mongolia is an autonomous province of Communist China. It has a population of 8,500,000, of whom 1,500,000 are Mongols. The overwhelming majority of the population is Chinese. The border between Inner and Outer Mongolia is tightly guarded.

Like Sinkiang, Mongolia spent many centuries under Chinese domination. The force of the Chinese Revolution of 1911 and the Russian Revolution of 1917 fractured Mongolia into three parts. Buryat-Mongolia was quickly absorbed into the Soviet Empire. Inner Mongolia was sucked into the Chinese Goliath. Outer Mongolia lived independently for a few years before it became Moscow's first political satellite. In fact, until 1949 the Soviet Union was the only country to recognize Outer Mongolia as a political entity, and Moscow exchanged ambassadors with Ulan Bator.

Recognition did not imply solicitude. During the 1930's Outer Mongolia was treated like a stepchild. Its magnificent horses were requisitioned by the Cavalry Corps of the Red Army. Its cattle were requisitioned to feed the Russian army based in Siberia.

Outer Mongolia was treated as little more than a military outpost against the possibility of Japanese attack.

Meanwhile, its leadership was trained in the ways of Moscow. Marshal Choibalsan, undisputed head of the Mongolian Communist Party since 1939, died in January, 1952, during a visit to Moscow. His successor, Y. Tsedenbal, was another Moscow-trained Communist, who still retains complete power despite a widespread purge in March, 1959. Tsedenbal's political lieutenants have all been groomed in Moscow, and they all speak Russian. In 1946 the Russians insisted that the Mongolians replace their ancient script with a modified Cyrillic alphabet that is now taught in schools and used in books. Still, it is believed that many Mongolian officials continue to use their ancient script.

Before 1953 the Russians did very little to develop Outer Mongolia. According to one report, they did set up a small tannery, a coal mine, and a vodka factory. After 1953 the Russians decided to help the Mongolians. They gave Ulan Bator full control over Soviet-Mongolian joint-stock companies. They also lent the Mongolians about 1,000,000,000 rubles for economic development.

Why did the Russians change their attitude toward Outer Mongolia in 1953? The answers all seem to revolve around Peking.

For one thing, the Chinese have been developing Inner Mongolia. It is now economically and culturally on a higher level than Outer Mongolia; the Russians may have felt the Chinese were trying to upstage them.

For another, Ulan Bator's leaders have been trying to escape from their diplomatic and political isolation—an isolation that they reportedly feel has been imposed by the Russians.

Finally, the Russians had to respond to China's closer relations with Outer Mongolia. Ever since the Chinese came to power, they have tried to cultivate ties with Ulan Bator. Almost immediately, they recognized the Mongolian People's Republic. On October 4, 1952, Peking and Ulan Bator signed a ten-year agreement on cultural and economic co-operation. In 1956 Peking gave Outer Mongolia 160,000,000 rubles, and sent its first contingent of technicians to Ulan Bator. In 1959 the Chinese and the Mongolians signed another economic agreement: more money, at a nominal interest rate, and a promise to help Outer Mongolia build two electric-power stations, three concrete highway bridges, a poultry farm, a starch and alcohol factory, a metal workshop, and a housing project. The Chinese added twenty thousand laborers, free of charge, to help with these projects.

Salisbury, a keen analyst, said that the Mongolians in Ulan Bator think Russia drives a hard bargain on economic matters. "But not China," he added. "The Chinese are considered fair traders who seem to want to help Mongolia without any strings."

"Wherever there is a construction project," Salisbury continued, "the Chinese are building it. A rush job to replace a bridge torn out by floods? The Chinese are working hard on it under arc lights at 2:30 A.M. A new irrigation project to turn a semidesert into agricultural land? The Chinese, five hundred strong, are carrying it out."

The dynamism of China has begun to attract Mongolian intellectuals. Many of them return from Peking with a crusading spirit they cannot find in Moscow; they feel Peking has an ideological *élan* that is magnetic. A few hundred years ago, Mongolia detested China. In the nineteenth century, Mongolia welcomed Russia. Now, Salisbury believes, "the position seems to be reversed." Russia is detested; China is admired.

"The momentum of the Chinese initiative is so great, the attractive force of Chinese dynamism is so overpowering," an Asian diplomat is quoted as saying, "that it is hard to see how, over the long run, Russia can maintain her position here. She is still the first power in Outer Mongolia. But five years from now this may well no longer be true."

Shortly after talking with Salisbury, I met two Mongols who confirmed his impression that Russia and China are presently engaged in a rough "competition" for Mongolia. They said China has been building many factories; Russia, many schools. "This is not a helpful kind of co-operation," one of them said in Russian. "This is competition."

I mentioned to them that Mao once told Edgar Snow that he regarded Mongolia as part of China, and I suggested the possibility that Mao may be trying to guide a "Greater Mongolia" movement that would eventually bring the three parts of Mongolia together under Chinese suzerainty. "That is an old story," one of the Mongolian students said, sadly. "Certainly the Chinese want to get Outer Mongolia, and they may. The tragedy is that we cannot do anything about it. It would be wonderful if we could establish diplomatic relations with other Asian nations. And we might really be able to break out of our isolation if the United States would recognize us, or offer us some kind of technical aid. As it is now, our people are becoming more aware of Mongolian nationalism, but we are helpless to assert even a Polish kind of national socialism."

When I mentioned that Gomulka was beginning to look and act more like Kádár every day, the Mongolians said: "That is all right; we would settle for Kádár's status." One of the students then told me that a conference of Mongolian specialists would soon be held in Ulan Bator and that a group of American scholars had been invited. "That will be the first time that we have ever been able to hold such a conference," the other student said.

Another story about the emergence of Mongolian nationalism concerned Rimchin. "Who," I asked, "is Rimchin?"

"Rimchin," the student answered, "is one of our greatest writers. When Stalin lived, Rimchin was attacked as a cosmopolitan and later as a bourgeois nationalist. But they couldn't get rid of him because he was so popular in Ulan Bator. Well, a few months ago he arrived in Leningrad, looking every bit as though he was Genghis Khan, with a flowing, colorful robe and a bright beaded hat. The Russians told him to dress more properly, but he only laughed at them. He demanded that the Russians return all of Mongolia's classical literature—the ancient manuscripts that they had taken about twenty years before. Of course, the Russians wouldn't return the manuscripts, but Rimchin caused quite a stir in Leningrad. Eventually he went home, back to Ulan Bator."

Was there any large-scale co-operation between Mongolian and Soviet scholars?

"No, there is very little co-operation. The Russians run our Academy of Science, and they do not permit us to do a great deal of research on the 'golden age' of Mongolian history. They keep all the source material in Moscow or Leningrad. I guess they have a feeling we may get ideas." The Mongolian student laughed. "Imagine—another Mongol invasion of Russia!" Both students burst into laughter.

* * *

The Mongolian students had raised an interesting problem—How good was the co-operation between Soviet and Chinese scholars? A few days later, I put this question to a few veteran Western diplomats in Moscow. "Surprisingly poor" was the general impression.

A few years ago, one of them said, a scholarly journal called *Soviet Union and China* was published in Moscow. After the first issue appeared, the Chinese sent a formal request to the Soviet Institute of Chinese Studies. They wanted the right to censor the journal before publication. The Soviet Institute was stunned. "Was there anything wrong?" "No," the Chinese answered, but they still insisted on the right of censorship.

Soviet Sinologists realized that the issue had suddenly acquired a political dimension, and they asked the Academy of Science for guidance. The Academy asked the Minister of Culture for guidance. The Minister of Culture asked Premier Khrushchev for guidance. Premier Khrushchev, who could not turn to anyone for guidance, grew angry. "Tell the Chinese," he reportedly muttered, "that they have no business censoring a Soviet journal."

"Is that what you want us to tell the Chinese?" the Minister of Culture asked, somewhat skeptically.

Khrushchev thought for a moment. He did not wish to antagonize the Chinese, but he did not want to lose face. "Let's drop the journal," he decided at last.

For the next few months the Russians tried to convince the Chinese that a scholarly journal was no cause for anxiety. On the contrary, it was a good showcase for historical and sociological studies that were devoid of political content. Apparently, the Chinese agreed. In late 1957 the Institute of Chinese studies announced that a new journal would soon be published.

Early in 1958 the new journal appeared in bookstores throughout the country. It was called *Sovetskoe Kitaevedenie—the Soviet Journal of Chinese Studies*—a quarterly devoted to scholarly treatises about China. The first three issues, published on schedule, were concerned principally with prerevolutionary Chinese society. Rarely did an article appear that concerned contemporary China.

A young Soviet Sinologist explained that it was "safer" to work on the past than to play with the present. "The Chinese revolution," he said, "is so volatile, it moves so quickly, that we are not sure what the developments signify."

"You mean the line hasn't been set, don't you?"

"Yes, if you want to put it that way—the line hasn't been set. Too many things are happening in China, and our relations are so touchy that we feel it's safer to write only about the past. For example, a friend of mine is now writing a study of Russian diplomat Lawrence Lang's six voyages to China between 1717 and 1737. Another friend will soon come out with an article on Russian doctors in the clerical mission in Peking in the eighteenth century."

With a gay twinkle in his eye, he added, "You don't get into any trouble writing about those subjects."

One day, in a bookstore on Gorki Street, I spotted the fourth issue of the *Soviet Journal of Chinese Studies* for 1958. I had heard that Number 4 should have been published in December, 1958, but that it was late. There was even a story that the *Journal* would not be published any more.

"When did this *Journal* appear?" I asked the salesman.

"This month," he answered.

The *Journal* was seven months late. I asked him why.

"Technical difficulties," he replied.

"Technical difficulties," I knew, was an all-encompassing excuse for economic failure, political uncertainty, bureaucratic mismanagement, and even technical difficulties. I started to glance through the *Journal*. The lead article offered an excellent reason for the unusual delay in publication. It was called "The Great Leap in the Economic and Cultural Development of the People's Republic of China," and it was written by A. V. Meliksetov, a leading Soviet Sinologist. Judging by the footnotes, I surmised that Meliksetov had written the article in 1959—after Premier Khrushchev had established the official Soviet reaction to the Chinese communes at the twenty-first Party Congress in January and February. Meliksetov's point was that the communes were not for export.

The *Journal* also offered some insight into Communist scholarship. About 60 per cent of the footnotes came from official Communist sources—mostly from Mao Tse-tung, Liu Shao-chi, and Lenin. Thirty per cent came from Western Sinologists, such as J. L. Buck, and 10 per cent from prerevolutionary Russian and Chinese scholars.

I thought it would be a good idea to go to the Institute of Chinese Studies. Its address was printed in the *Journal:* 7 Chinese Boulevard—exactly a ten-minute walk from the Kremlin. The institute was large and impressive. No one asked me for identification. I entered the director's office, identified myself, and asked if I could speak to a Soviet Sinologist. A secretary politely asked me to take a seat. She returned five minutes later. A meeting had been arranged.

I was ushered into a small, comfortable office, where I met two Sinologists. They were both pleasant, and they were both nervous. After a perfunctory exchange of niceties, I asked them why the *Journal* had been delayed for seven months before publication.

Could the delay have had anything to do with the communes?

"Oh, no," one of them answered firmly.

"Well, then, why the delay?"

"Technical difficulties," he answered.

I smiled, realizing that I had better change the subject.

How many people work at the institute? "About one hundred professional Sinologists."

Do they all speak Chinese? "Yes, now they do—almost all of them do." The other Sinologist nodded enthusiastically. "Almost all of them."

Where are they trained? "In the universities. Moscow University just last year opened a Chinese Institute, where students enroll for six years of graduate work in the Chinese language and culture."

The atmosphere in the small office was beginning to warm.

What about co-operation between Chinese and Russian scholars?

"Excellent," one Sinologist said; "Superb," the other Sinologist echoed. Then each proceeded to define "excellent" and "superb."

"Of course, we have had only one Chinese scholar lecture at the institute this year, but that is because they are so busy."

The other said: "Of course, only a few of us have been permitted to go to China in an official capacity; but don't get the wrong idea; if we want to go to China as tourists, we can. There are very few obstructions."

Were there any established exchanges between Russian and Chinese Sinologists? "Not yet."

I thought this was a good time to tell the Sinologists the Polish joke about how wonderful it was to have Russia as a "buffer" between eastern Europe and China. One Sinologist laughed coldly, while the other said: "That is nonsense. Nonsense. We are very pleased by the successes of our Chinese comrades." He started to sound like a *Pravda* editorial. "We delight in their successes, because their successes are blows against imperialism."

"Besides," the first Sinologist added, playfully, "we are now spending so much money to help develop China. When China gets to be self-sufficient, really powerful, we won't have to spend that much. We'll have more for ourselves."

When I mentioned that he sounded a little like an isolationist American senator, he said, "That is no compliment!" We all laughed. Then he added: "People in the West have a curious way of studying only the peculiarities of a given situation rather than the general movement of mankind. They permit the peculiarities to dominate their understanding of the over-all truth." This was the dialectical way of saying that Westerners study specifics—such as the commune controversy—as keys to an understanding of the whole. The Marxist scholar normally makes an assumption about the whole, before he delves into the specifics to substantiate his original assumption.

This was also the dialectical way of saying that our interview was over. I thanked both Sinologists. Before leaving their office, I glanced quickly at their bookcase. About half of the books were the works of American scholars. The Russians, who are supposed to have "excellent" and "superb" contacts with the Chinese, have to rely on the works of Americans, who have "hostile" relations with Peking. An irony of contemporary politics.

* * *

The Russians and the Chinese have had difficulties—over ideology, over borderlands, over journals, even over the conduct of foreign affairs. By the summer of 1959, it was becoming apparent that Peking and Moscow had begun to disagree on the direction of international policy.

Moscow was the capital of an industrialized nation that had begun to long for better clothing, reliable trains, and color television. Peking was the capital of a convulsed nation that seethed with terror and tension. Moscow was bourgeois; Peking was revolutionary. In short, Moscow's needs were different from Peking's, and these needs were expressed in the conduct of foreign policy. Moscow preached peaceful coexistence; Peking preached revolutionary war.

For example, Moscow and Peking differed sharply on Communist strategy in Iraq during the summer of 1959. In late spring, 1959, it was an open secret in Baghdad that Communist strength was growing very rapidly. Skillful agitators incited Iraqi crowds against General Abdul Karim Qassim; they accused the general of treason, and they demanded a voice in the government. Dispassionate observers believed that Qassim would have been helpless against a major Communist assault. But the assault never materialized. On urgent orders from Moscow, the Iraqi Communist Party was forced to change its tactics. Khrushchev feared that a successful Communist coup in Baghdad would wreck his policy of "peaceful coexistence"; moreover, he was already hoping that he would soon be able to visit the United States. So the Iraqi Communist Party was pressured into demoting "leftist deviationists," abandoning "mob violence and hysteria," and acknowledging General Qassim as a "national revolutionary leader," which, in a Marxist context, is high praise.

The Chinese disagreed with Moscow's tactics. They felt the

Iraqi Communists should have intensified their anti-Qassim agitation—hoping to create favorable conditions for a Communist *coup d'état*. Such a coup would have thrown the Middle East into total confusion.

Many diplomats in Moscow have attempted to explain this divergence in Communist policy toward Iraq. They say Khrushchev believes in the superiority of the socialist system. Moscow's booming rates of economic growth, he feels, guarantee the eventual triumph of Communism over capitalism. The image of Soviet abundance will attract the underdeveloped nations to the banner of Marxism; the sphere of capitalist influence will gradually shrink; and Moscow, armed with hydrogen warheads and long-range missiles, will be able to dictate the terms of Washington's surrender.

The Chinese see global strategy through the prism of poverty, racial bitterness, and nationalistic fervor. Capitalism, they feel, must not be pampered into defeat; it must be crushed—irrevocably. White, imperialistic Washington must be brought to its knees; it must kowtow before the dragon throne. If Algeria's rebels disturb France, and thus the United States, so much the better. If Iraq's Communists can throw the Middle East into economic and political turmoil, so much the better. If Communism's rockets can demolish the West, so much the better.

A striking manifestation of these divergencies is Moscow's comparative hospitality toward foreigners and Peking's hostility. In the Chinese capital foreign diplomats have been given the cold shoulder by Chinese officialdom. They have little contact—even on a professional level—with Peking politicians, and virtually no contact with the Chinese people. One British diplomat, passing through Moscow after a tour in China, said: "We are the prisoners of Peking. We are not really wanted there by the Chinese. Many of us feel the best thing that could happen to us would be if we were all thrown out." A Mongolian diplomat, now in Moscow, told me how thrilled he had been, after a tour of duty in Peking, to "get back to Ulan Bator—and the West again."

Even in Moscow, Chinese Communists maintain a frigid distance from foreigners. It used to be that the Burmese, Ceylonese, and Indians had cordial relations with the Chinese; now even they have trouble discussing more than the weather with Peking.

The other face of Communism is Russian—merrier in 1959 than in 1956. Suitcase diplomacy has changed Moscow from an overgrown village into a world capital. More hotels and restaurants have been opened. More buildings have been constructed. Neon lights brighten the broad boulevards of the city, and women look a bit more chic. G.U.M., the big department store in Red Square, has a much bigger selection of ladies' fashions, television sets, and household gadgets, and I had the feeling that Moscow was even beginning to develop a traffic problem. Moscow is no Stockholm—it certainly is no Paris—but it was looking better than I had ever seen it. Moscow had become bourgeois.

Even Russian Communism had become bourgeois. One afternoon, in one of Moscow's more fashionable restaurants, I met a young Komsomol, named Sasha, who was willing to discuss Communism—an unusual topic of conversation in a country which, contrary to popular belief, rarely indulges in public ideological debate.

"Oh, it is going to be just glorious," Sasha prophesied, his dark eyes alive with anticipation.

"What is?"

"Why, Communism, of course," Sasha snapped, obviously annoyed by my ideological obtuseness. "You wait; you'll see. When we have Communism in Russia, every family will have its own car. And that's inevitable; it will happen in your country too."

His prognosis was too priceless to deflate with facts, so I did not bother to mention that almost every American family already had its own car—and under capitalism.

For six weeks in the summer of 1959, many of those American cars were on exhibit in Moscow. The place—Sokolniki Park, a lovely patch of greenery across Moscow's grayness. The occasion—the American National Exhibition, a glittering display of television, art, motion pictures, books, automobiles, even a model of of the paddle-wheel Explorer VI satellite. The significance—another illustration of Moscow's rapprochement with the West and its un-Chinese receptivity to bourgeois comforts. The value—the first relatively uncensored picture of American life to appear in the Soviet Union since the Bolshevik Revolution.

It was a success.

Seventy thousand Russians saw the exhibition every day. The architectural antithesis of the usual Soviet exhibit, the American Fair looked radiant and curvaceous, like a shapely model out for a Fifth Avenue stroll. Inside a golden geodesic dome, featuring a spectacular twenty-minute film about America projected on seven gigantic television screens; inside the glass pavilion, where modern chairs were suspended from the ceiling and brightly colored shoes hung from an eye-catching Ferris wheel; and inside a light green plastic pavilion, where the Sandburg-Steichen "Family of Man" exhibit slowly "grew" on the Russian people; the wonder of American abundance and imagination was on display.

Every exhibit was a classroom. The students were the Russian people; intensely curious and culturally starved, they had been given their first chance to ask questions about the United States without having to glance fearfully over their shoulder. The teachers were seventy-five Russian-speaking American guides, who indefatigably explained, "sold," and defended the United States. For ten hours every day, class was in session.

The message of American prosperity must have been getting through to the Russian people, because, for a time, the Soviet press attacked the fair and the guides. "Less Boasting—More Deeds," *Izvestia* cautioned Washington. "Myth of the Average American," *Pravda* scorned. From long experience, the Russian people knew the "careerists" were busy.

"Please don't believe everything you read," a Russian confided. "My friends and I love America, and we love to hear about America. Listen, I'll tell you a secret." He peered cautiously over his shoulder. "There are many careerists in our country—bad people, who say terrible things about the United States. But don't pay them any mind; they're in the Party; they have to say such things."

The fact is, the exhibition did raise some fundamental questions about the Soviet system for thinking Russians. One day a young Russian student left the book exhibit, shaking his head in anger.

"What's wrong?" I asked.

"It's so frustrating, so terrible," he said. "We can see all these books—and the shoes and the cars—and we can touch them. But now, under our system, we can't have them, and that's wrong."

"Well, there has been some improvement in the Russian standard of living; maybe someday soon you'll be able to have them."

"I hope so, but I can't make myself believe it. You know the way it's been with us. Changes have taken place—they do now—but they all take place so slowly. And besides, there's never any guarantee that the changes will be good ones for us."

If the exhibition did anger, disturb, frustrate, and excite some Russians, then Washington should not be too disturbed by the fact that *Pravda* attacked it. In fact, in the context of global politics, Washington should be glad that it has had the chance to talk to the Russian people and to show them the variety and choice in American life. The exhibition was an important step in Russia's mushrooming rapprochement with the West. It was also further proof that Moscow and Peking are out of step. For it will be a long time before China entertains an American exhibition!

Vice President Richard Nixon, for whom the Russians have little affection, was invited to Moscow to open the exhibition. In television blue, the Vice President addressed the opening-day throngs, telling them about American prosperity in a mood of high-pitched optimism. Then, for a week, he toured the Soviet Union, visiting Novosibirsk, Sverdlovsk, and Leningrad. Everywhere, he smiled, debated, and learned, as he unofficially opened his campaign for the Presidency.

When the Vice President returned to Moscow from his handshaking swing through Soviet Siberia, I learned from a highly informed source that Premier Khrushchev would soon visit the United States. I reported this story from Moscow for CBS News. The day after Vice President Nixon left Moscow for a triumphant tour of Poland, the Soviet press suddenly stopped its propaganda attack against the American Exhibition. I suspected the reason. That night, in a simultaneous release from Moscow and Washington, the news was made official. Krushchev would visit the United States; Eisenhower would visit the Soviet Union.

The exchange made stunning headlines in Russia. Overnight, the press became friendly, gushing with warm stories about "traditional" United States–Russian friendship. The people, sniffing at the grapevine, relaxed; they realized that relations between Washington and Moscow had to improve.

What about relations between Washington and Peking? A few days later, I read the translations of recent issues of the Chinese Communist press. All Peking newspapers acknowledged the "peaceful" intentions of the Soviet Union, mentioned the "exchange" of visits as a "contribution to the easing of international tensions," and continued their tirade against "American imperialism," "Wall Street colonialism," and the "paper-tiger defense" of the United States. Clearly, Peking was unenthusiastic about Khrushchev's forthcoming visit to the United States; clearly, Peking had not changed the vicious tone of its anti-American attack.

How would Peking express its displeasure?

What would Peking do?

CHAPTER EIGHT New Delhi

ASIA.

When we arrived at Palam Airport, New Delhi, after a spectacular flight over the Himalayas from Tashkent, Uzbekistan, the thermometer in the waiting room registered 98.7 degrees.

"Welcome to New Delhi," an airline hostess chirped, as she greeted sixteen of India's most uncomfortable tourists.

"Awful warm," a young American remarked, as he slowly peeled off his jacket.

"Warm?" she replied. "Why, this is cool! Last week, before the rains, it was 108 degrees every afternoon." She smiled sympathetically. "Please be patient. Your bags will be along in a few moments."

Indian porters, sweating profusely, hurried through the room, lugging heavy grips, while customs officials, wearing white shirts and black caps, mopped their brows. Huge fans rotated slowly overhead, providing little relief from the heavy heat. An elderly Englishman in a faded white suit and floppy straw hat sat in a wicker chair near a screen door. Oblivious to the heat and the commotion, he looked like a character from a Maugham novel, smoking a pipe and reading the London *Times*.

There were eight Russians, two Indians, and a handful of Americans among the passengers. The Indians, bright-eyed and ecstatic, said they were returning from London, where they had been studying at the School of Economics. The Russians, who said nothing, were apparently beginning a diplomatic tour. The Americans, obvious in white sneakers and khaki trousers, were "hitting" India "for a couple of weeks before school starts."

In fifteen minutes the porters brought our bags into customs. Spontaneously, a line formed. I slipped behind a tall, silent Sikh.

One of the Russians, impatient, aggressive, bulled his way past me, elbowing in the best Moscow tradition. When he tried to force his way past the Sikh, the turbaned Indian impassively straight-armed him and then shoved him to the rear of the line. "That's not the way it's done here," he said quietly.

The Russian, trembling with anger, clenched his fists. A hush fell over the room. Quickly another Russian jumped to his side and whispered something in his ear. He nodded. A few tense moments passed. Then, brushing back a shock of brown hair, he approached the Sikh, and apologized. He spoke fluent English.

Later, in the evening, over a hot curry dinner, I told this story to a group of Indian journalists. "I am not surprised," one of them commented, "that the Russian spoke good English. I am surprised only at his behavior." He lit a British cigarette. "You see, in India, the Russians, unlike the Chinese, want to be liked, and they work hard for that affection."

* * *

One of the most popular stories in New Delhi is about the American, British, and Russian diplomats who arrive for a tour of duty. The American, the story goes, quickly drops his baggage at the embassy and rushes off to the market place—the native one, of course—to buy his mother a beaded bag. The Englishman checks his valises at the Imperial Hotel, luxurious with air conditioning and Scotch whisky, corners a bearer, tips him generously, and asks where he can find a friendly Indian girl. ("You know the way the British are when they leave London," an Indian said.) The Russian, though, has a different goal. He leaves his luggage at the Soviet Embassy, and then takes a public bus to a museum where he tells Indian students in fluent Hindi how Russia has always admired Indian culture.

Moscow began to woo India in 1954—first with smiles, then with delegations, and finally with money. This courtship symbolized a major change in Soviet foreign policy. Nikita Khrushchev, a new occupant of the Kremlin, realized that Stalin, a former occupant, had become so obsessed with Europe that he had ignored the potentialities of Asia and Africa. Nationalist leaders, such as Nehru and Sukarno, had been branded as "bourgeois" by the Soviet press, and their neutralist policy had been vilified by Stalin's propagandists. Khrushchev understood that Moscow could no longer afford a Stalinist orientation toward the underdeveloped areas of the world. In an age of rising nationalism, Khrushchev turned a Kremlin grimace into a grin, and Moscow began to reach over Turkey to shake hands with Nasserism and over the Himalayas to beam at Asia.

First, India—and Khrushchev refocused the propaganda image of Nehru in Russia. The Soviet press gradually began to applaud Nehru's support of Communist China and V. K. Krishna Menon's neutralism in the United Nations. Then Moscow informed the erratic Indian Communist Party that it would have to get along for a while without any overt Russian aid. Finally, in late 1954, Russia convinced Nehru that India needed Soviet economic assistance: low interest, long term, no strings.

In January, 1955, the Russians announced that they were going to help the Hindustan Gas Company, a private Calcutta concern, to build a file-manufacturing plant. The cost—about $2,000,000, in credits.

In February the Russians said that they would help India build a million-ton steel mill at Bhilai. The cost—approximately $280,000,000, of which Moscow would supply half, in credits.

The Soviet press promptly hailed this agreement as an "example" of "selfless, disinterested" Russian help. Unlike Washington's support of underdeveloped nations, Khrushchev boasted, Moscow's had no ulterior motive. "We want India to prosper as an independent country."

The words were sweet, and they made spectacular headlines—not only in India but also throughout Asia, where Bhilai became a symbol of Russian generosity. Radio Tashkent, Moscow's propaganda voice in Asia, said that Russia had plenty of Bhilais—more than enough to go around.

Later in the year, Russian engineers began to arrive in New Delhi. They were always courteous and efficient—never overbearing or supercilious. They were joined by Indian engineers. Together they journeyed to Bhilai, a hot, sleepy village that Russian and Indian muscle later converted into an industrial boom town of 65,000 steel workers. The Russians, who lived simply and worked hard, gradually gained Indian respect. This pleased Khrushchev. By 1959 Bhilai was producing pig iron; by 1961 Bhilai would produce one million tons of steel, one-sixth of India's planned output.

For Khrushchev, Bhilai was worth every ruble. In November, 1955, he crowned a year of aggressive courtship with a triumphant tour of India—a tour that was prompted by two major considerations. First, Khrushchev was anxious to strengthen Indian-Russian relations, and, second, he wanted to make certain that China's enhanced stature in Asia after the Bandung Conference had not eclipsed Russia's leadership of the Asian Communist movement.

On his arrival at Palam Airport, Khrushchev showed India that he was not only wealthy; he was also a regular fellow. With Premier Bulganin, a goateed sidekick who has since been relieved of political responsibility, Khrushchev greeted a cheering crowd of 500,000 Indians by pressing his hands together, Indian-style. He smiled broadly, and he looked and acted like a munificent uncle from the big city. The Indians roared their approval, and Nehru thanked Khrushchev for Bhilai.

Khrushchev seemed to enjoy India. A sturdy, rubbernecking tourist, he visited many historical shrines and impressive landmarks. He took every occasion to praise his hosts. On farms, he displayed a peasant's familiarity with crops and seeds, and he delighted the constant crowd by drinking milk from a coconut. In cities, he always managed to spot an Indian child when a cameraman needed a picture, and he could rarely suppress a speech when he saw a microphone.

Sometimes Khrushchev violated diplomatic convention. For example, he badly ruffled Nehru's sense of neutrality by attacking Britain and the United States on Indian soil, and he deeply disturbed many officials by using New Delhi as a platform for assailing SEATO, the Southeast Asia Treaty Organization. Still, Khrushchev's odyssey to India was assessed as a diplomatic success. He promised Nehru more economic assistance; in 1956 this amounted to $220,000,000—fertilizer plants, oil refineries, diamond-mining equipment, drilling rigs—and many, many Soviet technicians. India was grateful. Khrushchev also paraded Moscow's technological progress before Asia's hungry eyes; and although he occasionally mentioned China, he was selling the Russian model for economic development to the backward countries of Asia and Africa—none of which could have failed to be impressed. His message was simple; forty years ago, he seemed to say, Russia was underdeveloped, too, just as you are. Today, we are building Bhilais throughout Asia.

Since Khrushchev's 1955 tour of India, Moscow's friendship with New Delhi has blossomed, and Russia has shown repeatedly that it values India's affection very highly. At a nominal charge —sometimes at no charge at all—thousands of Indian technicians have been trained in Russian factories and schools, and cultural delegations have been swapped with increasing frequency. Moscow has been liberal in support of India's neutralism. In turn, Soviet propaganda has had a chance to flood India, bringing reflected respectability to its Communist Party, which, in February, 1957, parlayed respectability into power. In the hot, dusty streets of Cochin, in Kerala, I witnessed a historic Communist triumph—historic, because it was the first time that a Communist Party had ever been swept into power legally in a major election. Communist slogans were whitewashed on clay huts, and the symbol of a hammer-and-sickle was carved into many peasant bullock wagons.

Communism became more acceptable in India, as Nehru continued to praise Russia's "strides" toward "democracy." In November, 1956, it took the Indian Prime Minister almost three weeks to denounce the Soviet suppression of the Hungarian Revolution—much to the disgust of many Indian intellectuals. It took Nehru only one day to condemn the British, French, and Israeli assault against Egypt.

To many veteran observers in New Delhi, this time difference was eloquent proof that Russia and India had cultivated a firm diplomatic friendship.

* * *

In early August, 1959, the same observers were beginning to question the firmness of India's friendship with China. "Until last year," one of them commented, "I thought that we were getting on very well with the Chinese. Then, with the news of the communes, we sensed a great storm in China. We did not know exactly what was going to happen, but we hoped that our relations with China would not be harmed."

Actually, Indian intellectuals had good reason for optimism. Ever since October, 1949, when Mao Tse-tung took power on the Chinese mainland, Prime Minister Nehru has seized every opportunity to applaud Peking and to support its "legitimate interests" in the United Nations, and he could rightfully have expected Mao to cherish the close relationship that had developed between Delhi and Peking. After all, India was one of the first nations to extend diplomatic recognition to the Chinese Communist regime. And, in October, 1950, when Mao ordered the Red Army to occupy Tibet, Nehru agreed somewhat reluctantly that Tibet fell "within the Chinese sphere of influence," but he added that he did not think Peking had to "invade" Tibet. Nevertheless, four years later, he recognized Tibet as an "integral part of China."

In November, 1950, when Mao ordered the Red Army across the Yalu River, Nehru instructed the Indian delegate to the United Nations, Sir Benegal Rau, to sponsor a resolution in the General Assembly proposing the establishment of a committee to explore the possibility of a cease-fire. Peking quickly rejected a cease-fire until "all foreign forces," meaning the United States, withdrew from Korea. Mao's negativism chilled the General Assembly, but Sir Benegal Rau continued his efforts to mediate China's quarrel with the United Nations. In effect, India became Peking's attorney before the bar of world public opinion.

Delhi's ambassador to Peking discussed the Korean "police action" with Chou En-lai, and he informed Sir Benegal that China's rejection of the cease-fire proposal was not absolute. The United States, stoutly committed to the defense of South Korea and to the maintenance of a strong anti-Peking position, demanded that China withdraw from North Korea. China refused. The United States then proposed that the General Assembly condemn China as an "aggressor" in Korea. In firm defense, India contended that China was not an "aggressor" and that the United States should adopt a more "accommodating" attitude toward China's "interests" and "susceptibilities."

Despite India's efforts, China was condemned.

A few months later, in May, 1951, the General Assembly considered another United States proposal—that the United Nations should surround the Chinese mainland with an embargo on all military and strategic materials. The proposal was adopted 47 to 0. India abstained.

Until an acceptable cease-fire agreement was reached in 1953, India continued to serve as Peking's spokesman in the United Nations—a far more effective spokesman than the Soviet Union, because India was respected and neutral.

In June, 1954, the bonds of China's diplomatic isolation were broken. Chou En-lai agreed to discuss the future of Indo-China at an international gathering in Geneva. On his way back to Peking, he stopped in New Delhi, where he met Nehru. This meeting clearly established them as the towering spokesmen of Asia, and it further strengthened Indian-Chinese relations.

First, they agreed that peace was important for backward Asia, and they formulated the doctrine of *Panchshila*—the five principles of mutual respect, nonaggression, noninterference, recognition of equality, and peaceful coexistence that have become the ideological backbone of Asian diplomatic neutralism. Both leaders acknowledged the economic, political, and social differences between India and China, but they maintained that these differences need not injure a friendship that was already two thousand years old. (Cynical observers noted that India and China had had "good relations" for two thousand years because, during this time, they never had anything to do with each other.)

Second, Chou invited Nehru to visit Peking, and Nehru accepted. In October, 1954, Nehru attended the celebration of the fifth anniversary of the Chinese People's Republic. Before klieg lights and whirring cameras, Chou embraced Nehru and the Dalai Lama—a symbolic ratification of India's approval of China's control over Tibet.

In April, 1955, Nehru met Chou once again—in the clean, cool town of Bandung, in West Java. Twenty-nine Asian and African nations, excluding Israel, Nationalist China, and the Soviet Union, praised the principles of *Panchshila,* attacked atomic and hydrogen tests, criticized colonialism, and supported movements for national independence. A third force was born, in which Nehru and Chou emerged as leading figures.

Chou visited New Delhi again in late December, 1956, and in mid-January, 1957. On both occasions, he reiterated Peking's support of *Panchshila,* attacked "great-power chauvinism," and soothed Asia about Russia's suppression of the Hungarian Revolution. China, he said, would never use its force to impose a political solution anywhere in Asia. Nehru must have remembered Tibet, but he did not say a word. Apparently, he was convinced that China was too preoccupied with "economic reconstruction" to bother with external expansion.

By late 1958, Indian intellectuals, possibly Nehru himself, were beginning to question this hypothesis. Suddenly, as Mao launched his commune drive, the Indians sensed a stiffened Chinese attitude —on trade, on manners, on diplomacy, and on cartography.

* * *

"The Chinese wanted to drive us out of our traditional markets in Southeast Asia." The speaker was an Indian businessman, and he was angry. "For years we have tried to get on with the Chinese. Now I am not so sure we can. Recently, in Kuala Lumpur, the Chinese began to undersell us. They flooded the market with cheap bicycles and silks. They knew they would be hurting us, but they did not care."

Another Indian businessman had a similar complaint. "The Chinese," he said, "have even forced us out of the Himalayan trade. In 1958 they announced, without explanation, that we could no longer maintain offices in Lhasa—or even along Tibet's borders with Bhutan and Sikkim. So we have lost yet another valuable source of revenue."

Indian officials, returning from China, were equally disturbed by Peking's diplomatic behavior. They felt that Chinese officials had deliberately snubbed them. One well-known Delhi professor described Peking's attitude toward India as one of "absolute contempt."

In Delhi, the Chinese conferred with Indian officials—but only on matters of business. Otherwise, they kept their distance. The

Chinese Communist Embassy reduced its social activities to a bare minimum, and Peking officials even refused to attend Ceylonese parties. The Ceylonese had been their closest confreres.

Why? Indians were frankly puzzled.

In July, 1958, the Chinese provided an important clue. In *China Pictorial,* Peking's version of *Life,* they published a map of the Sino-Indian border that brazenly claimed about 40,000 square miles of Indian territory. The claim had been made before —but never in a mass magazine. The Indians suspected trouble.

Madame Lakshmi Menon, Deputy Minister for External Affairs, fired a strong note of protest to Peking. The Chinese retorted in vague terms. "The map has been drawn," they said, "on the basis of agreements reached before the Communists took power."

Nehru responded: "The Chinese Communist Government have revised many things since they took over power from Marshal Chiang Kai-shek. But they have not revised Chiang's maps of China yet." Peking did not answer.

In September, 1958, the Chinese accused the Indians of "intruding" into Sinkiang—near Tahungliutan, a village along the Tibet-Sinkiang highway. The Indians denied the accusation.

In October, 1958, Indian border guards discovered that the Chinese had constructed part of this highway across Aksai Chin, the northeastern corner of Ladakh. Delhi protested. Again, Peking did not answer.

These incidents were not publicized, but they had important repercussions. First, Nehru postponed a scheduled visit to Lhasa. His explanation was that he had heard that eastern Tibet was in revolt. Instead, he journeyed to the hermit kingdom of Bhutan, where he offered the maharaja economic help. The maharaja was reportedly reluctant to accept India's help, but he did agree to permit India, Bhutan's protector, to build a highway from Bhutan to Sikkim through India. The highway, a quarter of which had been completed by August, 1959, would facilitate trade between India's tiny protectorates—without either of them having to ask Tibet for permission to cut through Yatung, a trading center along the existing overland pass between Bhutan and Sikkim.

Second, Nehru instructed his ambassador in Katmandu to ex-

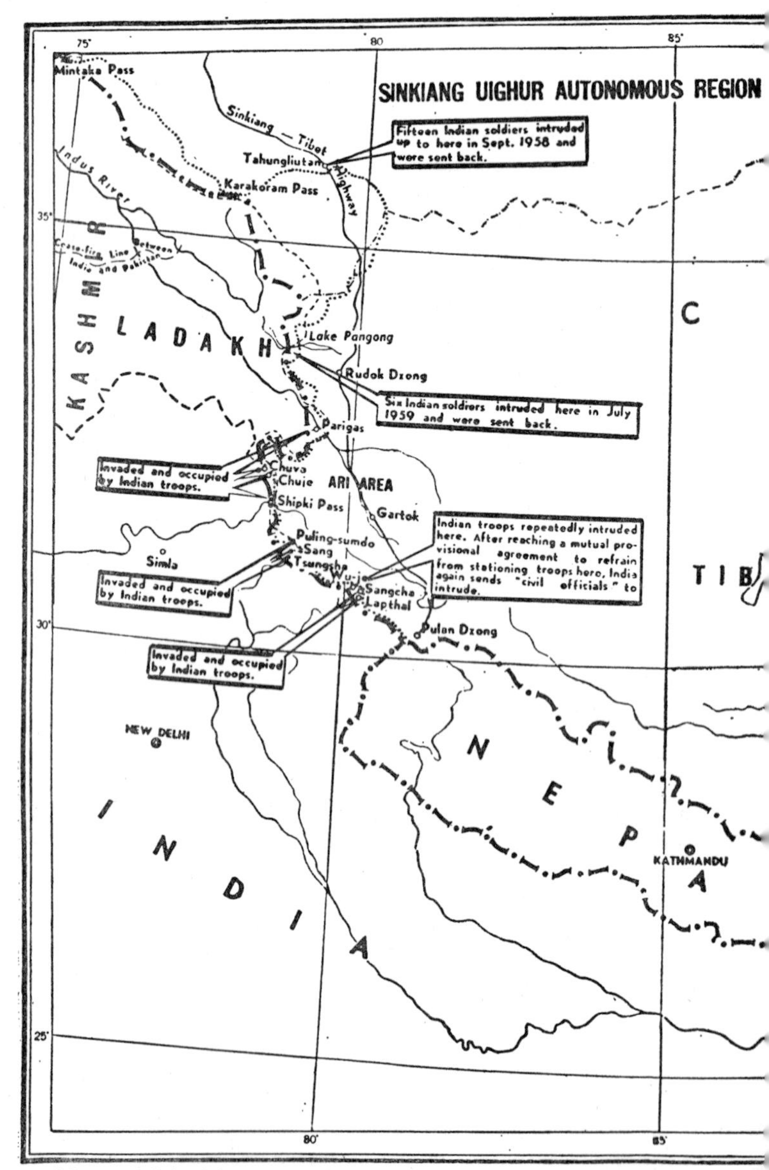

Map published in connection with the China-India boundary questi
in the English-language propaganda magazine *China Reconstructs* (F
king), 1959. While blandly annexing big areas of Indian territory a

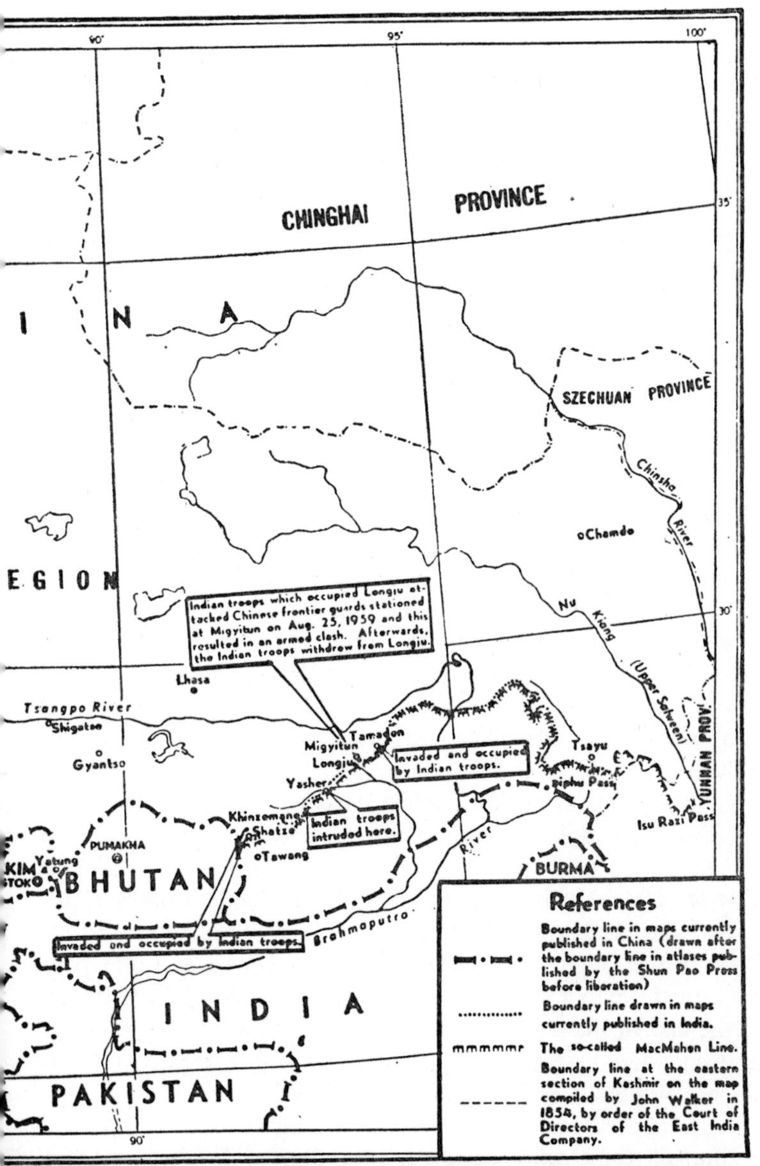

arging India with aggressions, the map ignores actions by Chinese rces, and Indian protests. (*Reproduced courtesy of* East Europe *magine*)

plore the possibility of a tighter union between Nepal and India. At the same time, he sent gentle feelers toward Pakistan about the feasibility of a diplomatic rapprochement between Karachi and Delhi, after a decade of open hostility.

Finally, Nehru asked his cartographic experts to examine the background of the Sino-Indian border dispute in Ladakh and in the Northeast Frontier—the two areas where he expected trouble if the unrest in Tibet should erupt into open revolt.

* * *

Ladakh: India meets Russia and China in northern Jammu and Kashmir—an ancient, barren wedge of Buddhist-Hindu culture that history has thrust into Central Asia. For over a thousand years this remote, mountainous enclave was the crossroads of Asia. Through its dangerous passes Buddhism journeyed to China, pausing in Tibet and Burma; in its dusty market places merchants bartered the silks of Peking for the rugs of Persia.

In the seventh century Hsuan Tsang, a Chinese pilgrim, wandered through Kashmir. He marveled at the grandeur of Buddhist shrines and the asceticism of Hindu monks. Later in the century, T'ang ambitions drove Chinese armies across the plains of Sinkiang to the foothills of the Pamirs.

K. P. S. Menon, India's distinguished ambassador to Moscow, described this moment in Chinese military history. "The T'ang Emperors," he said, "performed the remarkable feat of sending an army of 100,000 men, which marched up the Pamirs from Kashgar, crossed the Barkot Pass (15,400 feet) into Yasin, occupied the whole of the Gilgit and Hunza valley, then known as Little Polu, and turned it into a military district with a garrison of 10,000 men. By the end of the eighth century, Chinese authority in this region declined—and indeed, disappeared forever; but the tradition of Chinese dominion over Kanjut has survived."

Four hundred years later, Kashmir was again invaded, this time by Mongol troops who scaled the steep face of the Pamirs. Occasionally, too, nomadic tribesmen from Tibet scourged Ladakh, an eastern province of Kashmir that was ruled by *gumpas,* Buddhist monasteries. In fact, for a time, Ladakh was incorporated into

Tibet; and, under Lhasa's supervision, Ladakh absorbed Tibet's culture, trade, and religion.

In the fifteenth century Ladakh became independent, but its new rulers still recognized the Dalai Lama as their suzerain. Commerce continued to flourish. From China came silk and rice; from Tibet came salt, tea, butter, and wool; from Central Asia came exotic rugs. Then, in the sixteenth century, Kashmir suddenly lost its strategic significance as a hub of Asian trade. Maritime Europe had discovered a new route to the Orient—around the Cape of Good Hope. The overland trails through Central Asia became romantic memories. As commerce died, Kashmir sank into splendid stagnation; and for three hundred years Kashmir, composed of Ladakh, Baltistan, Gilgit, Nagar, and Hunza, slept like a contented vacuum between Russia, China, and India.

In the last century these three giants began to eye Kashmir. China, weak and corrupt, still proclaimed its historic suzerainty over Tibet and Sinkiang, Kashmir's neighbor. Czarist Russia, aggressive and expansionist, swept through Central Asia, and Britain, alarmed by Moscow's dreams, ordered its lancers into Kashmir. The vacuum had to be filled. In 1840 Zorawar Singh, an outstanding Indian soldier, conquered Ladakh, Baltistan, and Gilgit, and in 1846 Gulab Singh, his leader, was invested by London with supreme power over Jammu and Kashmir. Quickly, Singh fixed Kashmir's borders with Tibet. Lhasa agreed, but Peking, Lhasa's master, did not. Convulsed in internal disorder, Peking simply could not adjust to the modern, "barbarian" concept of borders. China believed it was the "middle kingdom," surrounded by "tributary states." If Tibet was a tributary of China, and Ladakh a tributary of Tibet, then Ladakh was also a tributary of China.

This is the basis of the Chinese claim to about 8,000 square miles of Ladakh. So, in February, 1959, Nehru knew why a group of Indian officers, skiing in Ladakh's snow-capped mountains, was arrested. Peking said they had violated the "borders" of China.

Northeast Frontier: "Pahar" is a big word in Hindu mythology, for "pahar" means "mountain." In India, there is only one "pahar" —the Himalayas, "the whitest, snowiest, and iciest range" in the world. "The crown of India," Nehru called it.

To Indians, the Himalayas are more than a geographic expression; they symbolize the highest aspirations of man. Even the illiterate peasant in Bangalore knows the "pahar," for, in India, there is an old saying: "We all have a desire to see the Himalayas at least once in our lives, so we can look upon the face of our creator."

From the dawn of Indian history, the Himalayas have carved their lofty imprint into Hindu psychology. Indian merchants have traded with Tibet for several thousand years, and the legends of Lhasa have climbed into the mountains of Nepal, Sikkim, and Bhutan—India's "buffers" against China. In the thriving trading towns, perched on the Himalayan crests, the mysteries of Tibetan life intrigued Nepalese priests, and Lamaism was incorporated into the faith. Intermarriages were frequent, and, until recently, the tribesmen of the Northeast Frontier, or of Bhutan or Sikkim, wandered through the passes between Tibet and India as nonchalantly as the donkeys.

When the British ruled India, they became concerned about the Himalayas. They realized that this mighty massif was undefended and undefined, and, periodically, the Tibetans did invade the hermit kingdoms of Sikkim and Bhutan; sometimes the Tibetans even ravaged parts of India. In 1887, for example, the Tibetans drove into Sikkim, occupied Gangtok, its capital, and then moved toward India. In 1888 the British helped the Indians drive the Tibetans back across the border.

Still, the issue was not pressing, and the British waited until 1914 to fix the border between their Northeast Frontier and Tibet—a border that ran over 850 miles of uncharted Himalayan peaks from Bhutan to Burma. The demarcation was agreed upon at Simla, a mountain resort in northeast India. Sir Arthur Henry McMahon represented Britain in a tripartite conference with China and Tibet. The border—the McMahon Line—was named after Sir Arthur. Britain formally ratified the agreement; so did Tibet; China merely initialed it.

For the next few decades, Indian and British diplomats realized that the Chinese were dissatisfied with the McMahon Line. Both Nationalist and Communist maps ignored the line, incorporating about 32,000 miles of Indian territory into Tibet. Chinese intellectuals, Nationalists and Communists alike, filled political brochures with "irredenta" promises. Moreover, Indian scholars, conscious of their border history, knew that Sikkim and Bhutan could easily be Tibetanized—if Tibet were modernized and militarized.

Dr. K. M. Panikkar, diplomat, scholar, and politician, once wrote: "Why it [the Himalaya] has so far not been penetrated for an attack on the Indian plains is not because there are no passes which open out to India, but because the Tibetan plateau was never in the past organized as a military state. . . . The fact that the Chinese were unable in the past to organize a strong military area in Tibet should not blind us to such possibilities in the future. It may not be a danger in the immediate present, but there is no doubt that an organized modern state will alter the character of the Himalayan problem."

When the Chinese Communists invaded Tibet in 1950, Nehru conceded that Tibet fell "within the Chinese sphere of influence"; but he could not conceal his anxiety. On November 20, 1950, Nehru told the Indian Parliament that India would protect Nepal, Sikkim, and Bhutan; then he added that the McMahon Line "is our boundary, map or no map. We will not allow anyone to come across that boundary."

* * *

The Tibetan revolt in March, 1959 heightened the Panikkar analysis. From a scholarly hypothesis, the border dilemma was alchemized into a national threat. On March 17, 1959, when the Dalai Lama slipped into India, the Peking press opened a vicious assault against Delhi. "For a while," an Indian journalist recalled, "the Chinese sounded the way they did in 1949, when they called Nehru 'the running dog of American imperialism.' *Panchshila* was discarded as an old-fashioned doctrine, and the Chinese got tough all over Asia—not only here."

The Chinese also turned the border dispute—dormant for half a century—into an international crisis. Chou En-lai returned to his history texts. The McMahon Line, he said, was the "product of British aggression against Tibet." Surely, India could not "reasonably" expect "liberated" China to accept Sir Arthur's conception of the Tibetan-Indian border.

Nehru's retort was a curious mixture of diplomatic restraint and undiplomatic sarcasm. "There is nothing to indicate," he said, "that the Tibetan authorities were in any way dissatisfied with the agreed boundary. Moreover, although the Chinese plenipotentiary at the Conference objected to the boundaries between Inner and Outer Tibet, there is no mention of any Chinese reservation in respect to the Indian-Tibet frontier during the discussions or at any time of their initialing of the Convention." Nehru then added another thought: he said that during Chou En-lai's journey to New Delhi in January, 1957, he, Nehru, had been assured that China accepted the McMahon Line. It was "disappointing," Nehru remarked, that Peking had apparently changed its mind.

By August, 1959, New Delhi appeared frightened—even to a newcomer. Before the border dispute had burst into world headlines, it was already the major topic of conversation in Indian offices and parlors.

"They've already booted us out of Tibet," a businessman lamented. "Hundreds of thousands of rupees—lost."

"They've even banned Indian money from Lhasa," another businessman cried.

"They've begun to move heavy artillery toward the border," an official exclaimed.

"They've started to occupy Indian territory—not only in the Northeast Frontier but also in Ladakh," a diplomat gasped.

Everyone knew who "they" were, apparently—even the Russians. One evening, during a reception, a Soviet diplomat cornered two Indian journalists. "We know how you must feel about *them,*" he confided, "but don't worry. You may not be able to get along with them, but you can get along with us. We're two completely different kinds of Communists—we and they." The Soviet official added that Moscow felt the time had come to improve Indian-Russian relations "in a big way."

"How?" one of the journalists asked.

The Russian made two promises. First, he said, the Soviet Union would soon extend a major economic loan to India—"over $300,-

000,000." Second, Moscow would redraw its Asian maps according to Indian specifications. Since 1949 the Russians had followed the Chinese example.

Moscow seems to have kept both promises. A major credit was formally granted in February, 1960, and at least one new Soviet map defines the Tibetan-Indian border with a dot-dash line, indicating a move toward India's position.

But the Russians did not stop at political concessions. They became the social butterflies of Delhi during the summer of 1959. "They're throwing as many parties as the Americans," an Indian said. "This peaceful competition in cocktails is wonderful. No objections—none at all."

As Indian sentiment against China mounted—students stoned the Peking Embassy and newspapers shouted for "retaliation," a Dullesian word in Delhi—the Russians made another pitch for Indian affection. They opened an impressive "cultural" office in downtown Delhi—a kind of Russian USIS—where Indians were invited to read Soviet and Hindu literature in any of five languages, or to see Disneyish cartoons free of charge.

Meanwhile, *Pravda* drummed a steady propaganda beat: India and Russia have always been good friends, and, China notwithstanding, they will always remain good friends. Indeed, during the heat of the Tibetan revolt, the Soviet press consistently softpedaled the Indian-Chinese rift—so effectively, in fact, that the rift appeared to be a "lovers' quarrel" and the revolt a "minor uprising of feudal, reactionary landlords." Undisturbed by a fact, when a national policy is involved, *Pravda* simply ignored the mass character of the Tibetan rebellion.

* * *

The obvious differences between Russian and Chinese policy toward India raised a basic question about the Moscow-Peking alliance: Were Russia's smiles and China's frowns really two faces of a well-integrated Communist policy, or were they manifestations of two independent foreign policies? I asked India's experts.

"The key to the question," an Indian diplomat with Moscow and Peking experience suggested, "is the degree of co-ordination between Russia and China on international problems. I believe that these two Communist countries do not agree on a unified policy toward India. I would even go further: I think they tried, but they found they could not agree."

"Why not?"

"Well," he began, filling a British pipe with American tobacco, "there are two major hypotheses—not only in India, but in the West, too. The first might be called the 'phases' explanation—that is, Russia is in an advanced industrial phase of development and therefore wants peace, and China is in a primitive phase of development and therefore feeds on tension. The second hypothesis is concerned more with *Realpolitik* than with theory. China feels that it has a few unresolved territorial disputes with the United States, such as Formosa, which must be settled before it can even dream of getting on with Washington. And, naturally, China has produced the appropriate ideological rationalizations. You know—the United States is a 'decaying capitalist power,' a 'paper tiger' that will fight to the last gasp any peaceful rapprochement between the socialist and capitalist camps.

"But the Russians disagree. They feel—especially Khrushchev—that the United States will not fight, particularly now that it sees the increasing might and rocket power of the Soviet system. Moreover, mind you, Russia does not have any outstanding territorial problems—except that of Berlin, which may actually be more of a diplomatic tool for negotiation than a burning issue in itself."

"Which hypothesis do you buy?" I asked.

"A little bit of both," he answered smilingly. "After all, what would you expect from a neutral?"

Other diplomats, both Indian and foreign, elaborated on both hypotheses, some offering illustrative insights into a particularly tricky question. For example, a British official believed that the apparent divergencies between Russian and Chinese policy could be traced to a bitter struggle for power within the Chinese Communist Party—a struggle that pivoted on the crucial problem of how much Soviet assistance China needed to industrialize in the shortest possible time.

According to this official, who has had a long career in Asia,

Mao represents a hard "China-first" position. He is a devout Communist, but he does not fancy too chummy a relationship with Moscow. And he does not think China really needs Russia as much as Russia believes. Ranged against Mao is Liu Shao-chi, China's Number Two man, portrayed as a "Russia-firster," a Communist who would be willing to bend Chinese interests to fit the Soviet hold. This struggle between Liu and Mao reportedly became more acute after August, 1958, when Mao got his way and launched the commune program against Liu's wishes. Liu's faction was said to have staged a comeback during the fall of 1958, when China admitted the shortcomings of the communes and Mao stepped down as President of the Republic. Since then, Mao was pictured as having regained some of his former strength.

To my mind, the specific features of the "power struggle" may be questionable, but the existence of a struggle may prove to be one of the important explanations for the contradictions that have arisen in the alliance.

Most of the diplomats sought the key to Chinese foreign policy elsewhere. For example, they believed that China really did not want to sour relations with India—certainly not over Tibet. "China's hand was forced; even we can see that," an Indian said. "Ever since 1956, China has been trying to suppress a revolt of Tibetan tribesmen. Unfortunately, China couldn't suppress the revolt, which got worse, until, in early 1959, it spread throughout the country, forcing the Dalai Lama to seek asylum in India. That was the straw that broke the camel's back. That made China act as belligerently toward us as she did."

"Is that the only reason?"

"I believe so. But, unfortunately, soon afterward, the Chinese began to see that the revolt gave them a golden opportunity to 'solve' the whole Tibetan problem. The Tibetans, you know, are a rather plucky people who have lived in the shadow of Chinese domination for centuries. In 1950, when the Chinese invaded Tibet, they tried to overhaul the social and economic structure of Tibetan society. But they couldn't. They tried again in 1954—and again they failed. In 1956, during the antichauvinism campaign, they apparently decided to withdraw their Chinese cadres and hope in time to persuade the Dalai Lama to agree to Chinese reform.

"But the Khamba tribesmen of eastern Tibet wanted to rid Tibet of Chinese influence. And they staged numerous raids on Chinese outposts—many of them quite successful raids. In March, angry nomadic tribesmen arrived in Lhasa to celebrate the Tibetan New Year. They did not like the way the Chinese had been curtailing the Dalai Lama's authority, and skirmishes broke out on the outskirts of town. Soon these clashes got out of hand, and the revolt against the Chinese spread throughout Tibet. The Chinese were forced to bring in reinforcements—just as they were forced to respond viciously when India granted the Dalai Lama sanctuary.

"The rebellion, however, did give them the chance, finally, to crush Tibetan resistance to Chinese authority. And when the shooting stops, the Chinese will be in a good position to solve the whole problem of Tibet. I think Mao realizes this—and I also think he values this opportunity more than he does Indian friendship."

"What does this opportunity mean for India?"

"As I see it," he continued, "it means that we now have to live under the constant threat that the Chinese may try to Tibetanize our protectorates of Sikkim, Bhutan, and Nepal. And also, I might add, Ladakh, a large part of which they consider to be theirs. This threat will force us, I fear, to arm more than we would like to, but it may be a good thing, too. It may have opened Nehru's eyes to the danger that many of us feel China represents."

"What about Russia?"

"There is no threat from Russia."

This diplomat may have been right, especially about Nehru. On August 26th, when Chinese troops occupied Longju, an Indian outpost in the Northeast Frontier, Nehru said that although he saw a desire for peace in Russia he did not see the same desire in Communist China. He described Moscow as "satisfied territorially," but he indicated that the Chinese had not yet "got over their first flush of revolutionary mentality." A few months later, after Chinese troops moved into Ladakh, Nehru said: "I doubt that there is any country that cares more for peace than the Soviet Union. I doubt that there is any country that cares less for peace than China." The Peking leaders, he continued, know very little about the outside world; so they count their claims against it—and sit at home, and brood.

While it is doubtful that there is no other country in the world that "cares more for peace than the Soviet Union," it appears likely that Moscow is delighted to pose as India's "eternal friend," even if this pose distresses the Chinese. At a cocktail party in Moscow, Khrushchev himself described the Indian-Chinese border dispute as "incomprehensible," since "nobody lives in those mountains." He also expressed the hope that India and China would settle their differences peacefully. This fence-sitting must have upset the Chinese, who could reasonably have expected the Russians to support them. Instead, Moscow "hoped" for a "peaceful" settlement.

No, the experts seemed to agree, there was no co-ordination between Moscow and Peking on the Indian border dispute—or, for that matter, on an integrated policy toward Asia. "It's no easy topic you're pursuing," an Indian friend commiserated; "it has had all of us baffled—even the Indian Communists, poor fellows!"

* * *

The Indian Communists were indeed "poor fellows."

They have had to develop in the shadow of two towering, magnetic figures who have dominated India's political and social life: Gandhi and Nehru. They never could cope with Gandhi's campaign of nonviolence, which ran counter to a basic Marxist precept of class war, and they never could understand Nehru's strict neutralism, which frustrated their Moscow inclinations. Thus, their leaders constantly sought to cloak their ideological vacillation and psychological insecurity with a blind, clumsy allegiance to Moscow.

In 1939, when Stalin signed his pact with Hitler, the Indian Communist Party opened a strong attack against "imperialist war." In 1941, when Hitler betrayed Stalin, the "imperialist war" was transformed overnight into a "liberation war"; and the Indian Communist Party swung its weight behind Russia so blatantly that the Congress Party began to suspect that its prime motivation was ideological loyalty rather than Indian patriotism. In fact, Congress leaders chided the Communists on their "international nationalism."

After the war, as Gandhi and Nehru led India to independence, the Indian Communists made a major effort to gain influence in the trade unions. They failed, and their national prestige plummeted. But, through patient propagandizing, Soviet solicitude, and clever connivance, the Indian Communists managed to attract a sizable vote in the general elections of 1951–1952. For the next five years they basked in the reflected warmth of Nehru's love affair with China, and, in the general elections of 1957, they gained broad popular support in Kerala, West Bengal, and Andhra—enough in Kerala to take power. They also picked up thirty seats in the Lok Sabha (India's Lower House of Parliament) and sufficient self-confidence to voice their opinion on important issues of domestic and foreign policy.

By August, 1959, the Indian Communist Party was again in trouble. President Rajendra Prasad had just ousted E. M. S. Namboodiripad's Communist government in Kerala for "subverting" the Indian Constitution, and the Communists had brazenly supported the Chinese during the Tibetan uprising. When Peking accused Delhi of "inspiring" the revolt, the Indian Communist Party foolishly supported China. In the Lok Sabha, Indian Communists admitted that "the peoples' Government of China, in all sincerity, has asked us to look into this matter." "How?" the Lok Sabha demanded. Gradually, the link between the Indian Communist Party and Peking was uncovered.

Apparently, a leading member of the Central Committee of the Indian CP received an urgent message from the Chinese Embassy in New Delhi after the Dalai Lama escaped into India. Peking wanted him to serve as China's spokesman in the Lok Sabha; he agreed.

This infuriated India. The Election Commissioner was petitioned to cancel the Communist Party's accreditation as a national party. Nehru angrily stated that the "Communists cease to be Indians, having shown a total absence of feelings of decency and nationality." University students stoned the Chinese Embassy and denounced Indian Communism.

In this environment, I had a long talk with one of the leaders of the Indian Communist Party, a dark, mustached man in dhoti, leggings, and a white shirt, who did not want his name disclosed. We discussed Indian Communism in a mutual friend's office. "X" spoke in Churchillian prose. An Oxford scholar who worships Marx, he referred frequently to Cromwell, Robespierre, and Lenin. Leaning back in a straight, wooden chair, he spoke with remarkable candor. "The Indian Communist Party is very weak, very weak indeed. After we won power in Kerala, we thought we had a good chance to extend our influence to West Bengal and Andhra. Now, in the wake of the Tibetan revolt, we have not only lost power in Kerala; we have also lost influence throughout the country. Tibet has set us back ten years."

He got up from his chair. Nervously, he cracked his knuckles, and began to pace. "We know that we lack popular support. Therefore we must follow a program of sane opposition. We call Nehru 'progressive'; there are Chinese who call him 'reactionary.' We also follow the general outlines of his domestic program: no violence, no passive resistance. Generally speaking, we even support his foreign policy."

"Your support of the Chinese during the Tibetan uprising wasn't exactly 'sane opposition,' was it?"

"That," he exclaimed, pointing a finger at me for emphasis, "was probably a mistake, for the Party has been split on that question ever since. In Bombay, S. A. Dange, and in Kerala, E. M. S. Namboodiripad feel that we should support India and the McMahon Line. Tactically, they believe support makes more sense. I tend to agree. But, here in Delhi, Ajoy Ghosh and others seem to support the Chinese. They think that we would be betraying the cause of Communism if we behaved like the German Social-Democrats in 1914.

"Tibet," he continued, "has broken the discipline of our Party, because now we are under two great pressures. We want to improve our stature in India. Naturally. We want to come to power

—preferably through peaceful means. But we also want to remain faithful to the world Communist movement. And this presents a grave dilemma. I am beginning to question whether these two desires can be reconciled."

Was it possible that this dilemma was deepened by the emergence of Peking as an alternate focus of Marxist power?

Yes, "X" said, that was possible.

"Take the communes, for example. At first we decided to say nothing, although we studied this development with intense interest. After a while we agreed to publish only reprints of the official Chinese version—with no comment. This was difficult. Here was Mao, the leading Marxist theorist, propounding a new dogma which might, after all, be applicable in India, though I doubt it. And here was Khrushchev implicitly attacking the dogma as 'old-fashioned.' Since our allegiance is closer to Moscow than to Peking, we came to believe, officially, that the communes represent only a phase of economic development."

Nothing more than that?

"No, just a phase. The communes are too radical a departure from traditional Marxist lines of development. Soon, the Chinese will abandon them."

At that moment "X" darted to the door and swung it open. No one was there. He turned toward me and smiled sheepishly. He closed the door. "I guess I am a little nervous," he conceded.

"Last fall," he continued, "Yudin, the Russian ambassador in Peking, told our ambassador that Moscow would not comment officially about the communes until it had had a chance to see how they would develop. And he indicated that the Chinese had told them very little about the communes. So, since the Russians were not going to comment, we decided we had better not comment either."

Was there any conflict in the Indian CP between the Moscow and Peking brands of Communism?

"Not really. I think most of us agree that the Russian model is more appropriate for India."

Was there any feeling that Peking was beginning to steal Moscow's ideological thunder?

"Ye-es," he began hesitatingly, "I think so. I was in China in 1956, and I could feel the country alive with ideological excitement."

Didn't this represent a challenge to Moscow?

"Definitely. These days the challenge comes from the East—for Russia as well as for the West. For example, the Indian Communists who attended the twenty-first Congress of the Soviet Communist Party in Moscow were very disappointed by Khrushchev's pep talk. They felt he tried to highlight his advanced industry and technology—as though this were a substitute for ideology. But it is not, and I think Khrushchev knows this."

"Then why don't you side with China rather than with Russia?"

"Because we are Indians."

Apparently, in the underdeveloped areas of the world, nationalism still involves a deeper commitment that any ideology. His *nation* was confronted by a military threat from China; his *ideology* thus became secondary.

CHAPTER NINE Bangkok

SOUTHEAST ASIA—HOT, JUNGLED, TEEMING, RICH, NATIONALISTIC, and pivotal; eleven different governments—eight of them born in war, baptized by passion; one of them convulsed in Communist transformation; another balanced nervously between imperial dominion and self-rule; one an oil-spouting colonial relic; a variety of political theories—democracy, communism, autocracy, monarchy, dictatorship, and medicine-manism; almost 190,000,000 people—brown, tan, and yellow worshipers of idols, Buddha, Mohammed, Christ, Tao, and the sun; eye-catching in grass skirts, batik dresses, silk shirts, Brooks Brothers slacks, or nothing; and battlers for atomic prosperity and national dignity; contrasts in beauty and comfort—cities as breath-taking as Bangkok and as oppressive as Jakarta; islands as congested as Singapore and as barren as Borneo; lands as advanced as Thailand and as primitive as Sarawak. Southeast Asia—a stunning study in diversity, and an attractive new prize.

For this colorful collection of equatorial jungles and islands, World War Two was a historic moment. The old colonial ties binding Asia to Europe were cut by the disruption of war and the excitement of nationalism. Japan, hungry for conquest, rushed down the Malayan Peninsula toward the natural wealth of Indonesia. Patriotic leaders, such as Rangoon's Ba Maw and Jakarta's Sukarno, sensitive about race, anxious for independence, welcomed the rising sun. They tried to co-operate with the Japanese —for a time, successfully. They thought Tokyo would help them break the shackles of European domination, but they soon discovered that the Japanese had merely substituted yellow imperialism for white colonialism. The nationalists organized rebel bands, sabotaged Japanese supply lines, and dreamed of independence.

After the war the nationalists demanded their independence. Britain and the Netherlands, exhausted by the war, revolted by tyranny, gradually granted independence to Burma, Malaya, and Indonesia. France, still dreaming of *grandeur,* fought bitterly for Indo-China, but in 1954 she finally conceded defeat. The United States kept its word and freed the Philippines. Infants in a world of giants, the new nations were led by men who had had little experience with the responsibilities of government—though all were obsessed by a bright vision of independence and modernity.

In the postwar devastation and economic confusion of Southeast Asia, the Communists found a broad target for propaganda and subversion. They were heartened by Mao Tse-tung's victories over Chiang Kai-shek and by Stalin's successes in eastern Europe. As the Sukarnos treasured their independence, the Communists plotted their coups.

They had their instructions. In February, 1948, at the Communist Congress at Calcutta, the Soviet delegates had voiced Stalin's wish, and Stalin's wish was their command. Armed insurrection!

The Communists staged a bloody uprising against the British in Malaya; and although the uprising did not produce a Communist victory, it did touch off a guerilla war that still rages in the Malayan jungles. In Medan, Indonesia, the Communists tried to seize power, but Sukarno crushed them. In Burma, Thailand, and Indo-China there were more Communist-inspired revolts. Although none of these was immediately successful, they did set the stage for five years of political instability and economic turmoil throughout Southeast Asia. After Mao's victory in China, they proved conclusively that the Communists considered this region fair game. The only problem appeared to be tactical: *How* would the Communists take power? They never doubted that they would!

* * *

It is the considered opinion of experts—from New Delhi to Hong Kong—that Stalin's death marked a major turning point in Communist tactics in Southeast Asia.

Before 1953 Moscow and Peking seemed to be closely co-ordinated in their policy toward the newly independent nations of Southeast Asia. Rebel Communist bands, operating just across China's southern borders, were armed, supported, and inspired by Peking; legal propaganda fronts, operating in Rangoon, Bangkok, and Jakarta, were supported by Moscow. Their goal was to attract the new nations to Communism by applauding Asian nationalism and denouncing Caucasian colonialism.

When Stalin died, Moscow and Peking both realized that their insurrectionist tactic had not paid handsome dividends. Ho Chi-Minh had done well in North Vietnam, humiliating the French and establishing a Communist government; but Vietminh somehow did not seem like sufficient reward. Moreover, Burma and Thailand, among others, had outlawed the Communist Party, which had come to be regarded by local nationalists as "foreign." This action followed Mao's deep involvement in the Korean War—an involvement that kindled old Asian fears of Chinese expansionism and touched off a rash of anti-Communist acts throughout the area. In September, 1954, the Southeast Asia Treaty Organization was created as a defensive bulwark against the possibility of future Communist aggression. The membership consisted of the United States, Britain, France, Australia, New Zealand, Thailand, Pakistan, and the Philippines. A special protocol brought South Vietnam, Laos, and Cambodia behind the SEATO shield.

A change in Communist tactics seemed dictated, and the catalyst of change emerged in the short, stubby figure of Nikita Khrushchev. He journeyed to Peking in October, 1954. There, in the Chinese capital, an agreement was apparently reached to ditch insurrection in favor of limited co-operation. The Communist parties of Southeast Asia—those that remained legal—were ordered to behave like other political parties. They were to continue to try to take power—but by legal means. If they were offered an opportunity to join a "united front," they were to take it and say "Thank you." They were also instructed to sing the praises of their "bourgeois nationalist" leaders; no longer, for example, was Sukarno a "reactionary"; overnight he became a "progressive."

The illegal Communist parties received similar instructions. They were to limit their guerrilla warfare except where they were assured an easy triumph. They were to maintain close contact with the Russian and Communist Chinese embassies, and they were to enhance the stature of the "progressive" forces of their countries in every possible way—even if this meant an occasional sacrifice of Communist interests.

In the diplomatic arena the Communists were to become "reasonable" advocates of "peaceful coexistence." The Chinese quickly doffed their cloak of aggressiveness and donned a smiling mask of friendship. At Bandung, in April, 1955, Chou En-lai acted as though he were running in a Wisconsin primary. He smiled while others frowned, and he whispered while others ranted. His suave placidity won friends for China and for local Communist parties who were jockeying for political power.

Meanwhile, the Russians complemented the Chinese very deftly. They sent technical missions to Southeast Asia, and offered economic assistance. No strings, they mentioned for the *n*th time. They also took advantage of the liberal atmosphere to unload inexpensive propaganda that glorified the "peaceful" achievements of the Soviet system.

The happy face of this co-ordinated Communist policy reaped considerable advantages in Asia. In 1956 Communist-front parties in Burma did well in local elections. In 1957 the Communist Party of Indonesia, which claimed a membership of over one million, became the fourth largest vote-getting party in the country. Moreover, I heard from experts throughout Asia in 1957 that the Communist tide had swelled to such proportions that a Marxist victory appeared inevitable. "Maybe five or ten years, then the whole area will go Communist," they agreed.

In 1958 there was another change in Communist tactics in Southeast Asia—a change that took many Westerners by surprise. Although the Russians apparently wanted to maintain their friendly relations with the new nations of this area, the Chinese began to behave with their old supercilious crudeness. The probable reasons for this change have already been suggested—although, in Southeast Asia, two other reasons could be added. First, it has been stated that the Chinese were miffed in 1958 when the Russians proposed the inclusion of India, rather than China, in a summit meeting; and, second, the Chinese reportedly were annoyed by the general tone of Soviet propaganda in Asia. They felt that the Russians had not paid sufficient attention to the Chinese Revolution.

In any case, the Russians and the Chinese began to differ on tactics in Asia. The basic disagreement revolved around the concept of "friendly neutrality." The Chinese now believe that Communist governments should be brought to power throughout Asia as quickly as possible, while the Russians maintain that "friendship" has proved to be a more successful approach than truculence. According to Aleksandr Y. Kaznachayev, a young Soviet diplomat in Rangoon who defected to the West, the "Chinese Communists don't believe in a policy of friendly neutrality. In the eyes of Chinese, the Soviet policy of friendly neutrality practically destroyed the natural base for installing Communism in those countries. The natural base for installing Communism in those countries is poverty—lack of political experience of peoples. The policy of friendly neutrality provides the possibility for governments of those countries to obtain the help of Western countries, and at the same time the help of the Soviet bloc, to improve the living conditions of the people and to reconstruct their economy. At the same time, it gives them the opportunity to gain a definite amount of political experience. In the eyes of the Chinese, this is criminal destruction. This is a losing of time, valuable time and valuable conditions."

Kaznachayev also disclosed that the Chinese and the Russians had "probably" divided Asia into "unofficial" spheres of influence. Burma, Thailand, Malaya, Cambodia, Laos, Vietnam, and "possibly" Indonesia, he felt, fell within Peking's sphere, while Afghanistan, India, and Ceylon fell within Moscow's.

This neat division was not accepted by many Western specialists on Communist affairs. In 1957, during a trip through Asia, I heard their reasoning. A sphere of influence, they said, could be interpreted in two ways; Moscow and Peking might have agreed to a highly general formula for a Communist Asia ("Burma is yours, but India is mine"); or they might have agreed to a division of authority among the Asian CP's ("The Thai Party listens to you, but the Indian CP obeys me"). This kind of cynical manipulation, the specialists continued, sounded too unorthodox for normal inter-Party communication. Moreover, it seemed to ignore the historical antecedents of the Southeast Asian CP's.

Most of them had strong ties with Moscow because they were the offshoots of European CP's. For instance, the Indonesian CP was inspired by the Dutch CP, which naturally took its orders from Moscow. Likewise, the Vietnamese CP was created by the French CP, which has always been loyal to Moscow. Thus, the origin of an Asian party could normally be traced to its colonial source.

In this way, the specialists said, the Kremlin exercised the major influence over all of the Asian CP's—except possibly the Malayan and Thai parties, which had begun as Chinese satellites. It was unlikely that Russia would have forfeited this influence to China without a struggle.

Neither Moscow nor Peking has given any indication of having reached an agreement on sharing the ideological spoils of world Communism. In fact, since 1954 the Russians and the Chinese have been maneuvering for the loyalty of Asia's CP's; and, the specialists concluded, the Chinese appear to be gaining the upper hand. Before 1957 the Russians seemed to have supplied the guiding light for Asian Communism. In 1957 it was a tossup.

So, how did the alignment of Asian CP's look in 1959?

* * *

Thailand is an attractive exception in the colonial history of Asia. Never was this small monarchic, Buddhist nation of 20,800,000 people occupied by a European power. The Chakri Dynasty has ruled serenely and supremely over a happy people in a fertile land. Thais believe in fun. "Mai bien bai," they would tell me, whenever confronted with a dilemma. "Mai bien bai" means "What the heck," and Thais would choose the path of least resistance.

In 1932 a new Constitution was proclaimed. Its aim was to put an end to absolutism, which was reckoned "old-fashioned," and to introduce democracy, which was considered "modern." In 1933 the new democracy outlawed the Communist Party. Thai political life revolved around two men: Field Marshal Luang Pibul

Songgram, who represented economic conservatism, personal authoritarianism, and military glory, and Nai Pridi Panomyong (Pridi to his followers), who represented socialism, liberalism, and a bit of authoritarianism.

When World War Two erupted, Pibul, who admired German militarism, joined the Axis and supplied the Japanese. Pridi organized an anti-Tokyo underground that harassed the Nipponese. In July, 1944, Pibul's government collapsed, and Pridi stormed to power. When the war ended, Pridi legalized the Thai Communist Party and promised a democratic government. In 1947 Pibul staged a *coup d'état,* which, in Thailand, is a political way of life. He, too, promised a democratic government, while Pridi, attracted by Mao's success in China, fled to the north, where he hoped to organize a Free Thai Movement. Since 1953 the Chinese Communists have given this movement their full support and active encouragement.

Pridi frightened Pibul; so did Communism—both domestic and foreign. Pibul surrounded himself with military strong men—Generals Phao and Sarit, who governed and chiseled unscrupulously. This triumvirate loudly proclaimed their anti-Communism. In 1947 Thailand was permitted to join the United Nations. In 1949 Pibul suddenly found an aggressive Communist China hovering over his northern borders; he vowed that he would never recognize Peking—a vow that endeared him to Washington.

In 1950 he denounced North Korea's attack against South Korea; and in 1951 Thailand voted with the majority of the General Assembly in condemning China as an "aggressor nation." After the establishment of Ho Chi-Minh's regime in 1954, Pibul was anxious to join SEATO, which, at his invitation, established its headquarters in Bangkok.

Thus, on foreign affairs, Thailand has consistently followed a United States line in Asia: anti-Communism and nonrecognition. The effect has been twofold: the Communists have attacked Thailand as the "lackey of American imperialism," and the United States has pumped hundreds of millions of dollars of economic aid into Bangkok, making it the most prosperous "Western" area in Asia.

Although there are some disgruntled intellectuals who resent the "lackey" accusation, most Thais do not seem to mind the Communist insults. They live well—very well, by Asian standards—and they have not lost their traditional sense of humor. They are warm and hospitable. Their dress is Western in Bangkok and Thai in the villages. Many speak English, which they study in school.

In fact, as one Thai told me, "We would have a paradise on earth, if it weren't for three things." He listed them as political corruption, Communist subversion, and 2,300,000 overseas Chinese. "Unfortunately, we can't do anything—not yet—about the political corruption, but I think there is a good deal less of it now than there was two or three years ago. Communism and the overseas Chinese," he added, "those are our problems!"

* * *

In Thailand the overseas Chinese have extraordinary economic power. They are easily the best businessmen in the country. Thrifty and industrious, they control a large percentage of Thailand's working capital. At least one-half of all the stores on Bangkok's busy boulevards are owned by Chinese merchants. All of the street-corner stands, selling cigarettes, chewing gum, and post cards, are owned by Chinese businessmen, most of them under ten years of age. They speak Thai, Chinese, and English, and all drive a hard bargain.

One afternoon, at Wat Aron, a spectacular Buddhist monument of red, blue, green, yellow, and brown mosaics that the tourist books call the "temple of dawn," a young Asian boy wanted to sell us some post cards.

"No, thank you," I said. We had had enough of postcard beauty.

"Okay," he said in slightly accented English. "How about a straw hat?"

"No, thanks."

"Okay," he persisted, "how about some good rubbings of Wat Aron?"

We marveled at his salesmanship.

"Cheap," he added.

"Okay," I mimicked, "I'll have ten *bhat* worth of whatever you have."

He handed me three post cards, and laughed.

"Are you Thai?" I asked.

"I am Chinese," he answered, and his voice seemed to burst with pride.

A Thai friend who accompanied us to Wat Aron patted him lightly on the arm and said, "The Chinese are smart, very smart."

"Aren't you a little concerned about the economic power that the Chinese have?"

"No," he answered calmly, a warm smile playing across his open face, "you don't understand. You see, whenever we need anything, on Sundays or holidays, any hour of the day or night, they have it for us. There is no need to go into competition with the Chinese and open other stores. They do everything for us. It is a wonderful system."

His attitude was not necessarily typical, for many Thais have become alarmed by the increasing importance of the Chinese minority. They are slowly beginning to realize that 2,300,000 Chinese, voting as a single bloc, voicing a single wish, can swing the political balance of power—either in a free election or in a seizure of power. So far, the Chinese have shown no inclination to capitalize on their political potential, but the possibility exists.

In Thailand, the Chinese are not very sociable. They are clannish. They do not belong to many clubs. Many of them are not even Thai citizens. They are a tough, commercial group. Their newspapers devote considerably more space to events in China, or to events within the Chinese community in Bangkok, than to general developments affecting all Thais. They do not consider themselves Thai; they consider themselves Chinese who have a primary national loyalty to China. As one American observed: "The Chinese work in Thailand; they don't live here."

Of course, they are aware of constant government pressure, and they are highly suspect. Ever since the mainland fell to Mao, they have come to be regarded as his personal agents in Thailand—a dangerous fifth column that sends chills down Pibul's spine.

In 1952 Pibul again outlawed the Communist Party and hounded every Chinese suspected of leftist leanings. One hundred and fifty Chinese business firms were raided, and two hundred and fifty

Chinese businessmen were arrested. This vicious drive lasted until 1954; apparently, it so intimidated the Chinese that most of them were eager to become associated with Chiang's regime, regardless of their personal feelings. In fact, many Chinese families made it a steady practice to send at least one son to study on Formosa.

In 1955, when the Chinese Communist regime began to smile, the Chinese in Bangkok began to swing toward Peking. They had family on the mainland, and, besides, the Chinese Communists encouraged their business. This pro-Communist drift again frightened Pibul, but he did not respond with his characteristic brutality. Instead, he passed a series of laws aimed at reducing Chinese control over the Thai economy. Any firm, he decreed, employing more than ten persons, had to hire at least 50 per cent of its force from among ethnic Thais, and he tried to stimulate Thais to go into business.

"Pibul and his successors probably feel that they can still control the Chinese because they control the army and the police. They have been ugly with the Chinese before, and they can be ugly with them again." The speaker was a British diplomat, who had witnessed the cruelty of an anti-Chinese raid in Bangkok.

Anxiety about the Chinese is always just beneath the surface. One day, I was discussing Bangkok's refusal to recognize the Peking regime with one of Thailand's most distinguished diplomats. "The reason," he said, "is simple. The Chinese. The pressure toward recognition is very great. Remember, we are a small country, and China is very large and ominous. We should recognize Peking, perhaps, but we cannot. If we recognized Mao's regime, the Chinese Communists would set up a large embassy here in Bangkok, certainly as large as the Soviet Embassy was before 1955. They would wield tremendous power, especially among the Chinese businessmen. Now, can you imagine what would happen if we tried to put any pressure on them, and they rushed for help to the Peking Embassy? The Communists would offer that help, and we would be lost."

"Do the Russians exercise any influence over the Thai Communist Party, illegal though it may be?"

"No, but the Chinese do."

* * *

Actually, there are four Communist parties in Thailand—all of them illegal. First, the Chinese Communist Party of Thailand; then, the Communist Party of Thailand; and, finally, the Communist Party of Vietnam and the Chinese Communist Party of Malaya. All four parties probably never had a following of more than several thousand, but, as one student of Communism observed, "it took only several thousand Communists to start the Bolshevik Revolution."

The CCPT, the largest, was formed in 1923 in Bangkok as an offshoot of the Chinese Communist Party. Its membership is solely Chinese. It has tried—without much success—to influence the curricula of the Chinese schools in Bangkok. During the war it organized its own underground, refusing to have anything to do with Pridi's Thai underground.

The CPT is the only Communist Party in which Thais participate. It operates mainly through front organizations. Its leadership is said to be highly nationalistic, but this is not supported by the facts. In 1951 the CPT worked enthusiastically to send a delegation to Peking for the "world peace meeting." At that time it was believed likely that the CPT leadership established close ties to Peking.

Very little is known about the CPVN and the CCPM. The CPVN was organized by Ho Chi-Minh in 1928, when he visited Bangkok. In Thailand's northeast 70,000 Vietnamese refugees live—most of whom are loyal to Ho's regime. They provide support for the CPVN.

The CCPM draws its strength from the "Malayan Races Liberation Army," which is stationed in the jungles between Thailand and Malaya. No statistics are available on CCPM strength, and it is believed that Chin Peng, Secretary-General of the Malayan Communist Party, is in effective control.

With the possible exception of the CPT, these parties are more concerned with China, Vietnam, and Malaya than with Thailand.

They are all said to be supported by Communist China, and they are all said to owe allegiance to Peking.

The Russians do not seem to have any control over their activities. Thailand—and its CP's—belong to China.

CHAPTER TEN Jakarta

IN 1811 A YOUNG ENGLISHMAN NAMED STOCKDALE VISITED JAkarta, which was then called Batavia. Afterward, he penned his impressions:

"Most of the people who live here and even many of the rich who might be supposed to have attained the summit of their wishes have something in their countenance expressive of discontent and dejection which seems a certain sign that all is not right within. After a short residence in this debilitating atmosphere a state of languor and love of inactivity soon overcome all the active powers of the mind and, occasioning a total neglect of exercise, ruin the constitution and induce an absolute repugnance to every kind of occupation. The only resource for those who are in this state of listlessness approaching to torpidity is to seek for relief in society and to endeavor to kill the heavy hours in the most frivolous manner. Smoking tobacco, uninteresting and useless conversation, drinking and card-playing form the sum of their amusements—utterly at a loss how to pass the many tedious hours of the day, only solicitous to make choice of such ways of killing time as least interfere with their beloved state of motionless repose."

One hundred and forty-eight years later, I felt as though I were viewing Jakarta through Stockdale's eyes: for, on the surface, things have not changed very much.

Jakarta's pace is maddeningly slow. The tropical sun, the heavy humidity, and the killer mosquitoes seem to have mesmerized the sprawling city into a state of "motionless repose." Westerners rarely stray from their air-conditioned immunity, and humor obviously requires too great an effort. A "listlessness" hangs over the city like a moist cloud. No one rushes, for in Jakarta energy is precious and patience saintly. In fact, Indonesians distrust speed. A few years ago, I was told, somewhat apocryphally, a Westerner was arrested for running. He was fined 100 rupees. "But why?" he objected angrily. "For disturbing the peace," the judge explained.

Even business cannot be hurried. In Jakarta's steaming market places, where meats, fish, umbrellas, birds, hats, and Lux soap hang in the equatorial sun, a sale is a day's pleasure. The barefooted dealer, in narrow dark trousers and broad-brimmed straw hat, would not dream of selling me a yard of batik cloth at his asking price. First, I had to understand how the cloth was made; then, how it was transported to Jakarta; and, finally, how it could be used. His explanation, which was carefully translated, could not be rushed. He wanted 1,500 rupees for a batik cloth, two yards long and one yard wide. "Sold," I said firmly, as I reached into my wallet. "Sold?" he replied suspiciously. "But we have not discussed it. Come over here. Sit down. Let us talk about it." We talked "about it" for a few hours—"it" encompassing the weather, the United States, President Sukarno, and Istana Merdeka, the White House of Jakarta. I finally bought the batik, when he was convinced "we" had agreed on a price—1,000 rupees.

The price of a *betjak* ride (a *betjak* is a kind of bicycle-rickshaw) is also negotiated in a leisurely manner. For example, it is standard procedure for the driver to ask for twice what he really expects. A normal ride in downtown Jakarta, which is crowded with 38,000 *betjaks,* named Paris, Sin-Sin, or even Morris, costs about five rupees. Therefore, according to the unwritten rules of Jakartan mobility, the driver asks for ten rupees. The passenger shakes his head vigorously and walks away. The driver cycles after him. "Eight rupees," he bargains playfully. "No," the passenger argues, looking at him with feigned anger, "three rupees, and that's final!" The negotiation continues. "Six rupees," the driver concedes, "six rupees is a good price." The passenger again shakes his head; then he stops, usually smiles and asks, "How about five?" "Excellent," the driver says, and the two negotiators, both highly satisfied with another successful "deal," drive off.

Indonesians enjoy negotiations—but they have to be conducted on Indonesian terms. In a nation where the temperature and humidity maintain an irritating constancy, habits do not change easily. For hundreds of years, a *kali,* or canal, has cut through the center of Jakarta. To Westerners—and many, many Indonesians—the *kali* is an extraordinary eyesore. It is an unusual combination of washing machine, swimming pool, and toilet. Its odors are sickening; some of them waft over to nearby restaurants, which, astonishingly, continue to do a good business. A few brave politicians have ventured to suggest that the *kali* be buried, but public indignation (rare in Indonesia) has stymied any such attempt. About five years ago, when Indonesia entered the world of suitcase diplomacy, a compromise was reached, which may enter the history texts as the "great compromise of 1955." It was agreed that a temporary parking lot be built over the *kali* whenever a foreign dignitary visits Jakarta, but it was explicitly stated that the lot was to be removed when he leaves. "You just don't get rid of the *kali* that quickly," an American commented; "it's a part of the local scene, and change in Indonesia comes hard."

* * *

But in the last fifteen years Indonesia has changed—Indonesia notwithstanding. The Dutch are gone. Three hundred years of foreign rule have been brought to an end. Three thousand islands, scattered formlessly around the equator, have been united into a sovereign state. Ninety million people from the Celebes to Sumatra have become Indonesians, speaking Bahasa Indonesia, a Malay-rooted language, and saluting a national flag of red and white. A revolutionary firebrand named Sukarno, inspiring as an orator and cunning as a politician, has assumed virtually dictatorial powers to lead Indonesia through the uncharted jungle of "guided democracy," his personal political concoction. A doctrine called "independent neutrality" governs Jakarta's foreign policy.

I had visited Jakarta in March, 1957, when a rebellion against "Javanese domination" was erupting in the outer islands. At that time Jakarta looked like a particularly unattractive welcome mat for Indonesia. But in August, 1959, when I returned, the capital looked fairly presentable. Its hot, narrow streets had obviously been cleared of rubbish, and red-and-white banners had been strung from cottage to cottage. Telegraph poles were dressed like peppermint sticks, and trees and ashcans were whitewashed.

All over the city, six numbers were painted on trees, trucks, and government buildings: 17-8-45-17-8-59. These six numbers told the political story of this island republic, which, once a colonial hinterland, has begun to attract Moscow's and Washington's increasing interest by its bold, stumbling, independent strides toward national honor—an honor, Sukarno states, that exists free of Eastern or Western influence.

By 17-8-45 was meant August 17, 1945—the day Indonesia defiantly proclaimed its independence from Dutch colonialism—and 17-8-59 meant August 17, 1959—the fourteenth anniversary of Indonesia's July Fourth. From the awninged terrace of Istana Merdeka, President Sukarno told tens of thousands of cheering Indonesians that prosperity and modernity were just around the corner. In his usually flamboyant way, Sukarno denounced colonialism and imperialism; he shook his fist at an imaginary enemy; he upbraided "military alliances"; he cajoled the Indonesians; he scolded the "slackers"; he promised the sky. "If they object," he screamed, "let the dogs bark! Our caravan marches on!"

After three hours of speechmaking, Sukarno, resplendent in a white uniform, sat down to watch his "people" march across the broad lawn in neat, colorful brigades—each, a symbol of another handicraft or region.

"From Sukarno's behavior this morning," I said later to a group of diplomats and journalists, "you would think this country did not have a care in the world."

"That is one of Sukarno's great gifts; he's a splendid orator and a splendid actor," an American diplomat remarked. "Actually, the country is in very bad shape. And that is the real tragedy of Indonesia, because it is one of the richest countries in the world. It could be a paradise." The others nodded in agreement, as they sipped gin and tonic, the orange juice of Jakarta.

"First of all," he elaborated, "democracy does not really work. Sukarno calls it 'guided,' but the political life of the country begins and ends with Sukarno. Last month, under army supervision, he was vested with virtually dictatorial powers. One of his first acts was to disband Parliament. Second, he has coddled the Communist Party so much—and attacked Western imperialism so consistently—that the Partai Komunis Indonesia (PKI) now claims a membership of 1,500,000. And if it wasn't for the fact that General Abdul Nasution is so anti-Communist—he's a devout Moslem—it's possible that Indonesia might already have gone Communist. Third, a very costly, damaging rebellion against the Jakarta government continues in the outer islands, where it is felt that Sukarno has favored Javanese development to the economic detriment of the outer islands, especially Sumatra. You know, for example, that Sumatra supplies Indonesia with about 70 per cent of its total foreign currency, in exchange for which she gets only a small portion of the national budget. And Sumatrans don't think this system is just. But the most important problem facing Sukarno's government is the poor state of the nation's economic health."

Another diplomat interrupted his colleague. "Right!" he exclaimed, the exclamation mark in his voice. "If this nation functioned properly from an economic viewpoint, it could take care of its other problems. But now I don't think it can. The best Indonesian economists are in Sumatra with the rebellion, and the poorer ones, here in Jakarta, are not doing anything."

"They can't!" a journalist interjected. "Whenever they suggest a sensible remedy to stop the inflation, or to provide more jobs, or to bring the Chinese into a national effort, Sukarno says they sound like the rebels, and he stops them. Two years ago, the inflation wasn't so bad; you could get only 65 rupees to the dollar. Now, you can get 140 rupees without any trouble."

"The fact is," another journalist concluded, "the whole economy is faltering—and faltering badly."

* * *

One day, we decided to leave the Indonesian doormat of Jakarta for a drive to Bandung, the cool, mountain-cradled city in West

Java where the first Afro-Asian Conference was held in 1955. "We" were my brother and his wife, my wife and I. "Jakarta," Bernard observed, "is not Indonesia."

The ride from Jakarta to Bandung, which takes about five hours, was breath-takingly beautiful. The delicate blue-green panorama of sky, mountain, and paddy was the most spectacular scenery I had ever seen. The narrow highway had been cut through the jungled mountains, and, in the distance, it looked unreal—like a snake frozen into the landscape. Terraced rice fields with neat rows of green shoots reflected the blue and white of the clouded sky and the brown and green of the mountains, as they climbed toward the horizon.

Against this lush tropical backdrop, Indonesian farmers toiled, paying no attention to our noisy Dodge as it honked its way through sleepy villages that seemed to cliff-hang around every turn. Water buffalo stood motionless in the rice fields. Occasionally, a monkey swung down from a tree, and we tossed him a banana, which we had bought from a peasant woman in Tjipanas.

These idyllic images fleeted past our windows, and it was difficult to believe that Jakarta, ugly, old Batavia, was the capital of this extraordinary wonder. After a few more bumpy hours of Javanese grandeur, we arrived in Bandung. White, scrubbed, almost efficient, Bandung seemed like the more natural capital of Indonesia. New construction was widespread, and the people appeared to have more verve. I hoped that Stockdale had got to Bandung.

"Where shall we have dinner tonight?" I asked.

"There's a fine Chinese restaurant not too far from the hotel," Bernard suggested.

"But we had Chinese food last night," I objected. "How about eating right here at the hotel?"

"All right," he consented, "but I warned you."

The food, which was neither Indonesian nor Western, was cold and pasty. After a few courses, I asked: "Where's the Chinese restaurant?" Bernard laughed. "Right around the corner; let's go." We paid our check, and left.

The Chinese dinner was not only superb; it was also symbolic.

For, it highlighted one of the most profound truths about economic life in Indonesia—the critical role of 3,000,000 overseas Chinese. They are the cooks and businessmen of Indonesia; they control the economy of this rich, strategic island republic.

In Bandung, when I wanted to buy a shirt, I had to go to a Chinese haberdasher. When I wanted to buy a book, I had to go to a Chinese bookstore, one of many prominently displaying Peking propaganda. When I wanted to buy an aspirin, I had to go to a Chinese druggist. When I wanted to buy ice cream, I had to go to a Chinese ice-cream parlor. I was completely dependent upon the Chinese businessman, the middleman of the Indonesian economy. So were the 87,000,000 Indonesians, who had begun to resent this dependence.

They realized that many Chinese had Indonesian roots, two or three centuries old. But they also knew that the Chinese did not think of Indonesia as home. Thrifty and clannish, they had retained their language and their culture, and they had withstood the mounting pressure for assimilation. In a nation rampant with nationalism, they represented an indigestible, despised lump of Chinese culture.

Although facts are foreign to Jakarta, it has been estimated that approximately 1,000,000 Chinese businessmen have a stranglehold on the collection of produce and the distribution of consumer goods in "rural" Indonesia. For example, in Tjibadak, a small town in West Java, the shopkeepers, middlemen, transport operators, contractors, doctors, dentists, and moneylenders are all Chinese. A shopkeeper in Tjibadak probably earns about 5,000 rupees a month, of which he could easily save half for investment or loans. The average Indonesian worker earns 500 rupees a month. A high government official earns 2,500 rupees a month. President Sukarno's base income is only 5,000 rupees a month. In contrast to the relatively poor Chinese shopkeeper in Tjibadak, who still earns ten times more than the average Indonesian worker, the wealthy Chinese merchant, of whom there are thousands throughout the archipelago, earns up to 500,000 rupees a month.

These statistics provide the economic explanation for the anti-Chinese prejudice that has developed throughout the islands, especially since independence. To the sensitive, ultranationalistic Indonesian, it appeared as though one brand of foreign exploitation had been replaced by another.

One Indonesian said: "They're interested only in money. They'd sell themselves, or you, or us to the Communists or to any other bidder. Since they always manage to accumulate most of the money, we have to get part of it back. Actually, it's a game—they expect it."

The "game" began during the Bandung Conference. According to authoritative Indonesian sources, Communist China signed a treaty with Jakarta in 1955 about the nationality of the overseas Chinese in Indonesia. In effect, the treaty stated that within four years these Chinese would have to choose between Communist Chinese and Indonesian citizenship. Chiang Kai-shek's China was ignored.

By 1957 the Jakarta government began to suspect that most of the Chinese would opt for Peking citizenship. A law was passed on July 1, 1957, requiring all "aliens" to pay a stiff annual tax of about 3,000 rupees per family. "In Indonesia," a veteran newspaperman told me, "an 'alien' is a Chinese." On September 15, 1958, Jakarta accused a large number of Chinese residents of political and economic subversion; their clubs, schools, banks, and homes were nationalized. As it happened, most of them were anti-Communists who might well have opted for Indonesian citizenship and helped the economy. On May 14, 1959, Jakarta banned all "aliens" from retail trade in rural Indonesia. The ban was to go into effect on January 1, 1960.

The Chinese were not concerned. If the ban were implemented, they could easily bribe the enforcement agencies. Corruption was commonplace. Besides, the Chinese realized that the ban could disrupt the entire Indonesian economy, and as a result they could not imagine that the Indonesians were serious. Finally, the Chinese felt that they could always rely on the Indonesian Communist Party and the Chinese Communist Embassy to support their plea for exemption from the ban.

By August, 1959, when I arrived in Indonesia, it was clear that the Indonesians meant business. The overwhelming majority of the Chinese had selected Peking citizenship, and Jakarta had become terrified. It suspected every Chinese shopkeeper of espionage —or, at the very least, of subversion.

As an Indonesian politician told me: "Look in their homes. Most of the time, you find pictures of Mao Tse-tung, or the Chinese Communist flag pinned to a map of Indonesia."

Another Indonesian politician said: "They are a fifth column, and now that the Chinese Communists have begun to push their weight around as though they owned Southeast Asia, these Indonesian Chinese can do their bidding right here."

An Indonesian diplomat: "Put it any way you like. The problem is very simple. Peking can use the overseas Chinese for their own national ends. Remember, China gets stronger every day. Russia knows this, too. I tell you that if we do not break the Chinese grip on our economy—and get rid of the Chinese—no matter what the cost—Chinese warships will appear off the shores of Indonesia within five years to support the Chinese here. And we will have to reshape our nation as they wish."

Prompted by these fears, the Indonesians forced all Chinese businessmen—many of whom still wore black, baggy silk pants and pigtails—to remove Chinese characters from store fronts. In Jakarta and Bandung I saw only the outlines of the characters—haunting symbols of a major economic clash. Then, on August 25th, the major action: President Sukarno cut the value of 500-rupee and 1,000-rupee bank notes by 90 per cent, froze 90 per cent of all bank balances over 25,000 rupees, and warned that the move was taken against "speculators," "corruptors," and "holders of hot money." Whom did he mean but the Chinese?

Foreign Minister Subandrio sped to Peking to "explain"; but Foreign Minister Chen Yi was in no mood for explanations. He demanded that Jakarta call off its anti-Chinese offensive. In Indonesia, Chinese Ambassador Huang Chen sent embassy officials into the countryside to advise Chinese residents to ignore the ban. Several clashes were reported between the Chinese and the Indonesians. Relations between Peking and Jakarta froze in a state of mutual antagonism.

Peking accused Indonesia of "subjecting" overseas Chinese "to the most cruel treatment . . . as nationals of a hostile country." Jakarta retorted angrily: the overseas Chinese were charged with "hoarding, smuggling, speculation . . . and reactionary behavior." Subandrio explained that Indonesia wanted only to change "a liberal economic system into a socialist system"—an aim which Communist China surely should be able to understand!

* * *

Although many observers of the Indonesian scene felt that Jakarta had acted hastily (as one Western economist observed, "Until such time as the Indonesians have a substitute for the Chinese middleman in the economy, they are hurting only themselves by forcibly ejecting the Chinese"), they understood Jakarta's motivation. Indonesia was faced by a double Chinese threat: at home a powerful Chinese fifth column, supported by the Chinese Communist Embassy and the Indonesian Communist Party; abroad, Communist China, a powerful and demanding neighbor whose policy throughout Asia was beginning to reflect traditional Chinese haughtiness. Jakarta decided that it had better act before Peking did.

In its haste, Jakarta unexpectedly found a friend in the Soviet Union. Its relations with the United States had become more cordial—especially after Ambassador Howard Jones arrived in Jakarta in 1958. Now, as it faced the overpowering threat of Communist China's intrusion into Indonesian affairs, Jakarta received a polite, unpublicized call from the Soviet Embassy. This call focused attention once again on the duality of Communist foreign policy.

As the Chinese huffed, the Russians smiled.

Was this a co-ordinated effort? Not in the opinion of experts in Jakarta.

They cited this evidence.

The Russians, they said, told the Indonesian Foreign Ministry at a private meeting that Moscow did not share Peking's opposition to the retail ban. Indeed, Moscow did not wish to be associated with Peking's belligerence. Moreover, Russian diplomats told

Indonesians that the time had come for a "radical" improvement in Moscow-Jakarta relations. They said they wanted to sign a cultural and trade agreement with Indonesia, and they hinted that Soviet Premier Khrushchev might soon decide to pay a state visit to Jakarta.

"These are the actions of a nation," a Western expert suggested, "that is more nationalist than Communist. Of course, it could be argued that Russia is trying to offset some of Asia's disillusionment with Communism since the Tibetan revolt, and China's troubles with India and Indonesia. Actually, I think I'd put it another way: I think Khrushchev realizes that Russia has become so closely linked with China as an ally that in the eyes of Asians Russia must share the sins of China. If China is tough, then Asia thinks Communism is tough and therefore that Russia is tough. This is a difficult burden for Moscow to bear at this point, and Khrushchev wants to convince Asia that China is one thing and Russia is another. If at the same time this brings reflected glory to Communism, then so much the better. But the major consideration in Khrushchev's actions is Russia—not China, not Communism."

* * *

The Chinese-Indonesian dispute provided an excellent opportunity to listen to the reflections of many astute Indonesian diplomats and politicians who had journeyed to or served in Moscow and Peking. These reflections involved not only insights into the alliance but fascinating observations about Chinese psychology.

For example, an Indonesian diplomat who once served in London and Moscow, said: "The Chinese have an inner dignity that one must respect. It comes, I think, from a self-assurance, even a sense of superiority, that dates back thousands of years, when the Chinese *were* the most cultured race on earth. At a diplomatic reception, a Chinese ambassador looks dignified and self-sufficient even when he is standing off to one side, alone, a bit aloof. Any other ambassador might look a bit self-conscious, but not the Chinese.

"Even when they spit, they do it with dignity.

"The Russians, on the other hand, are not refined. Neither are most of their goods. I remember that the last time I was in China I heard that the Chinese had sent a large order of Russian goods back to Moscow because they did not think the quality was good enough. The Chinese understand good quality. They are an intelligent people with a long heritage of technology. I think they will acquire all the refinements of modern technology in a very short time.

"In Chinese villages even the lowliest peasant ridicules the Russians. He draws an imaginary figure in the air with his hands—a figure with square shoulders and bell-bottom pants—and then he laughs.

"Still, the Chinese need the Russians desperately at this stage of their development, but they do not like the way the Russians always boast about *their* level of technological achievement.

"And I am convinced that the Chinese do not like the drift of Russia's comparatively warmer relations with the West. The Chinese argue ideologically; they tell the Russians that as their economic level rises, as they become more like the West, they will become contaminated by bourgeois ideas. The Chinese say that the Russians will not be able to convince the West to lay down their arms without a fight. Khrushchev tells the Chinese he can sell the West on a *status quo* in Europe and then go out for the rest of the world. Mao is not so sure this tactic will work. Besides, he needs a tough domestic line now, and, if need be, I feel Mao will go it alone—break off from the rest of the Communist world."

Another Indonesian diplomat remarked: "When Malenkov became Premier, he told the Chinese he wanted to get along with the United States. The Chinese objected strenuously. Their objections were used by Malenkov's opponents to force his resignation. Chou En-lai repeatedly cold-shouldered Malenkov at official receptions. When Khrushchev first rose to power, the Chinese were pleased. Now that he's beginning to espouse many of Malenkov's ideas, the Chinese have begun to cool toward him, too. They maintain a working relationship with Khrushchev, but that's all. They cannot support a Russian leader who wants to get along with the bourgeois world. There's the rub."

An Indonesian politician, a former diplomat, said: "At Khrushchev's meeting with Mao, in August, 1958, some kind of agreement was apparently reached that Russia will not—cannot—speak for China when China's national interests or foreign policy are involved in an international dispute. I am convinced Mao insisted on this in those talks."

A Marxist scholar was of the opinion that Russia is swiftly becoming a "have" nation: "China is very definitely a 'have-not' nation. For Marxists, this makes a basic difference which cannot be ignored. This leads to antagonism and conflict, and I believe that a break between the Russians and the Chinese is inevitable.

"You see, both nations are governed by Communist dictatorships, and differences of opinion on important matters of policy—such as how to deal with the United States—cannot be tolerated. This is true between nations of the same race; it is especially true between nations of different races—especially if one of those races resents what it considers a tradition of exploitation at the hands of the other.

"Yes, there will be a split. There has to be. And it need not await the time when China will be economically self-sufficient. It can come at any time; and when it does it will come suddenly, dramatically, without any warning!"

* * *

A Balinese prince, who once served in the Indonesian government but now prefers the political exile of his parlor to participation in a "stumbling," "directionless" regime, ruminated one afternoon about the possible effects of Sino-Soviet tensions on the PKI, the most powerful, influential, dreaded Asian CP after Mao's.

"It must be exceedingly difficult," he said, sipping tea in the warm comfort of his aristocratic parlor, "for the PKI to make up its mind whether its primary ideological loyalty should be to Russia or to China. After all, men like Aidit [Dipa N. Aidit, Secretary-General of the PKI] have visited Moscow and Peking—many of them were trained in either of the two Communist capitals, some in both—and they can see that there is a tug of war between Moscow and Peking, with strong undercurrents of tension and hostility."

"What do you think will happen?"

"It's hard to say. Take, for example, this current squabble over the resident Chinese in Indonesia. Peking supports them fully; Russia tries to keep a 'hands-off' policy. What is the PKI to do? Support the implied Russian position that these are just a bunch of Chinese capitalists, and thus run the risk of offending the Chinese Communists, or help the Chinese capitalists, and defy the wishes of the strongest Communist nation on earth? It's a dilemma."

"Well, what has the PKI done?"

"From the drift of *Harian Rakjat,* the Communist newspaper in Jakarta, I would guess that the PKI has decided to ride with Peking on this issue. I have noticed articles supporting the Chinese capitalists against the Indonesian government—a most peculiar position for a local Communist Party to take."

Why did the PKI support Peking?

Jakarta's experts all seemed to agree that the Chinese merchants of Indonesia—ironically, the richest people in the country—have contributed handsomely to the PKI treasury. Recently, the PKI received a windfall—presumably from the Chinese merchants—to open a new headquarters on one of Jakarta's broadest, busiest boulevards and to intensify Marxist propaganda throughout the country. The headquarters building is impressive, boasting large pictures of Aidit and Marx—strange bedfellows—and bright red posters with redder hammers and sickles. When these Chinese merchants suspected that Jakarta meant to enforce its new anti-Chinese regulations, they appealed to the PKI for support against the government. The PKI, feeling that it could not afford to turn its back on its financial angels, swung its broad support behind the Chinese capitalists.

The shift to Peking's line, however, was not abrupt. Very gradually, ever since 1957, the PKI has begun to follow Peking's lead in ideological and foreign policy questions. At that time I had heard in Jakarta that the PKI was ambivalent about its ideological commitment. Moscow or Peking—it was a tossup, although for years the PKI had unquestionably been an obedient Moscow booster. A serious factional struggle was said to have developed within the Party over the question of Moscow versus Peking loyalty.

By 1959 the views of the pro-Peking faction, reportedly headed by Aidit, appeared to be winning out. Observers in Jakarta cited this evidence:

First, on ideological and party issues: the PKI has emphasized the "broad, mass character" of its movement. This approach was introduced after Aidit returned from a long stay in China to take control of the Party and to implement the lessons he had learned from Mao. For a long time the Chinese Communist Party has recognized the necessity of a broadly based movement in a primitive country, while the Soviet Communist Party has continued to stress an "élitist" principle.

The PKI has always applauded the Chinese tactic of establishing "liberated areas," that is, areas within a country which have fallen under Communist control and have been transformed into military bases for further expansion. The Russians have always had mixed feelings about "liberated areas." The Chinese have not; they came to power from "liberated areas." The Indonesian Communists hope that they can, in the same way.

The emphasis in the PKI propaganda prominently displayed throughout Indonesia is increasingly on China. Russia's rockets are praised, and so is Russia's economic progress—but without *Pravda*'s grandiose exaggerations. Instead, the stress is on Communist China's achievements: China's "unprecedented" economic and technological strides; China's "growing" military strength; China's "increasing" number of schools, homes, and offices; China's "tolerance" toward Moslems (Indonesia is a Moslem country); China's this and China's that.

And, most recently, in September, 1959, the PKI Central Committee filled the Draft Thesis for its General Report to the sixth National Congress of the Party with laudatory descriptions of China's economic progress and quotations from Chinese Communist pronouncements on ideology. Liu Shao-chi and Mao Tse-tung were quoted liberally as oracles on Party organization and on Communist "contradictions." Although Khrushchev was mentioned, he was rarely quoted.

Second, on the foreign policy line:

The PKI has launched vicious attacks against the United States, echoing Peking's hard line and ignoring Moscow's soft one. The United States is described as "falling even deeper into the abyss of economic crisis." The "U.S. imperialists" are called "the Number One enemy of all the nations of the world," and, the PKI warns, "the entire world, including the Indonesian people, are already well acquainted with the aggressive, interventionist, and oppressive nature of American imperialism."

The PKI has wholeheartedly backed Peking's distrust of the concept of "friendly neutrality." The Russians, we know, have pushed this concept, although they realize that the Chinese disapprove of it. The Russians believe that a "friendly neutral," such as India, helps the strategic goals of Communism; the Chinese believe that Russia errs if she expects India to respond gratefully to Soviet economic and diplomatic support.

The PKI has consistently cheered the Algerian rebels—even after Khrushchev decided to back De Gaulle. The Chinese support the rebels, and have even extended diplomatic recognition to them. The Russians have only recently extended de facto recognition. The PKI—in a sense an Indonesian political rebel—backs China in this disagreement.

This evidence of a general shift provides an additional explanation for the PKI's support of Peking's line on the Chinese aliens in Indonesia—and underscores a major fact about the Russian-Chinese alliance: that the largest Communist Party in Asia next to Mao's has apparently swung toward Peking. This is a major shift in the ideological balance of power in Asia.

CHAPTER ELEVEN Singapore

OVERHEARD AT THE RAFFLES:

About Singapore: It is called the "Jewel of the South Seas," a strategically located, self-governing island within the British Commonwealth of Nations. Its population is 1,500,000, of whom 50 per cent are under the age of twenty-one. Ninety per cent are Chinese. Its Prime Minister is thirty-six-year-old Lee Kuan Yew, a Cambridge-educated Chinese attorney, openly leftist, anticolonial, and yet anti-Communist. "I come from a country," Lee once said, "where 90 per cent of the people don't speak English but where all the traffic signs say 'Halt.' "

Lee would like to merge Singapore with the multiracial Federation of Malaya, to which it is already connected by a causeway. He would also like to cultivate a primary loyalty to the Malay culture and language. This aim is elusive because Singapore is a Chinese city, carrying a red torch for Peking.

There are 250,000 students in Singapore. Most of them attend Chinese schools; most of them cherish Chinese culture; and most of them are inspired by an idealistic view of Chinese Communism.

"As far as they're concerned," an American teacher commented, "all of Southeast Asia will soon be 'liberated' by the Chinese Communists, and they await Mao as though he were a god, or some kind of infallible social genius."

In 1956 the Communist apparatus was shattered after Lim Yew-hock's government had forced a revision of the pro-Marxist curricula of the Chinese schools; but in the last four years the Communists have slowly and surreptitiously regained much of their former power in the schools and the trade unions. Indeed, it is felt that the Communists may again be in a position to stage a popular uprising against the government—and possibly seize power.

Will they?

Not immediately, the experts say. One shrewd Singapore politician recently told *Newsweek*'s Robert Elegant: "We may have a breathing spell because the Communists don't want an isolated Singapore. Their real problem is not taking power, but evading power until they've built up their strength in Malaya."

In the interim, the ideological influence of Singapore's Communists is predominantly Chinese. Their newspapers did not print a single word of criticism of the Peking suppression of the Tibetan revolt; their policy is praise, praise, and more praise for Peking's economic and political achievements. In contrast, the Soviet example strikes them as distant, foreign, and Caucasian.

* * *

About Malaya: More than one-third of Malaya's 6,200,000 inhabitants are Chinese, who, like Singapore's Chinese, have become increasingly fascinated by Peking's economic and diplomatic advances. They contribute handsomely to the illegal Malayan Communist Party.

The Malayan CP was formed in 1930—appropriately enough, as a result of meetings held in China. Its membership is almost exclusively Chinese; its orientation has always been toward China. Its early leaders were identified as followers of Mao Tse-tung—those Chinese Communists who were bitterly disillusioned by Stalin's "double-cross" in 1927.

When 30,000 Japanese troops swept down the Malayan Peninsula, routing four times as many British troops, many Malayan, Indian, and Chinese intellectuals, who had respected the British, shifted their allegiance to the Malayan Communists, the only organized anticolonial political body in the nation. The Communists, under Lai Teck, fought bitterly against the Japanese. When the war ended, the Malayan Communist Party emerged as the "broadest, most powerful nongovernmental organization in Malaya." Its aim was to establish a "People's Republic of Malaya," modeled along Maoist lines. Its opponent was the British, who returned to Kuala Lumpur in 1945.

In 1947 Chin Peng, a leading Malayan Communist, journeyed to Yenan. He returned with instructions to destroy the Lai Teck faction of the Malayan CP, which was accused of "complicity" with the Japanese. In May, 1948, after the Calcutta Congress ordered all Asian CP's to swing sharply to the left, the Malayan CP shattered the National Front, in which it had participated, and launched a campaign of terror. This campaign lasted for several years, after which Chin Peng ordered his guerrillas into the jungles where they now control a self-proclaimed "liberated area" near the Thai border.

The Party has no official newspaper; but, in the opinion of former Malayan Communists now residing in Singapore, this is unimportant in evaluating its attitude toward Russia and China. The Malayan CP, they say, is "a branch of the Chinese Communist Party." It obtains funds from the *hua-chiao,* the overseas Chinese, in Malaya, and ideological guidance from Peking. For example, the Malayan CP feels that "it is following in the footsteps of the Chinese Communist Party. It too has a small 'liberated area' from which it hopes to expand to total power in Malaya; and it too believes in the Maoist concept of 'protracted war': that is, no matter how long it may take, the Malayan CP will keep up the military pressure against the government while employing every psychological and propagandistic device to force the powerful, rich Chinese to swing their full allegiance behind the Communists." They hope that this tactic will swing Malaya's political pendulum toward Communism.

This tactic may be working; in the elections to the Legislative Council of August, 1959, the pro-Communist forces gained considerable strength. For the moment, there does not appear to be any doubt that the Malayan CP is a child of Peking—not Moscow.

* * *

About Burma: Rangoon shares a common problem with Jakarta. It has a Chinese Communist Embassy that represents 650,000,000 people on the march. If one of Burma's 300,000 *hua-chiao* has a grievance against the government—a rather common phenomenon in Southeast Asia where the Chinese businessman is distrusted and disliked—he can ask his embassy to intervene, which it generally does.

These interventions have frightened Burmese politicians, who recall a long history of Chinese intrusion into their affairs. They have come to regard the *hua-chiao* as a dangerous fifth column, and they cite this evidence.

In the last five years the Communists have gained control of approximately 70 per cent of the traditional secret Chinese societies that honeycomb the *hua-chiao* community. Moreover, they are believed to have acquired a virtual stranglehold over the curriculum of most of the Chinese schools. As one venerable Chinese merchant of Kuomintang persuasion recently confided to an American: "The worst thing is, we're losing our children. They either go to Communist-run schools or are crammed into dirty, overcrowded Nationalist schools. . . . The Communists don't care about us, but they're determined to steal our children—and they're succeeding."

Everywhere in Burma's *hua-chiao* ghetto, Kuomintang influence is shrinking—and shrinking quickly. Chinese shopkeepers who are thought to be sympathetic to Chiang Kai-shek have great difficulty in obtaining loans from any of the Chinese banks, whose purse strings are held in Peking. In addition, many Chinese shoppers have been intimidated into boycotting Kuomintang-oriented stores. So, these merchants have a tough choice: they can either go out of business, which is economic suicide, or they can "rectify" their views and support the Peking cause. Most of them naturally choose "rectification."

This process is accelerated by weekly, or daily seminars, during which Communist lecturers vilify Chiang and glorify Mao. They boast of Peking's economic progress, and they delight in China's growing stature in world politics. The "students" receive massive quantities of Communist propaganda, which flow into Rangoon through two principal sources: first, the Chinese and Soviet embassies; and, second, the Communist cadres smuggled across an undefined border from mainland China.

The embassies try to be discreet. Increasingly, in the last three years, the Soviet Embassy has become so discreet that it has virtually cut its ties to the Communist underground. On the other hand, the Chinese Embassy has repeatedly violated discretion in its frank and exuberant support of Communism in Burma. This difference has led many observers to the conclusion that Burma has been incorporated into Peking's ideological sphere of influence in Asia—a conclusion that has been verified by Aleksandr Kaznachayev.

The Communist cadres who infiltrate Burma have been described as a "new kind of conquest by a human sea of civilians, two thousand to four thousand a month." Sometimes, these cadres are staffed by Yunnanese—a tribal people who live along the Sino-Burmese border. At other times they consist of Cantonese and Fukienese who can blend into Burma's *hua-chiao* community without any difficulty. In either case, they are regarded as a menace. Rangoon itself does not know how many Chinese have infiltrated Burma, but Rangoon does know that they have inflamed a highly volatile situation. Possibly, this is one reason why General Ne Win accepted a wishy-washy solution of Burma's border dispute with China in February, 1960.

* * *

About North Vietnam: Whither Ho Chi-Minh? Is he a devotee of Moscow? Is he a student of Maoism? This is one of the biggest mysteries of Asian intelligence. Ho's career is shadowy, and facts are precious.

During the Second World War, Ho worked to build up an Indo-Chinese Communist Party. His pitch was extraordinarily simple. Ho promised that Tonkin, Annam, and Cochin China—the three counties of former French Indo-China—would become a unified independent state after the defeat of the Japanese. For a time, Ho organized his guerrilla force in China, and it is possible that he was supported by Mao. In 1944 he moved into the Red River delta; and, when the Japanese were defeated, Ho's troops occupied Hanoi and Saigon. He was acclaimed a national hero.

At the Potsdam Conference, however, the Allies decided that Nationalist China should occupy all of Indo-China north of the

16th parallel while Britain (later France) should occupy all of Indo-China south of this parallel. Ho agreed that he would permit "foreign" troops to "reoccupy" Indo-China—but only if they agreed to get out in five years. In the meantime the future of Cochin-China was to be settled by plebiscite.

In 1946 Ho visited Paris, which pleased the French and displeased the Indo-Chinese nationalists. Ho felt he had reached a *modus vivendi* with the French, but he was wrong. In October, 1946, Indo-China was incorporated into a far-flung French Union. Its new constituent parts—Vietnam, Laos, and Cambodia—were viewed as subordinate divisions of the French Republic. Ho again saw the hand of "French imperialism"; and, in December, 1946, French garrisons were attacked. A long, bloody civil war erupted. The French would not yield. Neither would Ho.

When the Chinese Communists occupied the mainland in late 1949, Ho's military ventures seemed to increase—suggesting that Mao did offer Ho some military assistance. There is no reliable estimate of "how much" assistance; but in December, 1950, the French invited the United States to help them. Already deeply involved in one anti-Communist war in Korea, Washington apparently felt that it was committed to stop aggression throughout Asia.

In 1953, a black year in Indo-China, although Laos and Cambodia were granted independence, there was a chance that Ho's war against the French could have exploded into a world war. Sensing the danger, Britain, France, Russia, and the United States invited Communist China to discuss a possible solution at Geneva in April, 1954. Chou En-lai accepted; in effect, he became Ho's broker; and North Vietnam was born.

Since 1954, experts feel that Ho's orientation toward Moscow and Peking has undergone a substantial change. Earlier, it was believed that Ho was an avid Moscow supporter—largely because he felt a kinship with the French Communist Party, an ideological satellite of Moscow. Moreover, Ho, a fiery nationalist, feared that China was so big—and so close—that North Vietnam would inevitably slip under Peking's suzerainty. Ever since 1954, as China's stature has grown domestically and diplomatically, Ho's fears have been substantiated. In the opinion of experts, Ho might have wished to retain a primary loyalty to Moscow, but he has been forced by the pressure of Peking's economic and political maneuvering to bring North Vietnam under its wing.

First, economic. Ho has entered into numerous economic arrangements with Peking, which increasingly have brought Hanoi into a position of dependence upon China for military weapons and technological equipment.

Second, political. Tran Van Giau, a Vietnamese Stalinist with the strongest commitment to Moscow, used to share power with Ho. Many students of Southeast Asian Communism considered him even more important than Ho. Then, last year, Tran mysteriously lost his authority in the Vietnamese Party. Many of his former functions have been taken over by Ho. It is believed that Peking forced this change to break the back of Tran's pro-Moscow following.

If this analysis is correct—and there are some experts who say that it may not be—then the Vietnamese Communist Party has also come under Peking's influence.

* * *

About the Alliance: Many highly qualified observers in the tricky world of Singapore diplomacy believe that Peking has become a red symbol of ideological fervor throughout Southeast Asia. They feel that Moscow has come to be regarded as a "bourgeois" nation.

"This is not our opinion," an English officer said; "it is the opinion of Asian Communists."

"Why so?" I asked.

"Well, there are two reasons, I suppose. For one thing, many Asian Communists never have acknowledged Moscow as the only core of the Marxist movement. They have always felt that Maoism can answer more of their problems than Stalinism. Now that they see Mao standing up to the Russians in so many ways, they think that he may have assumed the ideological leadership of the Communist world. At least, that is what they say.

"For another, Asian Communists have a way of assessing the merits of a situation in a purely theoretical framework. And, in this sense, they have begun to think of Russia as a 'bourgeois' country. After all, Khrushchev runs around the world boasting of more and better rockets and consumer goods, whereas Mao knows he has a revolution on his hands. And his decrees sound that way. No nonsense. No creampuff solutions. Just hard work—from the bottom up. And this impresses Asian Communists, because they realize better than anyone that to make their dreams come true they have one heck of a job to do."

His summary focused my own thinking on this subject. For, ever since my arrival in Asia, I had the feeling that Russia's pitch for these underdeveloped nations was off the mark. China's was clearly on the mark. Asia likes Asians who are working hard to bring dignity and prosperity to their countries, and they are frequently willing to overlook the human cost. Asia is suspicious of Europeans—especially gadget-conscious, prosperous Europeans.

* * *

So, with the possible exception of the Vietnamese Communist Party, all of Southeast Asia's CP's have swung their ideological allegiance to Peking. As I observed earlier, this is a change. Three years ago, I heard that Moscow and Peking were running neck and neck for their allegiance. Now the race is over. China has won.

I find this fact extremely important—for at least four reasons:

First, it proves that China has projected a more convincing picture of Communist orthodoxy to the Asian CP's. It has offered them a guide for action that is applicable in Asian circumstances.

Second, China can serve as a model for the implementation of Communist reforms following the seizure of power in any Southeast Asian nation. It can also help and support these new Communist nations, when and if they materialize.

Third, on the expectation that Southeast Asia will go Communist—and this is the basis of Peking's plans—the new pro-Peking countries would give China added stature within the Communist bloc. This would have the further effect of orientating Communist strategy more toward Asia than toward Europe.

And, finally, if it is true—as many experts say it is—that China may plan one day to go it alone without Russia, it will automatically have these states as satellites.

CHAPTER TWELVE Hong Kong

IN 1842 THE CELESTIAL EMPIRE OF CHINA REACHED A SOLEMN agreement with the "barbarian nation" of England about some "petty affairs of commerce." In Confucian China, commerce was beneath contempt. A small island, inhabited by a handful of hardy Chinese fishermen, would be ceded to Britain. Merchants would be allowed to establish their "lowly business ventures" on this irregular, mountainous rock that towered, like a magnificent angel, over one of the finest harbors in the world.

Soon, the merchant ships of Britain, France, Portugal, Spain, and the United States began to dock in the harbor. Businessmen opened shops and clubs. The island prospered, luring British merchants, Maine sea captains, and Spanish sailors to its swift trade.

In 1860 the British decided that they needed Kowloon—a small strip of the Chinese coast opposite the island. They took it. The Chinese, fighting internal rebellion and external greed, were in no position to object. Kowloon secured the harbor, and China trade skyrocketed. In 1898 the British also obtained the New Territories—356 square miles of protective hills around Kowloon—for which they signed a ninety-nine-year lease.

The island was called Hong Kong.

* * *

For the next few decades, Hong Kong prospered. Edwardian customs were transplanted to the granite slopes of Victoria Peak, which reached 1,800 feet into a misty sky. Impressive mansions were built around Repulse Bay; and elegant, if slightly stuffy, hotels attracted an elegant, if slightly stuffy, clientele.

In the 1920's this idyllic British island slowly began to realize that it was living on borrowed time. Chinese revolutionaries slipped through customs, and the passionate ideas of Asian nationalism began to eat into the *status quo*. Chiang Kai-shek distrusted British imperialism, and in 1925 he tried to force England to abandon Hong Kong. He threw a trade embargo around the island that almost stifled business. But, six months later, the pressures of revolution monopolized Chiang's attention, and he lifted the embargo. Hong Kong breathed a grateful sigh of relief.

Still, Asia was in desperate turmoil. "Asia for the Asians," the Japanese chanted. Trouble seemed to lurk behind every slogan. In 1937 the "rising sun" invaded China. Four years later, the Japanese attacked Pearl Harbor; and, within a few weeks, they were in Hong Kong. For the next three years they took full advantage of Hong Kong's harbor to supply their armies in China and Southeast Asia.

After the war the British returned to a troubled island. Victoria's residents were puzzled—and deeply disturbed. Would Britain's lease be revoked? Would Maoist agitation spark a Communist revolt? Actually, neither happened. The British slowly reintroduced order, and business quietly began to recover. In fact, 1948 was a boom year. Besides, Chiang could not possibly evict the British from Hong Kong, for he himself was then being evicted from China. Mao Tse-tung was crowning twenty years of civil war with victory.

In 1949 Mao finally defeated Chiang. As the Red Army, proud and triumphant, swept toward the relatively undefended border of the New Territories, Hong Kong panicked. Businesses closed. Dependents departed. Chinese refugees packed their belongings, scanning Asia for new roots. But the panic proved to be premature. The Chinese Communists did not invade Hong Kong; they thought it would serve the interests of China's industrialization more effectively as a source of needed technological imports. Instead, the Communists played a game of nerves. They fortified surrounding islands, flooded Hong Kong with propaganda, and chided the British about their "colonialism." The result was that Hong Kong was seized by a terrible feeling of impermanence, which, over the years, has been gradually transformed into a desperate fatalism. Everyone knows that 650,000,000 people cast a big shadow. Peking can take Hong Kong at any time; the only question is when.

* * *

Three million people live in Hong Kong—most of them, Chinese. Along the city's arcaded sidewalks, shapely, slender women in tight high-necked dresses with long side slits saunter on a perpetual shopping spree; other Chinese women in bell-bottom silk trousers and pajama jackets, bent under the weight of bamboo shoulder poles, make their way through the dense crowds. In the natural harbor, washed by mist, sleek destroyers sporting the British flag are docked. Small junks rowed by sinewy Chinese sailors angle past them with graceful boldness. On the island, small houses with pitched Chinese roofs are sandwiched between skyscrapers that seem to pop out of the mountainside at arresting angles. A tram climbs up the mountain to the Peak, which overlooks an unusually attractive city that seems forever to be bathed in misty splashes of blue and green. On certain days the scenery looks as though it might have been lifted from a Ming scroll.

Against this beautiful backdrop, the burning topic of conversation is China. In Hong Kong everyone understands that "China" is Communist China—not Formosa. The diplomatic and political repartee is always spiced with sophistication, perspective, and intelligence. Consulates are staffed by specialists on Chinese affairs. (In the United States Consulate there are no "ugly" Americans; they are all dedicated, serious students of Communist China.) Hong Kong's journalists, an elite corps, bring a scholar's understanding to their story; for the study of China today is similar to the study of Russia fifteen years ago.

At that time there were pitifully few opportunities to study Moscow at close range. The days of cultural exchange were still far in the future, and a handful of Western journalists struggled with a tough censor and severe restrictions to explain Russian reality to the outside world. The major task of analysis, therefore, fell to patient scholars and interpretive reporters who took the time to go through tedious newspapers and dull periodicals for the latest shifts in the Moscow line. This is roughly the same situation that analysts face today in understanding Chinese Communist policy and behavior, and it is encouraging to report that a great deal of information about China can be gleaned from the Chinese press.

But Hong Kong has an additional asset for the student of Communist China. In many world capitals, including London, New Delhi, even Moscow, experts are limited to the study of official publications; in Hong Kong they are able to add the human touch. Hong Kong is crowded with over a million refugees from Communist China. Each has a tale of personal reality.

Therefore, it is understandable that Hong Kong should be the one spot on earth where the focus of Chinese studies is directed inward. Is Communist China marching toward an earthly utopia as one man—as the experts in some parts of the world would have us believe? Or are there "internal contradictions" of considerable dimension? How successfully has Peking communized its youth? How secure are the communes?

Some of the answers are to be found in the mainland press; others, in the stories of the refugees.

For example, in a recent copy of *China Youth Daily,* Peking admitted that its plans were not foolproof. "Youth has suffered little in the past. It has no experience in the grave struggle for life and for the class struggle. It always has some sort of unreal ideas about a wonderful, happy life. In the communes, production has increased and income grown. Youth inevitably is anxious to indulge in entertainment and satisfaction. Therefore, after the 'rich harvest' some young people wrongly felt that 'the time has come to entertain themselves' and that they could freely spend their money. These are bourgeois ideas which make their appearance in the transition period and spoil the young people. That is why they must be educated, and bourgeois influence must be combated."

With a blush, Peking even discussed its "angry young men": "A great many young people do not know how to organize their lives. Some of the young people spend the greater part of their free time sleeping; others just roam the streets; still others—a small number—have been infected by bourgeois ideas and think only of better clothing and feeding themselves and even of abandoning themselves to immorality. These problems inflict serious harm on the sound spirit of the young workers and their attitude toward production."

One Chinese lady from Shanghai, a tailor by trade: "You ask do I love my country? I hate it. That's right," she added, defensively, "I hate it. How can anyone *love* what is going on in China? To love one's country—that means you must have pride in what is happening there. And I have no pride in what is happening in China now. I hate it. Husbands cannot live with their wives, and children are separated from their parents and families. Is that good?" she asked rhetorically.

"No!" she answered.

A Chinese waiter at the Foreign Correspondents' Club spoke about pride and humor: "You want to know about China—I'll tell you. I get letters from my family. There is not enough to eat, and they have no money. Everything has been taken away—everything. Even their pride. But the worst thing for me is that they also have taken away their sense of humor. My people do not laugh any more."

A Chinese cab driver, who wanted to talk about education: "It will be worse—much worse—with the next generation. They do not learn the way we did—although more people are learning to read and write. We had a book. And it had to be memorized in three months—and known. Now they take three years with one book, and the book is always about Mao. My people cannot think any more."

Their stories may have been tailored to fit their bitterness. They may be shallow and prejudiced. But they struck me as fresh and honest. I had been listening to descriptions of China that tested my imagination: 650,000,000 robots cheering Mao; a 14,000,000-strong Communist Party that is pure in purpose and untainted by purge; Maoist infallibility; diplomacy by direction; and a sinking feeling of inevitable Communist triumph. But here in Hong Kong, this propaganda myth seemed unreal.

* * *

If Hong Kong had a way of humanizing the dehumanized image of Communist China, it also had a way of humanizing the Russian-Chinese alliance. Experts still spoke in the traditional framework of "rifts" and "shifts" in the alliance, but they could also enjoy the luxury of adding a psychological interpretation. Russia and China were not just two nations, two histories, two cultures; they were also two psychologies—and two races.

A Chinese specialist on the staff of the Union Research Service, which translates and analyzes the Chinese press, sipped hot tea in his *People's-Daily* cluttered Kowloon office. "The Russian-Chinese alliance?" he sighed, stroking his whiskerless chin. "It'll never last!"

"A rash statement for a scholar, isn't it?" I remarked.

"It can't, I tell you. China has never been able to stand on its own feet. Never. And this irks the Chinese very much. Formosa—if you want to call that China—needs the United States to stand on its feet; and Communist China needs Russia. If the Chinese have to depend on a certain people, they tend not to like them. And most people don't like the Russians anyway. They think the Russians behave very badly. Besides, the alliance can't last, because the Chinese and Russian people are too different—in background and in race—and this is very important."

"They smile today," he concluded, "but they'll fight tomorrow. Just wait until the Chinese feel they don't have to depend upon the Russians. Just wait, and you'll see."

Father Ladany, a highly respected Catholic priest who had a parish in China until the early 1950's, agreed with this reading of Chinese psychology. Tall, thin, dark-eyed and sensitive to psychological nuance, Father Ladany reminisced about the "early days."

"In 1949," he said, "the Russians began arriving in Peking as advisers. They were all highly paid. The Chinese, by the way, pay very handsomely for Soviet aid. And they would have it no other way. Anyway, as soon as the Russians got there, they were welcomed by the Chinese people who really thought of them as friends. But the disillusionment set in very quickly. The Russians spent all their money buying up everything in the Chinese stores.

My God, the Chinese told me, here are all these advanced people, and they come to buy our clothing. Maybe they're not so wonderful as we thought."

Father Ladany laughed, and his laughter was infectious. "The Chinese didn't like the way the Russians isolated themselves. They occupied separate houses in Peking, and they had very little to do with the Chinese people. And very few of them spoke Chinese. Probably it was a regulation—I do not know for sure—that stopped the Russians from fraternizing with the Chinese. But from the beginning there have been deep feelings of suspicion."

The "suspicion," I discovered, has persisted. It was not until June 24, 1959, that the Russians and the Chinese finally reached an agreement on the establishment of Soviet consulates in China. The agreement did not specify the number, function, or location of the new consulates; but it is interesting that it took over nine years for the two allies to agree to set up consulates in China. There are no Chinese consulates anywhere in Russia—nor, for that matter, are there any other foreign consulates.

Peggy and Tillman Durdin, who have covered China for the *New York Times* for over twenty years, confirmed Father Ladany's impression that the Chinese have never liked the Russians. They both believed, however, that the Chinese leaders do not contemplate a break with the Russians, which they are said to feel would be disastrous for both nations. Peggy Durdin related an anecdote that showed how the Chinese feel about Russian advisers.

One day, she said, a flour mill in Shanghai received word from Peking that a Russian woman, a consultant on flour mills, planned to visit Shanghai and would probably tour the mill. Her reputation preceded her arrival. She was supposed to be a fanatic about cleanliness, who hated dust and despised cockroaches—especially in flour mills. "As you know," Peggy smiled, "roaches are a big problem—even here in Hong Kong." So, the Chinese, who were anxious to please her, took three hours off every day for over a month cleaning up the mill. The slogan was: War Against Roaches!

The "war" went well, and finally the Russian consultant arrived. On her tour of the mill, she did not see a single roach. But at the last moment a tiny one crawled out from under a table. The woman screamed. The mill's foreman, who had been controlling his temper, was furious. He picked up the roach—and ate it. "See, does it bother me?" he shouted in anger. "Was it so important to please you that we had to stop our work for three hours every day for over a month? No, damn it, no." The millworkers applauded their leader; the Russian left, unescorted.

An American diplomat, who has studied China for many years, described the alliance as a "marriage of incompatibles." "There are inevitable problems in our society," he said, "when a white marries a Negro. Well, in the Communist world, there are inevitable problems too when white Russia 'marries' yellow China. The race is different, and so is the psychology. There were major problems built into this alliance from the very beginning." He glanced out of the window, as he lit his pipe.

"But that doesn't mean there will be a break in the alliance. Not at all. They share a common world outlook; they are both Marxist; they see the world as moving in a certain direction, and they are pleased—their differences notwithstanding—that they are both going in that direction." Rather abruptly, the diplomat began to laugh. "You know, I say this, and I laugh because I'm really not sure I believe it. The Chinese have, in my view, taken over the ideological leadership of the world. And there is a school of thought that the Chinese may break off from the Russians even before they reach economic self-sufficiency. And, besides all this, the differences in foreign policy are becoming more pronounced every day."

I noted that the "differences" were apparent in India, Algeria, the Middle East, and Southeast Asia. "Where else?" I asked. "In Latin America," he answered.

"From 1949 on," he began, "the Chinese have tried to cultivate Latin America with trade and culture—well before the Russians adopted the soft sell themselves. Peking has invited many South American intellectuals. For instance, in 1951, Pablo Neruda, the Chilean poet, visited China."

Afterward, Neruda wrote an article for *People's Daily,* in which he poked fun at the American policy of nonrecognition: "They could not recognize the earth, yet the earth moves, moves forward, and not backward as they willed. . . . Let them ask of miners, of peasants by the thousands, of professors and poets, of old and young, from Alaska to the Antarctic, and they will have their answer: We recognize! We recognize! The great revolutionary Mao Tse-tung, we honor him!" This might have sounded like a straight Party-line attitude to Washington, but it made sweet music in Peking.

In March, 1952, José Ventureli, the Chilean painter, visited China; and a Chilean trade delegation signed a commercial agreement with Peking in October, 1952. An Argentine delegation also signed a trade agreement—in October, 1954.

In addition, the Chinese have staged numerous Latin-American art exhibitions; and frequently they have held "popular" rallies in Peking to denounce the United States as the "common enemy" of China and Latin America.

"Moreover," the American diplomat continued, "the Chinese have tripled the number of their Spanish and Portuguese broadcasts to Latin America in the last few years; and the Hsinhua News Agency has opened an office in Havana. Now, we know that the Russians have also stepped up the output of their Latin American propaganda; but we think there is a difference between the two. The Russians want to gain an economic foothold in Latin America. They would like to see many more Castro regimes. In essence, they would like to embarrass the United States. The Chinese want more than this. They think the United States is about to collapse because of 'internal contradictions.' So they reason that if the United States were suddenly deprived of its Latin American markets, our economy would fold up, and we would be thrown into a depression—we and the rest of the world.

"Furthermore, Peking's pitch to Latin America is very self-conscious. The propaganda is keyed to China—not Communism; and this disturbs the Russians—almost as much as the fact that the Chinese may be making independent contacts with various Latin American CP's at their expense."

He puffed thoughtfully on his pipe. "Are you coming around to the 'break' view yourself?" I asked. "It's an awfully attractive hypothesis," he said, "but, in answer to your question, not yet. There is still much more keeping them together than driving them apart."

A French diplomat, who admitted that he filed a report on China to Paris only "once every four or five months," discounted all hypotheses that speculated on the possibility of a break. Like other foreign diplomats in Hong Kong who took a conservative view of the alliance, he could cite a glowing Chinese appraisal of Khrushchev as "proof." The appraisal was made by Kuo Mo-jo, Chairman of the China Peace Committee, in Moscow on May 16, 1959. "Comrade Khrushchev," he reportedly said, "is an outstanding Marxist and a loyal successor to the cause of Lenin. He has contributed handsomely in his work during the past decades for the cause of safeguarding peace. As a supreme leader of the Soviet Union, he has employed his brilliant wisdom and ability in the building of the Soviet Union, the nucleus force of world peace, into a state more beautiful and stronger than ever."

The French diplomat also cited a statement by Soong Ching-ling, wife of Sun Yat-sen, who is president of the Sino-Soviet Friendship Society. "Recently, the imperialists and the revisionists have been resorting to all kinds of dirty tricks in an attempt to disturb the friendship between the Soviet Union and China, the two biggest socialist countries. In doing this, our enemies once again expose their ugly features, and can succeed in nothing."

These pats on the back have ritualistic meaning, but I am not convinced that they mean a break is impossible—certainly, not in themselves. A week before Stalin attacked Tito in 1948, the Soviet press was full of praise for Yugoslavia. Two weeks later, it was venomous in its attack.

Occasionally, it should be remembered, the Chinese press has contained blistering attacks against the Russians that serve as a sobering antidote to the saccharine professions of "boundless love." During the "rectification campaign" of 1957, when Mao encouraged his intellectuals to express their innermost thoughts, the Peking press published damning testimony about Moscow's "economic generosity."

For example, Lung Yun, Vice-Chairman of the National Defense Council, said: "It is unreasonable for China to bear all the expenses of the resist-America, aid-Korea war. . . . During the

Second World War, the United States granted loans and leases to her Allies. Later some of these Allies refused to pay back the loans while the United States excused some from repayment. It will take us more than ten years to repay the loans from the Soviet Union if we can ever repay them. *Besides, we have to pay interest to the Soviet Union.* China fought for socialism, but look at the results. . . . The Soviet Army dismantled and shipped away some of the machinery of our factories when it liberated northeast China. What was the price paid by the Soviet Union? Will the Soviet Union compensate us?"

These were provocative questions, and they had sparked provocative debates. Chinese economists apparently realized that Peking would have to pay Russia back in agricultural exports, which would produce dissatisfaction in China and would raise the question about whether Peking really needed so many Russian imports.

Yeh Chi-chuang, Minister of Foreign Trade, said in 1955: "Some people ask if the present volume of our exports is too large and has caused tension in the supply of our domestic market." Po I-po, Chairman of the National Economic Committee, said in 1956: "Our country is basically able to make our own equipment and build our own power plants, and . . . we are beginning to equip our own transportation and agricultural departments and to strengthen our defense with our own machines. . . . With the exception of certain enterprises with the most advanced technical level, our own equipment should be adopted, even if the quality is somewhat inferior."

Chinese scholars also objected to Soviet intrusion. Po Chueh-min, a leading geographer at Nankai University, protested: "Bound by certain dogma, I was forced to accept all things from the Soviet Union, lock, stock and barrel, despite the fact that some things were not persuasive to me. . . . They did not agree entirely with the reality of China. Yet I still had to follow them." Chi T'ao-ta, head of the Economics Department of Nankai University, agreed: "The discussion is based on conclusions drawn by other people rather than on our own concrete conditions and real data."

But, by June, 1957, these anti-Soviet sentiments were gagged.

Lu Ting-yi, director of the Propaganda Department of the CCP, attacked many scholars for "sowing discontent" between the Soviet Union and China. "These statements," he said, "are in fact reproductions of those of the imperialists and Chiang Kai-shek, wanting to brand the Soviet Union as 'red imperialism' and a nation that does not treat China on an equal footing." This attack was published on July 11, 1957—one of a series which ended the "rectification" campaign.

It would be interesting, I thought, to measure the praise and condemnation against the personal reflections of Percy Chen, an attorney who has been billed as Peking's official voice in Hong Kong. Chen, part-Trinidadian, part-Chinese, was born in Trinidad and educated in Great Britain. During the 1930's, while his father, Eugene Chen, served as Chiang's Foreign Minister, he represented General Motors in Russia. Later, he too worked for Chiang. In 1949, Chen, a charming, ambitious man, changed sides. He has worked for Mao ever since.

"How is the Russian-Chinese alliance getting along?" I asked. Chen had a personality that inspired informality. He showed me a picture of an attractive Caucasian woman. "Very lovely," I said.

"She's my wife," Chen responded. "She's a Russian, and we are now celebrating our thirtieth anniversary. That, my friend, is how well the Russian-Chinese alliance is getting along." Chen smiled engagingly.

I told Chen that many Hong Kong experts felt that China paid steep prices for Soviet aid. "That's right," Chen snapped; "we pay high prices, and we would not have it any other way." His voice had the kind of British accent that one frequently hears in the Caribbean. "We want our trade and our loans to be on a strictly business basis with the Russians. We do not want any favors. We do not want anything for which we cannot pay. And we do not want to feel dependent upon the Russians. In fact, I may say that we have already paid the Russians back for everything—except, of course, the new loan which we just obtained." This checked with what I had heard in London. "It's against Chinese psychology," Chen added, "to work out any business arrangement on any other basis."

I recalled what Alex Josey, a Singapore-based journalist, had told me at the Raffles about his meeting years earlier with Chou En-lai. Josey asked him about Russian economic aid. Chou praised the Russians for their generosity; then he added that Peking would soon pay back the Russians, implying that Peking did not want anything for nothing. Josey remarked that this sounded like a straight commercial transaction between capitalists. Yes, Chou was reported to have answered, it must be that way. We want to pay the Russians back for their help. We do not want to be indebted to anyone.

At this point, Chen changed topics. He started to talk in a broadly philosophical way about China. He said China has a civilization dating back five thousand years. "We've seen many civilizations come and go. But we are here, and we are doing quite well." He rattled off some impressive statistics. I told him I did not doubt for a moment that the Chinese Communists had made substantial economic strides. "The Chinese people like to have fun. They are a proud people, and they are superb workers. They will build Communism."

"Will they build it before the Russians do?" I asked.

Chen smiled. "You're raising another question."

"Perhaps," I conceded, "but will the Chinese build Communism before the Russians?"

"The communes," Chen began, "are the result of the grafting of urban methods on the framework of a rural society. It will obliterate differences between urban and rural work, and it will obliterate all other differences, too. It is our form for the transition to Communism or socialism; we will stick to it."

This was sophisticated ideological double talk. "But, Mr. Chen," I insisted, "will the Chinese get to Communism before the Russians?"

"You're stubborn," Chen said, as a playful smile came over his face, "but, if you insist, I would say it is entirely possible that the Chinese can arrive at Communism before any other nation."

"Why?"

Chen answered, with an expansive gesture that "there is not so much to get rid of. We can build on an almost virgin base and then go on to Communism without having to overcome many of the pitfalls of capitalist development that the Russians now face."

"How is Russia doing in overcoming these pitfalls?"

"Very well," Chen answered condescendingly. "Russia is slowly ridding itself of many basic antagonisms and pitfalls."

* * *

This kind of Chinese condescension must irritate the Russians—especially when it is focused on what is currently the most sensitive area of Moscow-Peking relations—the communes. Ever since August, 1958, when the Chinese defiantly announced a new social program based on rural and urban communes, a bitter dialogue between Mao and Khrushchev has occupied the attention of Communist ideologists and Western specialists. Peking said that every Chinese peasant would be moved into communes. The statement was simple, but a tremendous social revolution was involved.

"At daybreak, bells ring and whistles blow. . . . In about a quarter of an hour, the peasants line up. At the command of company and squad commanders, the teams march to the fields, holding flags. Here one no longer sees peasants in groups of two or three, smoking and going leisurely to the fields. What one hears are the sounds of measured steps and marching songs. The desultory living habits which have been with the peasants for thousands of years are gone forever. . . . All the ties that bind the peasants are broken. . . . The frames of individual families which had existed for thousands of years have been completely smashed. . . . Individualism has absolutely no market here."

This was the way Peking Radio described a typical morning on a new commune. A truly phenomenal campaign to force over 500,000,000 peasants into communes had been launched, and Chinese propagandists became so enthusiastic that they began to leapfrog whole stages of the Marxist blueprint of history. Said one propagandist: "At a time when the national economy and culture are developing at such a rate that 'twenty years are concentrated in a single day,' one can visualize the gradual transition of our country from socialism to Communism." Said another enthusiast: "Generally speaking, the transformation of collective ownership into ownership by the people as a whole is a process that will take three or four years—even five or six years, to complete in the rural areas." In the Soviet countryside, after forty-two years, private plots still existed—and thrived.

Thus, without having officially unfurled the flag of socialism, Peking was already waving the banner of Communism; and Moscow was upset. The Soviet press, which usually banner headlines every minor Chinese achievement, deliberately ignored the most colossal social revolution of the twentieth century; and Moscow Radio mentioned the communes three times in 215 broadcasts beamed to the Far East.

The Russians knew that the Chinese had hurled them a dramatic challenge for the ideological supremacy of the socialist world. With their communes, they had announced, in effect, that they would reach Communism first. It was a challenge the Russians were reluctantly forced to accept.

Pavel Yudin, Russia's former theoretician-ambassador to Peking, answered for Premier Khrushchev: "The basis of this unbreakable friendship between the peoples of the Soviet Union and China is the unity of our purpose in the struggle to build a *socialist* society in China and a *Communist* society in the Soviet Union at the greatest speed."

Early in December, 1958, Khrushchev decided he could speak for himself. As reported by Democratic Senator Hubert Humphrey of Minnesota, the Soviet leader was undiplomatically abusive about the communes. "Reactionary," "old-fashioned," he stormed.

A few weeks later, the Chinese Communists announced, somewhat shamefacedly, that they had become "dizzy with success." They made it clear that they were not building Communism in China—only socialism—and that it was still too early to institute communes in urban areas of the country. However, they repeated their "belief" that the communes remained the "basic transitional form to Communism" and would not be abandoned in rural regions. It was not yet clear whether the Chinese made this announcement because of Soviet pressure or administrative inefficiency—or both. In any case, in January, 1959, Soviet First Deputy Premier Anastas Mikoyan echoed Khrushchev's attack against the communes during his visit to the United States; and Khrushchev, addressing the twenty-first Party Congress in February, told the assembled delegates, Chou En-lai included, that *all* socialist countries would reach Communism "more or less at the same time." A week later, he signed an economic agreement with the Chinese, promising $1,250,000,000 in aid to be administered over a nine-year period; and he denounced Senator Humphrey as a "fabricator" of fairy tales. In addition, the celebration of the ninth anniversary of the Russian-Chinese alliance on February 14, 1959, seemed unusually warm.

Everyone would have thought that the commune squabble was over. It had been serious. Khrushchev had been maneuvered into an ideological corner by the Chinese assertion that an underdeveloped nation could reach Communism before an urban, industrialized society. He had swallowed his pride—as he has had to do before—and he had pronounced his new dictum on the simultaneous admission of all socialist states to the paradise of Communism. He had also given the Chinese a big financial boost. For their part, the Chinese had "backed down"—to use a Lowenthal expression. They no longer boasted of leapfrogging to Communism, and their ideological enthusiasts were brought under control.

But the controversy continued. In Soviet philosophical journals Khrushchev's new dictum was "explained." The idea was not that an underdeveloped nation would really become a Communist nation *at the same time* as an industrial nation. No, the idea was more general. It was that backward and advanced nations, which were either developing socialism or had already developed socialism, were in the vanguard of a broad historical movement toward Communism. Naturally, the argument continued, these nations would reach Communism "more or less at the same time," but this phrase had to be understood as a flexible time factor. Thus, "more or less" could mean a time difference of fifty to one hundred years.

Moreover, these journals alluded to an earlier analysis by T. S. Stepanyan. This Soviet philosopher had argued that European socialist states, including the Soviet Union, would reach Communism first, while Asian socialist states would reach Communism later. This viewpoint was never rejected.

It was against the background of this ideological debate between

Moscow and Peking that I began my legwork on the Russian-Chinese alliance in June, 1959. In every interview, in every capital, the commune question throbbed like an infected sore: in London, where experts were frankly bewildered; in Munich, where Ritvo speculated that the communes had forced Khrushchev to convene the twenty-first Party Congress merely to announce his new, vague formula on the simultaneous admission of all socialist states to Communism; in Vienna, where Rusisans themselves were prompted to criticize the Chinese "experiment"; and, in Warsaw, where the entire debate again burst into world headlines—without any apparent cause. For the first time, Khrushchev publicly attacked the communes. He argued that Russia had tried them soon after the Bolshevik Revolution, "but many people erroneously understood *even then* what Communism is and how it ought to be built." They failed, Khrushchev continued, because "there were not the appropriate conditions. . . . A situation arose in which everyone wanted to live well and at the same time to contribute as little work as possible to the common cause."

This frank attack puzzled many specialists. They could not understand what prompted Khrushchev to resurrect the issue in so dramatic a context—before a group of recalcitrant Catholic peasants in Poznań, scene of the 1956 uprising. They understood, however, that Khrushchev had brought the battle of the communes out of the obscurity of ideological jargon into the limelight of popular discussion. In his direct manner, Khrushchev was hurling the ideological challenge back in Peking's face.

Mao did not respond immediately. He needed time to think. He and his colleagues had been missing from Peking all summer, and experts in Singapore and Hong Kong wondered why. Only one thing was clear as we got closer to China: the communes had become a terribly irritating question—possibly the most irritating question ever to arise in the Russian-Chinese alliance.

One British journalist, based in Singapore, speculated one warm afternoon that the Chinese Communist Party had split over the issue of the communes. "I think Chou En-lai heads a so-called 'rightist' faction that believes the Russian-Chinese alliance is considerably more important than the irritating presence of the communes. Ranged against Chou are the 'leftists' such as Mao and Liu Shao-chi, who feel China's big problems of overpopulation and underproduction can only be solved within the framework of the communes."

An American diplomat, based in Hong Kong, represented another point of view. Gazing at Kowloon's hazy mountain tops, which seem to shelter Hong Kong's prosperity from the storm of the Chinese revolution just on the other side, he told me that he doesn't think there is any evidence of a high-level split in the Party. "I think the Chinese leaders have simply gone off somewhere in the hills—as they have so many times in the past—to take stock, to try to figure out what to do with the nation's serious economic problems."

Either school may yet be proved correct. When I arrived in Hong Kong, Peking had just announced that a meeting of the Chinese Communist Party had been held in August. Peripheral evidence also indicated that this meeting was only one of a series of high-echelon gatherings, at which, after considerable soul searching, the Chinese had made three characteristic announcements.

First, they admitted that production statistics for 1958 had been inflated. Only 250,000,000 tons of grain had been harvested—not, as previously reported, 375,000,000 tons. Only 8,000,000 tons of steel—not 11,000,000 tons. And those back-yard Bessemers did not produce "quality" steel. But the increases were stupendous, the statistical cutbacks notwithstanding.

Second, the Chinese said their production goals for 1959 had to be revised; they too had apparently been given an upward bias. Not 575,000,000 tons of grain—only 275,000,000 tons. The year 1959, it was sadly recalled, was one of "natural disasters such as floods and droughts."

Third, they decided to continue the "glorious task" of the "great leap forward" and to stick by the communes, which "not only have taken firm root but are ever more manifestly displaying their advantages."

And, finally, if Khrushchev was spoiling for a tussle over the communes, Mao was apparently willing to oblige. Early in September, I picked up a copy of *Red Flag,* the authoritative ideological journal of Chinese Communism on a newsstand in Hong Kong. (Hong Kong is saturated with Chinese Communist propaganda; there is little Russian propaganda.) Its lead editorial stunned all Western observers who kept a close check on the Chinese scene. It lashed out at "enemy agents" and "right opportunist ideas which hamper our advance." Then, in extraordinarily strong language, it defended the communes. In part, the editorial said that the Chinese peasants "are refashioning with *their own* hands *their own* destiny." "The difficulties are great." And "if . . . one thinks there are ready 'patterns' for everything and that things can be done according to 'patterns' and therefore everything goes as smoothly and calmly as plain sailing without any difficulty or setback, *this thinking, if it is not a bourgeois viewpoint toward mass movements, it is no more than the illusion of fools . . .*"

"Its a real puzzler," a journalist remarked. "After all, why should Khrushchev care how the Chinese peasants live? And, for that matter, why should Mao be concerned that Khrushchev, who may be just another 'foreign devil' to Mao, does not like his pet project?"

These are the questions I asked all the experts—not only in Hong Kong. Based on these interviews, I have come to these general conclusions. The Chinese Communists are realistic politicians. Soon after their 1949 triumph, they realized that they had a big problem on their hands. Their population was about to explode; they wanted to modernize, but they were plagued by China's perennial evils—poverty and hunger. Because they were devout Marxists, who had studied the Soviet example, they naturally turned to industrialization as the magic key. They would encourage industrialization, they reasoned, while an urban proletariat developed. In the meantime the peasants would be herded into collective farms where they hoped to produce enough food to feed themselves and the city folk.

But the supply of people was increasing much more rapidly than the supply of food—especially the food that was to feed the urban population. The Chinese tried birth control, which was suddenly proclaimed a social virtue, but it didn't work. It was just at this time—in late 1957—that Mao probably made a desperate decision. He would push China into a vast program of communization. There is no evidence that he considered communes before late 1957.

It appears that China's urban population faced the threat of starvation unless the entire agricultural setup was changed. And the change had to satisfy the demands of China's basic dilemmas —overpopulation and underproduction. The change was the communes. Mao hoped they would produce enough of a surplus on a regular basis to ensure the delivery of sufficient food to the cities.

In this "communal" setting Mao hoped to prove in China what Stalin had not been able to prove in Russia—that Communism could flower in an agrarian society. In 1952 Stalin had warned his colleagues that Russia could not advance to Communism until it had converted all of its collective farms into state farms. This was very difficult, Stalin said, because the peasants had grown accustomed to the luxury of private property on the collectives. In the transition to state farming, they would have to abandon the luxury, since no private property would be tolerated under this form of socialist agriculture. Mao hoped that the communes would hurry China toward socialist agriculture.

It was a gigantic job, but it was worth the effort. Thus, the communes were championed as the golden chariot for the ride to Communism, or, as it was later modified, to socialism. The ride might be bumpy, but it was a one-way road.

Khrushchev's reasons for attacking the communes are far more complicated than Mao's reasons for promoting them. First, Khrushchev did not like the way the Chinese jumped from one stage of the Marxist dialectic to another without waiting for the green light. The Chinese were supposed to be building socialism, and here they were talking as though they had discovered an independent short cut to Communism!

A second reason concerned Khrushchev's own agricultural program. In December, 1958, a plenary session of the Central Committee of the Soviet Communist Party met in Moscow. Khrushchev delivered the major address, and, interestingly, in fifteen thousand words he did not once mention China. Yet China's communes seem to have motivated his reasoning.

Khrushchev argued that it was a good idea to let the collective farms buy the farm machinery formerly owned by the Party-dominated Machine Tractor Stations, which had used this machinery as a level of control; to abolish the old system of forced deliveries of agricultural products from the farms to the state; and to pay the peasants primarily in cash rather than in kind. In other words, Khrushchev argued for a more liberal, money-conscious, profit-motivated agricultural organization. "Some comrades will ask: But if we want to go forward to Communism, how can it be a road to Communism if we extend relations of free sale . . . whereas we have learned in school that Communism is a state of affairs where there exists organized distribution and no market relations?" Khrushchev answered his own challenge: "You can't get to Communism unless you first have abundance, and you can't get abundance until you lower costs, and you can't lower costs unless you use the yardstick of the ruble."

As Khrushchev fought for this view, the Chinese appeared to have come upon a more orthodox, fundamentalist approach to Communism, using the commune as the basis for a Marxist system of incentive based upon community need rather than upon individual profit. This was thrown up to Khrushchev, and he did not like it.

Nor for that matter did Khrushchev like the haughtiness with which the Chinese announced the communes. It sounded too much like the classical Chinese story about the younger Confucian brother who deftly stole his elder's thunder. It sounded, in other words, like a repudiation of the entire Soviet experience, a refusal to follow Russia's example of forced collectivization and industrialization, and a claim to have discovered a far more effective way of reaching Communist goals.

Finally, the Chinese established a model of economic development and organization for the underdeveloped areas of the world —areas that the Russians had been cultivating for a longer time. The Russians justifiably felt that African and Asian nationalists, who welcome any short cut to prosperity, would begin to look to China for ideological leadership and social example. Thus, in one lightning stroke, the Chinese had stolen the underdeveloped market for ideas from the Russians—or so it appeared to the Kremlin—and Khrushchev was peeved.

For all of these reasons, the communes exercised an irritating influence on the Russian-Chinese alliance—for the moment, the most divisive influence that has ever affected the Moscow-Peking axis.

* * *

Against the background of this mushrooming disagreement on the communes, I had a chance to examine two other questions of vital concern to an understanding of the alliance: one involved the possibility that the Chinese Communist Party might actually have become divided in its loyalty to Moscow, and the other concerned a rash of speculation that Peking might be close to developing an atomic bomb. I had heard conflicting reports about both questions. I asked Hong Kong's experts where I could uncover more information. The concensus seemed to be—Formosa for politics, Japan for the bomb. "But be careful," a friend cautioned, "each nation has its own ax to grind."

CHAPTER THIRTEEN Taipei

BANGKOK WAS THE ONLY SOUTHEAST ASIAN CAPITAL WHERE I could get a visa to the Republic of China, or Taiwan, a small, lush, semitropical island about one hundred miles east of Amoy on the China coast. A diplomatic curiosity in Asia, the Chinese Embassy in Bangkok is impressive—but quiet, almost ghostly.

The green lawn surrounding the embassy, a two-tiered pagoda, is neatly cropped. Exotic shrubs take on a purple hue under the hot sun, and sky-blue flowers line the path to the visa office. There, officials are delighted to help an American. "How much?" I asked automatically. "No charge," a young Chinese diplomat replied. "Your visa expires in four years."

Everyone seems to speak in a whisper, although everyone knows that big decisions are no longer made at the embassy. Important conferences are seldom held under its pitched roof. In fact, the embassy is more of a political symbol than a diplomatic mission; it stands for Nationalist China—a huge nation, not a small island, free of Communist control, and for the hope that President Chiang Kai-shek will resume his authority over the mainland.

The ambassador, Dr. Han Lih-wu, is a cultured, soft-spoken educator who enjoys Plato as well as Confucius.

"The Chinese people will not tolerate the inhumanity of Communism much longer," Dr. Han said.

"They've tolerated it for ten years already," I commented.

"Yes," he replied, "but not much longer. Not much longer." His voice did not ring with conviction. He seemed to speak as much for himself as for me. He reached for a blue-and-white pamphlet that lay on his teakwood desk. He opened it.

"May I read you something?" Dr. Han asked.

"Please."

"This is from an Associated Press dispatch—filed from Taipei. 'People here don't seem to know what the word *defeat* means. The Chinese man in the street . . . does not doubt that Chiang Kai-shek's sunburst flag will eventually replace the Chinese Red's five yellow stars on red, but he likes to guess about just when the great event will be.' "

"What is your guess?" I wondered.

"Not much longer," Dr. Han repeated softly.

"Here. Take this pamphlet. I wrote it. It is about Taiwan."

* * *

The 158-page pamphlet is called *Taiwan Today*. A combination of apology, history, and propaganda, it contains a revealing Introduction. Dr. Han discusses the origins of Taiwan, which he describes as the size of Holland, about 13,800 square miles. Early Chinese records, he says, mention invasions from the mainland; they speak about the many Chinese fishermen who came to Taiwan, which means "terraced bay," from the coastal provinces of Fukien and Kwangtung. In the sixteenth century, Portuguese, Spanish, and Dutch merchants arrived on Taiwan, and they "made several attempts to colonize the island." The Dutch finally succeeded.

They ruled Taiwan from 1624 to 1661, an important date in Chinese history. The victorious Manchus had just conquered the mainland after a long and bloody struggle; the discredited and defeated Ming dynasty escaped to Taiwan. At this point, Dr. Han should be quoted in full:

"In 1661, Cheng Chen-kung, a Ming leader and patriot, was driven from the mainland and sailed for Taiwan. He was permitted to use the family name of the Ming dynasty and became known as Kuo Hsing Yeh, which sounded more like 'Koxinga' to the Dutch, and so he is known as Koxinga to most Europeans. He arrived on Taiwan with many thousands of Chinese, drove the Dutch from the island, and set up the last remnant of Ming rule. Many thousands of Chinese followed him to escape Manchu rule and the population grew to around 100,000. It was a population movement somewhat similar to the migration of settlers to America in search of political and religious freedom. But the Manchus finally took over Taiwan, too, in 1683."

I was struck by the extraordinary parallel. Chiang—the new Koxinga. Mao—the new Manchu. It was a credit to Dr. Han that he added the fateful conclusion of Koxinga's political career.

* * *

Taiwan lives prosperously behind the protective shield of the United States Seventh Fleet. Through the efficient offices of the International Co-operation Administration, hundreds of millions of dollars have been pumped into the Taiwanese economy. A well-conceived and administered land reform has given the peasant a personal stake in President Chiang's future, and nature has blessed the island with fertility and beauty. Taiwan produces three rice harvests a year—one of which can be earmarked for export to earn needed foreign currency. Private industry aimed at consumer production has increased, and education is free and compulsory. Dr. Han says that over 90 per cent of the children of school age attend classes.

Taipei, the capital, is an overgrown town, but it is clean and thriving. The influence of Main Street is omnipresent: jukeboxes and Coca-Cola, and dance halls and the strip tease. The Chinese women in Tiapei seem to prefer a matching skirt and blouse to the high-necked, side-slit dresses of Hong Kong. Although the Japanese ran Taiwan for half a century, the street signs are in English and Chinese.

An American military mission has opened its headquarters on Taipei's Fifth Avenue, and American automobiles dart through the city's traffic composed largely of rickshaws, bicycles, scooters, and an occasional horse and wagon.

In the center of Taipei is a big statue of Chiang Kai-shek, who wields dictatorial power behind a democratic façade. It was already clear in September, 1959, when we visited Taipei, that the constitutional prohibition against a third term would be lifted in 1960 to permit Chiang to "run" for the presidency. He exercises power through the political mechanism of the Kuomintang, which is modeled after the Soviet Communist Party. Chiang himself was trained in Moscow during the 1920's. His son, Chiang Ching-kuo, who is in charge of the secret police and the army, was educated in Russia. He was even a member of the Komsomol, and he speaks Russian fluently. Thus, both father and son represent a striking paradox: trained by Communism, they utilize some of its organizational techniques and fear its political consequences.

After a decade of China-on-Taiwan, many Nationalist Chinese have begun to abandon their dream of returning to the mainland. Some think of Taiwan as home; others plan to leave—possibly for Canada or the United States. Very few hope for a "return."

This attitude is reflected in the government's continuing re-evaluation of the possibility of a political return to the mainland. Of course, Chiang still denounces a "two-China" policy. "This cowardly and selfish attitude is like pacifying the tiger with one's own flesh and inviting the robber to become master of the house," he commented recently. But, seven or eight years ago, he would not have dignified the policy with any comment. At that time, he entertained the idea of "recapturing" the mainland. This obviously irritated the Communists, who regard Chiang as a "renegade," a "has-been." President Truman "leashed" Chiang. President Eisenhower "unleashed" him—and then "re-leashed" him. But neither Truman nor Eisenhower removed the Seventh Fleet, which serves the double function of keeping Mao out of Taiwan and Chiang out of China.

These days Chiang does not talk about "recapturing" the mainland; he knows the idea disturbs Washington; besides, he is no longer sure that it is possible. Instead, he limits his propaganda to a rather vague formula that includes uncertain proportions of popular uprising, national revolution, and Nationalist invasion. As Dr. Han writes: "Chinese Communism is bound to fail. Marxism has long been outmoded by economic development. It simply will not work in China—there isn't enough capital in China to communize the Chinese. If the Reds continue their practice of communizing consumer goods, the Chinese will be reduced to paupers. But against the tight control of the Communist Party, the secret service and the police, and by force of arms, a revolution would not be easy unless it were a widespread insurgence caused by general starvation. But revolution would be another matter when the Nationalists start to attack the mainland."

Chiang elaborates: "In choosing the right moment to launch our counteroffensive, it is better to deliberate carefully before moving than to act impulsively only to abandon the effort halfway." His deliberations have become so careful that many Chinese intellectuals on Taiwan have practically given up the notion of again raising the "sunburst" flag over Peking.

* * *

Just as Chiang's view of his return to the mainland has undergone a subtle metamorphosis, so too has his evaluation of the Russian-Chinese alliance. (Actually, Nationalist Chinese do not like to use the word "alliance"; in their minds, it connotes a kind of equality, which they do not officially see in the Moscow-Peking relationship.) It used to be that Taipei regarded the Chinese Communists merely as Russia's puppets—pathetic dolls which could be cynically manipulated by Moscow. For the record, even a scholar, such as Dr. Han, must repeat this line.

"By treaty and contract, by fetters and chains, Communist China is attached to Soviet Russia. In name, they are allies and comrades. The Russians have a tight grip on Red China, with agents and advisers all over the mainland. . . . Moscow is adept at pulling wires, at passing out orders, at making others do its work and fighting. When the time is ripe, according to Moscow's own calculation, it will strike if necessary. . . . Communist China is an important running dog in this plan. . . . Red China is a potent force at the service of Russia that can create a great deal of mischief. . . . The Chinese Communists are being equipped and trained for not only the defense of the Chinese mainland, but for the extension of Russian imperialism."

It suits Taipei's purposes to portray the Chinese Communists as the "running dogs" of Russian "imperialism." Thus Mao is stigmatized as the Chinese "puppet" of a "foreign power," while Chiang is glorified as a purely Chinese phenomenon.

Now, the Kuomintang's view of the "alliance" has changed—subtly, but substantially. After a week of interviews I am convinced that a measure of sophistication has been added to Taipei's official analysis of the Russian-Chinese alliance. The analysis is still motivated by political bias, but it is supported by sources—from the mainland and Taiwan—who have had intimate associations with the leading personalities of the Chinese Communist Party. These sources have been correct in the past; they called the Tibetan uprising and Liu's accession to the presidency of Communist China in December, 1958. They may again be proved correct in their analysis of the CCP's attitude toward Moscow. In any case, their opinions are valuable, and they should be heard and assessed.

* * *

First, Chiang's view. The Generalissimo, according to informed sources, believes that a personal feud between Premier Khrushchev and Chairman Mao has developed in the last few years, especially since the Chinese pronouncement on the communes. In fact, he says, it has touched off a chain reaction that has split the Chinese Communist Party into two factions: the pro-Moscow, or "internationalist," faction and the pro-Peking, or "native," faction.

Khrushchev's political strategy is supposedly aimed at "liquidating" Mao; presumably Russia would then be in a position to "control" the entire Chinese Party. Chiang describes Mao as a "fanatical Stalinist" who is battling heavy odds to retain his personal power. But, he says, Mao does not want to break China's ties with Russia; and neither does Khrushchev.

Ch'en Chien-chung's concept of the alliance is a mirrored reflection of Chiang's. Ch'en is one of the younger leaders of the Kuomintang, an "expert on mainland politics." Ch'en bears a striking physical resemblance to Chou En-lai, though his political orientation is somewhat different.

Ch'en believes that there is a major struggle for power in the Chinese Communist Party between Liu Shao-chi and Mao Tse-tung. Chou En-lai, he says, is only "peripherally involved." In 1955 Mao and Liu began to differ on policies for the solution of China's economic crisis. Ch'en suggested that while Mao felt China had to depend upon China—and only China—Liu was more sympathetic to the idea of increased Soviet economic aid.

Ch'en quickly sketched in some of the details of Liu's "Russian" background. Liu, he said, went to Moscow twice for intensive revolutionary training, first from 1922 to 1925, and then from 1928 to 1930. He studied at Sun Yat-sen University and took additional courses at the Red Army Academy. He participated in the 1929 Russian expedition against Manchuria, after which he was made secretary of the Manchurian regional committee of the Comintern. Thus, Liu was described as a Chinese Communist with a warm spot in his heart for Moscow.

Ch'en went on to explain that Liu strongly disapproved of Mao's commune policy but that Mao was able to override his objections because, between 1955 and 1958, he had replaced eleven provincial Party secretaries, supporters of Liu in key positions, with eleven of his own trusted lieutenants. These changes gave him the strength to proceed with the commune drive.

However, Ch'en continued, when the communes showed initial signs of sputtering, and when the Russians tacitly expressed their displeasure, Liu rallied enough forces within the Party to oppose Mao, to force him to relinquish his job as President of China, and to modify his commune claims. Since that time, Ch'en says, Mao's political power and prestige have been severely reduced. Now he can no longer decree legislation; he must seek the approval of the Party plenum.

Ch'en described Chou's position as that of conciliator between Mao and Liu, but pointed out that Chou was anxious to score political points at the expense of both Liu and Mao.

Liu, Ch'en emphasized, is not a Kremlin stooge, but his views on a more conservative approach to China's economic and social dilemmas happen to coincide at the moment with Khrushchev's.

This thought was frequently repeated by Ch'en's associates—one of whom, a former Communist, had known Liu very well, both in Moscow and in Peking. He said Liu loved China deeply. "In fact," he said, "I would go even further. I would say that Liu doesn't really like Russia very much, that he was a terrible student when he was in Moscow in the twenties, and that he never learned to speak Russian very well." Still, Liu has become the apple of Moscow's eye—at least, for the present.

The black sheep is Mao, whose "leftism" offends Khrushchev. Specifically, the Russians are said to dislike the ideological assumptions that supported the commune spurt and the warm friendship that Mao has allegedly cultivated with Molotov in Outer Mongolia. Moreover, Ch'en continues, Khrushchev is reported as "miffed" by Mao's cultural arrogance. "Khrushchev feels that Mao looks down on him," Ch'en said. "He may very well be right."

A few days before my talk with Ch'en, there had been a major change in the Chinese military hierarchy, involving two of the highest-ranking officers in the Chinese Red Army, Marshals Peng Teh-huai and Lin Piao. Marshal Peng had been replaced as Chinese Defense Minister by Marshal Lin. This change was accompanied by a high-level shakeup in the army and low-level switches in the Party, all of which sparked a vigorous debate over its possible political significance.

Ch'en analyzed the Defense Ministry switch in terms of the Mao-Liu struggle. He called Marshal Lin a Liu man and Marshal Peng a Mao man. He described Lin as a brilliant fifty-one-year-old military strategist who has disliked Mao ever since the early 1930's, when Lin, a precocious colonel, led the First Red Army Corps. He was in Moscow from 1938 to 1941, apparently recuperating from a war injury. His antagonism toward Mao developed further in 1946, when Lin commanded the Fourth Route Army in Manchuria. He not only worked closely with the Russians; he took his orders from them. This supposedly infuriated Mao, but he was unable to replace Lin. Again, in 1950, Lin, in command of the Chinese forces in Korea, reportedly "worked too closely" with the Russians, frequently ignoring Mao's orders. Despite his military successes Mao became more and more displeased with him.

Finally, when Mao could tolerate Lin's insubordination no longer, he removed him from his position of command. The youthful, brash marshal "disappeared" from public view until 1958.

At this point, according to Ch'en, Liu Shao-chi lifted him from political obscurity. A new faction, opposed to the extremist policies of Mao, crystallized around Liu and Lin. It was composed of army officers, trained in Moscow, who are assumed to feel a close tie to the Russians. By September, 1959, this faction had cut Mao's power to the point where Peng, whose loyalty to Mao was unquestioned, could be eased out of the Defense Ministry—and Lin eased in.

This, in brief, is the predominant Taipei theory about the pro-Russia and pro-China factions of the Chinese Communist Party—a theory that has been circulating within the ranks of the Kuomintang in a dizzy spiral of speculation.

* * *

But there is another version of the same story circulating in Taipei. Chinese Nationalist intellectuals, who swear their views are unblemished by political bias, discount the Liu-Lin versus Mao-Peng theory of Chinese Communist politics. Instead, they say that Mao stands above inner-Party squabbles. "To many Chinese Communists," a scholar said, "Mao is a father image, to whom competing factions come for advice. It would be decidedly beneath his dignity—indeed, he would lose face—to participate in a political struggle. The Communist Party is his Party, and none of its 14,000,000 members would raise a hand against him."

These intellectuals, however, do not discount the possibility of a Liu-Chou struggle for power. In fact, they believe that Liu represents a radical view—and Chou a conservative view—within Chinese Communism. Liu, they say, has a messianic faith in the resurgence of Chinese power. He feels that if the Russians are offended by the communes, disturbed by ideological leapfrogging, and irritated by an intransigent foreign policy, then they had better realize that China is not a satellite of Russia; it is a great world power embarking on an independent foreign and domestic policy that has only one aim: the enhancement of Chinese national power. This power will set an impressive example for the underdeveloped areas of the world. As these areas adopt the methods of Chinese Communism, the entire world will move irrevocably toward Communism. Marx will have been justified by Mao.

In November, 1949, the Nationalist scholars continue, Liu outlined this ideological scheme before the Asian and Australasian Trade Union Conference in Peking. The Chinese Revolution, he said, would serve as the blueprint for popular uprisings in all of the backward nations of Asia and Africa. His argument was so convincing that it has frequently been echoed in official Chinese pronouncements.

According to these Nationalist scholars, Chou has always taken a far more accommodating view of Russia than Liu. They contend that although he shares Liu's conviction that China has a special destiny, he feels that, for the moment, China must work closely with Russia; that it would be foolhardy for China to ignore Moscow's desires until it is economically and militarily self-sufficient. Therefore, once Chou became aware of Moscow's disapproval of the commune program and China's new hard foreign-policy line, he came out in opposition to both these policies. But Liu, who favored these policies, was the stronger, and by February, 1958, he was able to force Chou to give up his post as Foreign Minister, launch China on its commune drive, and press forward with a tough foreign policy.

A few months later, in August, 1958, when the communes were formally proclaimed, Liu's faction, now the dominant faction in the CCP, pressed their advantage home with a vicious "anti-rightist" campaign which, the scholars say, had an anti-Chou edge. The "rightists" were accused of "lacking enthusiasm" for the "great leap forward"; they "did not believe" in the "revolutionary upsurge" of the "working masses." Moreover, they "opposed" the general line of the Party.

Another target of the campaign was the Chinese intellectuals who believed in birth control. One of these intellectuals was Ma Yin-chu, the seventy-six-year-old president of Peking University, who was educated at Yale and Columbia. Ma openly disagreed with the government's view that China's teeming, unrestrained population was an economic asset. Ma said it was a liability that could bring ruin upon the Chinese people. He refused to "reexamine" his ideas—although his friend Chou En-lai pleaded with him to obey the general line of the Party, no matter what his personal feelings might be. Nationalist scholars say that Chou agrees with Ma but that he is too much of a politician to oppose the "general line" in a public debate. So, they say, Chou managed to gain a second term as Chinese Premier in April, 1959—although they feel that the low-level purge of government officials accompanying the announcement of Chou's second term signaled an influx into the government apparatus of Liu men.

Mao is portrayed as favoring Liu in his struggle with Chou, but Mao refuses to use his influence to crush Chou. He hopes to "remold" Chou, and he is confident that Chou "will see the error of his ways."

* * *

Even for Chinese Nationalist scholars, who believe in research and analysis, it is a hazardous game to delve into the murky maze of Chinese Communist politics—particularly if the major issues concern Peking's attitude toward Moscow. This is a topic of extreme sensitivity and paramount importance. For this reason, I have described the two principal theories; it is just possible that either, or parts of both, may yet be proved to be correct. But it must also be noted that there is evidence from reliable sources to refute the basic hypotheses of both theories. This evidence should be presented, even at the risk of confusing an already confusing picture.

Many Western students of Chinese Communism believe that Mao may have discovered a unique political formula for sidestepping the bitter internecine strife that has become the hallmark of the Soviet Communist Party. The formula seems to revolve around the conviction that bloody purges need not be the best method of political self-purification. Indeed, purges produce suspicion; suspicion produces distrust; distrust produces disloyalty; and disloyalty produces more purges. The cycle is vicious, ugly, un-Chinese. Mao apparently believes that political self-purification can be achieved only through a constant process of criticism and self-criticism. Thus, he has stressed the practice of discussing mistakes. Argue, debate, argue some more, debate some more—until, finally, the overpowering logic of the Party's position and Mao's charismatic personality destroy the will to oppose, and opposition, like the state, withers away.

This formula works; for, since 1921, when the CCP was founded, there have been only three purges in the Party—and only one which ultimately resulted in the death of the purged. This is a fantastic record for a Communist Party concerned about a civil war and government responsibility for forty years. The first purge took place in 1927, when Ch'en Tu-hsiu, the first Secretary-General of the Party, was expelled for "right deviationism." Then, in 1938, Chang Kuo-t'ao, a member of the Politburo, was expelled for "rebellion against the Party." Finally, in 1955, Kao Kong was purged. His crime—"violating Party discipline"; he was killed.

In contrast, the Soviet Communist Party (and the East European Communist parties, which emulate Moscow even in the instrumentality of terror) has been rocked by continuous purges. Some of them, such as the Great Purge of 1936–1938, reached into every home, and millions of Russians were destroyed in this cruel imposition of Party discipline. Only with the advent of Nikita Khrushchev's rule has the Soviet purge become more humane; now, the purged are not necessarily killed. They are not remolded —as happens in China—but they are permitted to contribute to the society in an extremely limited fashion. Thus, Molotov was made Soviet Ambassador to Outer Mongolia, and Shepilov teaches economics in Central Asia.

Against this background of a "purgeless" Party, it is possible to discount the reports of an inner-Party struggle for power—especially one that intimately involves Peking's relations with Moscow. The rarity of a Chinese political purge also underscores the unusual continuity of leadership in the Party. It is remarkable that two-thirds of the Central Committee of the Chinese Party joined the Party before 1927. Many of them have never left China. Thus, they comprise a homogeneous—and homespun—political group.

* * *

Several journalists who have covered Chinese politics for decades differ sharply with Taipei's analysis of the political significance of Marshal Lin Piao's promotion in the Defense Ministry. They are convinced that Lin is not aligned with Liu against Mao. In fact, they say that Lin worships Mao, and that Mao respects Lin.

In their version of Lin's career, in 1930, three years after he defected from Chiang Kai-shek's army, Lin was already one of Mao's trusted military leaders. In this capacity he commanded the First Red Army Corps with Soviet aid, developed a strong military base in Manchuria, and, always loyal to Mao, drove the Nationalists out of Manchuria. In 1950 Lin was one of the four ranking Chinese leaders who were glorified as "model Communists." Mao Tse-tung and Liu Shao-chi were among the others. After leading the Red Army into North Korea, Lin vanished from public view. The journalists attribute his long absence to the fact that Lin suffers from tuberculosis and that he required a long rest; and they attribute the Defense Ministry switch to a political dispute of relatively limited significance.

They claim that Marshal Peng was relieved of his responsibility because he disapproved of Mao's plan to employ the Red Army as a work force in the economic transformation of China. A hot-tempered man, who believes a soldier's job is war, Peng said that China could not be defended by an army of farmers; it could only be defended by an army of soldiers, who were well trained in the modern, complex weapons of war. One report indicated that the army lost more than two hundred days of training, while working in the communes. This "unmilitary" concept supposedly infuriated Peng. He communicated his discontent to his army friends who formed a faction in the army that opposed the predominant view of the Party.

Marshal Lin, on the other hand, did not oppose Mao's idea of incorporating the army into the economic and social life of the nation. In late 1959, Lin wrote in *Red Flag:* "Some years ago, there were comrades who regarded it as an extra burden for the army to participate in mass movements and assist the people in production. They held that only drilling and lectures constituted training, while participation in practical socialist struggles was not training but an obstruction to training which would bring 'more loss than gain.' Such a viewpoint is utterly wrong."

Such a viewpoint was Peng's; and Lin became Defense Minister. This explanation seemed to make more sense in the context of the history of continuity in the Chinese Communist Party; certainly it appeared less contrived than Taipei's official outlook.

* * *

Finally, the Liu-Chou leftist-rightist argument runs into factual difficulties—largely because it necessarily involves the exacting task of defining "rightist," one of the most elusive terms in the Communist lexicon. This argument is predicated on the assumption that Chou is a "rightist."

In 1957 the "rightists" who opposed the "general line" of the Party were permitted to speak their minds—at least, for a short time during the "hundred flowers" movement. These "rightists" attacked the Soviet Union. Thus, a "rightist" was someone who disliked Russia.

In 1958 the "rightists" who opposed the "general line" were not permitted to speak their minds, but, according to the Liu-Chou argument, Chou was a "rightist." Since the general line favored the communes, Chou, by definition, opposed the communes. So did the Russians. Thus, in 1957, a "rightist" disliked Moscow, but in 1958, a "rightist" sided with Moscow.

Moreover, in August, 1959, Chou launched the official Chinese CP attack against the "rightists"; and if he were a "rightist" he would hardly have launched the attack against himself. He said the "rightists" did not understand the importance of the communes, which, he said, "served the interests of socialism better than any other social form."

Since the Liu-Chou argument rested on the assumption that Chou was a "rightist," the argument seemed to make little sense.

These semantic problems have constructed a Chinese wall around Peking politics. Every argument seems to have its pitfalls, and every approach its inconsistencies. The fact is, we are dangerously ignorant of the role of Chinese politics in an understanding of the alliance. There is a great deal of work to be done in this area, and there is not much time in which to do it.

CHAPTER FOURTEEN Tokyo

JAPAN IS AN INTERESTING STUDY IN ACCOMMODATION. IT HAS beauty for the tourist, food for the gourmet, change for the sociologist, profit for the businessman, uncertainty for the politician, fascination for the scholar, and a story for the journalist.

The "story" in Japan simmers; it does not burn—not yet. Its components, carefully concealed behind scraping bows and polite smiles, are diplomatic neutralism, psychological apathy, and political instability. One day soon,* informed observers believe, these components will collide with shattering impact; and Japan will emerge from the resultant chaos with a "neutralist" foreign policy ("friendly" to China), encouraged by a leftist government and cheered by a bitter, deracinated generation of bomb babies who cannot shake off the horror of Hiroshima and Nagasaki. This prospect is frightening—and probable. "Remember one thing," a diplomat warned, "Japan is not a docile, contented ally who's learned her lesson and now wants to be friends with the United States—despite Prime Minister Kishi."

I arrived in Tokyo on September 20, 1959, hopeful that I might be able to uncover fresh evidence of Peking's ambitious drive toward developing an atomic bomb of its own. I had heard that Japanese scientists were keeping a close check on this drive. They had experienced the jolt of two atomic attacks; they had witnessed the ugly consequences of radiation poisoning; and they had expressed their obvious and understandable revulsion. Now they apparently realized that, if Japan were to be atomic-bombed again,

* This chapter was written in April, 1960. In June there were violent anti-American riots that forced Prime Minister Kishi to resign and to postpone the Eisenhower visit.

the guilt would undoubtedly be China's. So, they watched Peking's scientific progress with more than detached concern.

I would have begun to interview these scientists immediately, but I was sidetracked. September 20, 1959, was a special day in Japan's diplomatic life. Former Prime Minister Tanzan Ishibashi had just signed a joint communiqué with Premier Chou En-lai in Peking—a symbolic gesture that touched off a lively debate in Tokyo about the continued viability of Japan's military commitments to the United States. The communiqué itself envisaged the possibility that Japan and China might soon "normalize" their relations on the basis of the five principles of *Panchshila* (a Bandung doctrine that China resurrected for the moment), and it encouraged both nations to "promote mutual friendship, strengthen mutual trust, and improve the existing relations."

Ishibashi, who is more "liberal" than Kishi, had not gone to Peking as an "official" representative of the Japanese government, which was still committed to Washington's line of anti-Communism and nonrecognition. Indeed, the government quickly, though informally, disassociated itself from Ishibashi, and attacked the communiqué. Still, Ishibashi's mission struck a highly responsive chord among many Japanese intellectuals and diplomats, who believed, like Ishibashi, that Japan's future might best be served by reducing its military ties with the United States, cutting its defense appropriations, and warming its relations with China—a traditional source of raw materials and cultural inspiration and an eager market for Japanese industry. For a few days, this debate was an absorbing distraction, for it shed valuable light on Japan's attitude toward its probable role in Asian politics and toward the Russian-Chinese alliance.

* * *

Japanese political life is complicated and unstable. The ruling Liberal-Democratic Party is seriously divided over the controversial question of Japan's military treaty with the United States. The opposition Socialist Party is split over a program of domestic reform, and it strongly advocates a "neutral" foreign policy and recognition of Communist China. Splinter parties, including the

Communist Party of Japan, represent contrasting ideologies, ranging from Nipponese militarism to Zengakuren radicalism.

These differences are reflected in two fundamental attitudes toward Japan's role in Asian diplomacy. One attitude, expressed in the highest echelons of the Foreign Ministry, sees a resurgent, powerful Japan following an "independent" foreign policy that "reasserts" Tokyo's "traditional" claim to economic and political influence throughout Asia. The other attitude, expressed passionately by many Japanese intellectuals, students, and journalists, has a sad "leave us alone" quality; it sees a "neutral Japan" that has "warm" relations with Communist China. Neither attitude envisages Japan as a co-operative ally of the United States—a fact that has become a source of grave concern at the United States Embassy in Tokyo.

Japanese diplomats—many of them in high-ranking positions—have a pet expression. It is "for the time being"; and it is said with irritating frequency.

"For the time being," they say, "Japan is tied to the United States."

"For the time being, Japan cannot play its rightful role in Asian affairs."

"For the time being, Japan is forced into a second-rate status."

Listening to these undiplomatic diplomats, I had the uneasy feeling that the Second World War had never happened; they sounded like an eerie echo from the 1930's.

They agreed that Formosa was the key to Japan's role in Asia. In fact, one diplomat called Formosa the "basis of our relations with China." Another diplomat, his voice heavy with scorn, said: "We have renounced our legal claim to Formosa as part of our new constitution. According to that constitution, we cannot arm. We cannot exercise a military or political voice in Formosa. Chiang Kai-shek does not like us, but his time is limited. And, I must say —and the Taiwanese will support me in this—that we gave Taiwan a good government. We made it a better place than the mainland. Now we have no voice in its affairs."

Formosa, they continued, was the front line of Japan's defenses in Asia; and Formosa belonged to Japan. "The United States," a

Japanese diplomat said, "has never had a voice in Formosan politics before; now the United States runs Formosa. And we, who owned Formosa, have no voice in Formosa. Is that right? Is that fair?" The questions were rhetorical expressions of frustration and anger.

It was clear that the Foreign Ministry wants a rearmed Japan. The pitch for weapons is rooted in the belief that Germany, another defeated Axis power, is now permitted to rearm within the framework of a Western defense alliance. Why can't Japan?

The arms would be applied toward pressuring the government to adopt a tough foreign policy, aimed initially at "recapturing" Formosa and ultimately at "restoring" Japan to its "rightful role in Asian affairs." This policy immediately involves China—and, therefore, China's ally, Russia, the only "Far Eastern" nation that Japan fears. The angry militarists of the Foreign Ministry look upon Chiang's "occupation" of Formosa as a transient phase, but they are frankly disturbed by the prospect of a Chinese Communist occupation. "That would throw a Communist vise around Japan," a diplomat said. "Russia from the north, and China from the south. This must be stopped."

Thus, the "militarists" are in a dilemma. In their view, they can either blackmail the United States into supporting Japan's reoccupation of Formosa by threatening to reach an agreement with Peking or they can promise Peking an attractive economic and diplomatic deal in exchange for hegemony over Formosa. Both alternatives appear farfetched—and dangerous. "If the militarists have their way," an American observed, "we may be dragged into a war which we can only lose."

* * *

Possibly, it is the blind truculence of this "militarist" attitude that has frightened Japan's intellectuals and students into a nervous feeling of anxiety and unhappiness. They abhor the thought of war. They have been called an "orphan generation"—the offspring of Hiroshima, who believe in nothing and want to be left alone. "There is nothing, nothing in the world that I would die for," one student said. His nihilism is infectious. In the thousands of coffee-shops that dot Tokyo's landscape, teen-agers sip espresso and listen to jazz. They have no interest in treaties, wars, or dignity; and the suicide rate among them has skyrocketed.

A popular joke focuses attention on their desperate desire for diplomatic neutralism—a desire that has been exploited by the Socialist Party, which opposes rearmament and favors a "relaxation of tension." One young man tells another: "When and if another war breaks out, what are you going to do?" "Oh," his friend answers, "I will first serve in the Russian army and then get captured as quickly as possible by the United States army to sit out the war as an American POW."

Japan's intellectuals do not wish to offend anyone—especially the Chinese. When the Tibetan revolt erupted, many Liberal-Democrats expressed their indignation. The students sighed, sipped their coffee, and recalled the attempted Mongol invasion of Japan six hundred years ago. When they do discuss politics—and many do—their viewpoint is firmly leftist, almost utopian. When they feel the pressure of daily reality, they retreat to their protective shells and dream happy dreams.

Their sympathies are with the Socialist Party, and they are reflected in the splits within the Party—between those politicians who demand extreme domestic reform and those who merely favor reform. Still, if differences of opinion exist on domestic policy, there are no major differences on foreign policy. The Socialists—and the students—demand a "normalization" of relations with China. That means recognition, and the adoption of a "friendly" attitude toward Communism.

* * *

The Communist Party of Japan was billed throughout Indian and Southeast Asia as an ideological satellite of Russia. It was felt that Moscow valued the CPJ very highly, because Japan, unlike India, possessed a "class-conscious" proletariat who saw Marxism through the prism of classical dogma rather than Maoist perversion. Based on what I had heard, I expected to find a Moscow-bound CP that looked askance at Mao's peasant-oriented philosophy. After a couple of days of interviewing, I learned that I had been misinformed. The Communist Party of Japan seemed to be wedded to Mao's doctrine.

Sanzo Nozaka, First Secretary of the CPJ, studied in Russia for nine years. In 1939 he left Moscow for Yenan, Mao's headquarters in northwestern China. There he studied at Mao's feet until 1946, when he returned to a defeated Japan. He quickly assumed control of the CPJ and adopted a program based on Mao's *New Democracy*.

"The CPJ," Nozaka said in 1949, was learning "valuable theoretical and political lessons from the great Mao Tse-tung and from other Chinese Communist leaders."

The Cominform, Russian-controlled, criticized the popular-front tactics of the CPJ in 1950. Soon the *People's Daily* echoed this criticism; and the CPJ switched to a "militant" policy. On May 30, 1950, rioting erupted in Tokyo against the United States occupation. In June the United States demanded that Japan exclude "known Communists" from public works. Japan agreed, and thousands of CPJ members lost their jobs. The CPJ was almost destroyed.

In October, 1950, as Mao readied his troops for their "voluntary" intrusion into the Korean War, *People's Daily* suggested that the CPJ return to a "soft" policy. In February, 1951, the CPJ adopted a "new program," which emphasized co-operation and legality. This is the program the CPJ has maintained ever since.

Nozaka's relations with China have always been close. He has visited Peking many times. In 1959 he was once again in Peking, where he conferred with Mao Tse-tung and Liu Shao-chi. On October 20th the leaders of the CPJ and the CCP signed a joint communiqué in which the "glorious achievements" of Communist China were praised but in which not a single word appeared about the USSR.

A footnote to Nozaka's ties with Peking, according to Peter S. H. Tang, a Chinese-American student of Communist China with a pro-Formosa pitch: "In their overseas activities, the Chinese Communist secret police are said to be dispatched directly from the Central Committee of Overseas Affairs of the CCP. For example, the first group of thirty-nine Japanese Communists * was sent to Japan in 1949. By 1953 there were over one hundred Japanese Communists and over seventy Chinese Communist secret service personnel (including over twenty women) active in Japan under the supervision of the Overseas Department. And, in November, 1953, there were reportedly nine Chinese Communist secret police bases in Japan, each consisting of several working groups."

* * *

Perhaps it is a symbol of the complexity of Japanese politics that a radical fringe of youth consider the CPJ and the CPSU as "right-wing" and "infected" by "bourgeois ideology." This fringe is called Zengakuren, a wildly inflammable offshoot of the CPJ that once showed its disgust for parliamentary democracy by urinating on the walls of the Japanese Diet.

Zengakuren's methods are so extreme—even for the CPJ—that many of its sympathizers have been expelled from the Party. Mostly students, they have taken advantage of every occasion to demonstrate against the government. They consider Kishi or Hayato Ikeda, Minister of Trade and Industry †, a reactionary, and they are violently opposed to any Japanese treaty with the United States.

In this respect, Zengakuren, distrusted for its methods, not its viewpoint, has a strange rapport with the Chinese Communists, whose antiseptic aloofness from any "bourgeois influence" has divided them on foreign policy from Khrushchev's Russia.

* * *

In the opinion of Tokyo's experts—and this is an opinion that is shared by many other students of Communist China—Mao fervently believes that, as Kang Sheng, a Chinese Communist ideologist, recently stated in Moscow, "American imperialism is still the principal enemy of world peace." This belief, they say, is the

* Presumably, with a pro-China bias.
† Now Prime Minister of Japan.

philosophical backbone of Peking's foreign policy. Thus, Communist China instinctively opposes any "Communist" rapprochement with the West—especially the United States.

China feels that the United States "occupied" Taiwan and South Korea. This was "inadmissible intrusion" into Chinese domestic affairs. Moreover, the United States represents the "last bastion" of capitalist strength; it must be destroyed—quickly, mercilessly. It must not be coddled into defeat; for, according to the dogma, capitalism does not surrender to Communism. It dies in a final convulsive gasp. In 1929 Mao wrote: "Enemy advances; we retreat. Enemy retreats; we pursue. Enemy encamps; we agitate. Enemy tires; we attack." It is possible that Mao feels the time has come for an attack.

Therefore, when Premier Khrushchev announced in August, 1959, that he would soon exchange visits with President Eisenhower, the news must have struck Mao as an unnecessary capitulation. *People's Daily* reported the news, but with an extraordinary lack of enthusiasm. A few days later, the Chinese press "hailed" Khrushchev's "forthcoming visit to the United States" in September, 1959, as a "contribution to world peace"; but at the same time the press continued its blistering assaults upon "American imperialism."

This pattern of lukewarm praise for Khrushchev and cold contempt for Eisenhower was maintained during the Soviet leader's historic tour of the United States. Typically, when Khrushchev called Eisenhower a "man of peace," this compliment did not appear in the Chinese press.

Why?

Apparently, there were two explanations. I had heard one earlier—that China can never be friendly toward the United States until it feels that its territorial disputes with Washington have been solved. It seems unlikely that they ever will be solved to China's satisfaction, because they involve American bases (or, as the Chinese say, "occupation") in Taiwan, South Korea, Japan, and Bangkok, headquarters for SEATO, which is under constant Chinese fire.

The second explanation involves ideology. The Chinese take

their Marxism more seriously than do the Russians. At least, they think they do. Mao believes that the United States is a "paper tiger" —a military as well as economic pushover. To the underdeveloped nations of Southeast Asia, Peking boasts that Communist China held off the combined might of the United Nations, and "defeated" the United States. Moreover, Mao feels that the American economy is convulsed in crisis and that, in the final analysis, it has neither the capacity nor the will to support a major war against China. Thus, Mao dislikes the idea that Khrushchev journeys to the enemy, because, in a sense, he brings dignity to a regime that is tottering toward disaster.

Thus, while Russia's proletarian king toured Iowa's cornfields and lunched with Wall Street bankers, Chinese troops embarrassed him by infiltrating the loftiest peaks of the Himalayas and the rice paddies of Laos. While Russian peasants are gingerly spoonfed capitalist incentives (the more the better, according to Khrushchev), Chinese peasants are quartered in communes that are unofficially described as "short cuts to Communism." And, while millions of Russians ache for some of the "bourgeois" comforts of life, as they frankly admitted during America's glittering 1959 showcase of consumer goods in Moscow, Chinese ideologists confidently forecast the imminent collapse of America's "paper tiger" economy.

"These *are* contradictions," a French expert on China said in his Tokyo office, "and Khrushchev and Mao know they exist. I think that what Khrushchev fears most is that Mao is deliberately hardening these contradictions while he pushes ahead full force on the development of earth satellites and atomic bombs."

When will China get its satellites and atomic bombs?

The answer to this question holds the key to an understanding of Chinese domestic and foreign policy; for, as a British diplomat put it: "I personally think that when China has a bomb, the contradictions between Moscow and Peking will become considerably more acute. It is even possible that Khrushchev feels that at that time the balance of power may be decisively altered—not only in the Communist orbit, but throughout the world."

Meanwhile, it appears that Mao has more room for adventure

than Khrushchev. In a major speech in February, 1957, Mao strongly implied that he did not foresee a "general" war for at least eight years. However, he did not rule out the possibility of "limited" wars in the interim. This omission, whether it was deliberate or accidental, has put Moscow on the alert for any local hostility that could lead to a global war.

Poland used to be an excellent barometer for measuring the degree of Chinese influence on the bloc. It is still a pretty good one. In Warsaw a Polish journalist carried the French expert's argument one step further. In a moment of revealing frankness during a lively conversation in Warsaw's Bristol Hotel, he asked me: "Don't you sometimes wonder *why* Khrushchev is so insistent on closer cultural and commercial ties with the West, especially the United States? Well, there's your answer!" He pointed to three Chinese Communists who had just picked up their room keys from the old concierge. "It is bad enough now," he whispered, "but when they get the bomb . . ." His voice trailed off, and he raised his shoulders in a helpless gesture.

This theme was echoed in numerous conversations all over the world—that at least part of the reason (far from the whole reason) for Khrushchev's warmer relations with the West lies in his mounting anxiety that Peking may possibly start a "limited" war that could touch off a "general" war, in which nuclear weapons would be used. This could destroy the prosperity for which Russia has yearned for centuries.

The overwhelming majority of the world's experts say that Khrushchev does not want to risk any of this hard-won prosperity by igniting a "limited" or "general" war and that he is convinced of the inherent superiority of the Soviet system, which, he feels, will be adopted peacefully and inevitably by the entire world. The same experts say that Mao is not squeamish about triggering a nuclear war; that hungry and teeming China, hot with the fever of revolutionary transformation and fortunate in the broad dispersal of its yet limited industry, has little to lose; that, indeed, China in the long run could stand to gain in an atomic war.

Richard Crossman, a Labour MP, watched one million Chinese march through the streets of Peking in the summer of 1958, denouncing the landings of American and British troops in Lebanon and Jordan. He could not understand how the Chinese could call the United States a paper tiger. "After all," he told a large group of Chinese university students, "the United States might drop a hydrogen bomb on China." The young Chinese burst into laughter. The astonished British parliamentarian asked, "What's so funny?"

"The remark was so absurd," his interpreter explained, "that it was too funny to be answered by anything but polite laughter. After all, how could anyone be so foolish as to start a war that would wipe him out but leave many of us alive?"

This same reaction was echoed in New Delhi, where Chinese aggressiveness has finally provoked some Indian diplomats into back-yard gossip about the "good old days in Peking." One of them recently recalled what Chinese Foreign Minister Chen Yi had told him years before: "Remember, we are not afraid of a nuclear war. We do not share your moral compunction about the sacredness of life. If the United States were foolishly to attack the Chinese People's Republic, then atomic weapons would be used; Russia would be dragged into the war, whether she likes it or not; and do you know what would happen? The United States and Russia would be destroyed; we might even lose 300,000,000 people. But so what? We would still be left with over 300,000,000 people—and we would be the strongest power on earth."

The Indian added, in a quiet, deliberate voice, "Mind you, that's what he said two years ago—before they were even close to developing earth satellites or atomic bombs."

How close are the Chinese now?

First, on earth satellites. Robert Guillain, the brilliant French correspondent for *Le Monde,* who has studied Communist China for many years, said that Kuo Mo-jo, President of the Academy of Sciences, had boasted in October, 1957, that China would soon shoot a satellite into outer space. How reliable was Kuo's boast? Apparently, very reliable.

As head of the Academy of Sciences, Kuo should know the level of China's scientific achievement. Surely, no important project could be conducted without his knowledge. In addition, Kuo, who is not a member of the CCP, was rumored in Hong Kong to have told an Indian scientist that China would fire a satellite into orbit on October 1, 1959—the tenth anniversary of the Chinese People's Republic. Guillain echoed this rumor; so did the China experts in the United States Embassy. The fact that China did not fire a satellite into space on October 1st does not prove that China did not try and that China is not close to succeeding on another attempt. It is known, for example, that the Russians never broadcast their scientific failures. Why should the Chinese?

The evidence that China is close—as close as two years—to firing a satellite into orbit is not limited to Kuo's pronouncements or Hong Kong rumors. It also consists of intelligence estimates, based on the most carefully screened information and scientific interpolations, founded on technological and engineering opinion in non-Communist capitals around the world, including Washington.

First, Peking has said that it would enter the space race. According to scientists, the will to compete in space—and the knowledge that the achievement is feasible—supplies the motivation. Moreover, the Chinese are conscious of the immense prestige involved in launching a satellite; they feel, with good reason, that the psychological impact of a successful space probe on world opinion would be about as shocking as Russia's leap into space in October, 1957.

Second, the Chinese are said to have already constructed a satellite launching site near Lanchow in northwest China. This kind of construction would not necessarily involve Soviet participation, though it is considered possible that the Russians might be willing to help the Chinese launch an earth satellite, for propaganda purposes, without committing themselves to help Peking explode an atomic bomb.

Finally, the Chinese are known to have the technological ability to fire a satellite into orbit. The head of the Chinese satellite program is Dr. Tsien Hsue-shen, one of the world's leading experts on rocket power. Dr. Tsien was born in China and educated in the United States. In 1936 he joined the faculty of the California Institute of Technology, where he was eventually promoted to the leading research post of Goddard Professor of Jet Propulsion.

During World War Two he was a member of the Air Corps Scientific Advisory Board. In 1950, after Mao's victory on the mainland, Dr. Tsien was detained by American immigration officials. Five years later, he was deported from the United States on the grounds that he had been a member of the Communist Party before he came to this country.

It is believed that Dr. Tsien has visited the Soviet Union with other Chinese scientists and that he has had access to the latest scientific and technological information. It is further understood that China now possesses sufficient technological know-how to produce thirty jet fighters a month. Scientists say that there is little difference between the guidance devices used in rockets and the automatic pilots and gyroscopic mechanism used in jets. It is admitted that the development and production of the powerful rocket engines needed to shoot a satellite into orbit are difficult technological tasks; but it is agreed that if China started to build powerful rocket engines two or three years ago, it is entirely possible that China will be able to launch an earth satellite of its own—without outside assistance—within the next few years.

The best guess is two years; that is, by 1962.

* * *

Now, on atomic bombs.

There are no experts on this question—anywhere. There are only informed guesses.

One guess is that China would have had a bomb by now if the Russians had fully supported their effort. Clearly, they have not; for the Russians have given many foreign diplomats the distinct impression that they would just as soon restrict membership in the nuclear club to the three powers (Britain, Russia, and America) that now possess the bomb. In February, 1960, France exploded a nuclear device in the Sahara Desert. The Russians expressed their keen disapproval, but President de Gaulle would not be dissuaded. It is believed likely that the Chinese have seized on this explosion to put greater pressure on the Russians to supply them with the technical ability to set off a nuclear bomb as quickly as possible. The Russians may have reacted to this increased pressure with a greater will to reach a nuclear test ban agreement with the West—one that hopefully would force the Chinese to abandon their atomic-bomb efforts. The major difficulty with this effort is that the Chinese have already warned Russia and the West that they would not abide by any agreement reached at an international conference without the direct participation of the Peking government.

Victor Zorza, one of the most perceptive Russian experts in London, discovered some evidence in the spring of 1959 that seems to prove that the Chinese have set their sights on getting a bomb—no matter what obstacles Soviet diplomacy may throw in their path. A careful reading of Khrushchev's speech before the twenty-first Party Congress, Zorza says, indicates that the Soviet leader proposed a denuclearized zone in the Far East. This proposal was not approved by the Chinese; in fact, they merely reported the idea without any comment. A few months later, Zorza says, during Khrushchev's tour of Albania, the Soviet leader proposed a denuclearized zone in the Mediterranean area. This proposal was greeted with enthusiasm by the Chinese. The difference in response, Zorza believes, emphasizes the desire of the Chinese to develop an atomic bomb and the disappointment of the Chinese that the Russians apparently have not been willing to give them anything but verbal encouragement.

The encouragement started soon after Khrushchev's first visit to Peking, in October, 1954. At that time the Russians tried to convince the Chinese of their "unfailing support" for Peking's scientific and technological efforts to make a bomb.

In January, 1955, Moscow announced its willingness to help "friendly" nations develop atomic energy for peaceful purposes. Chou En-lai applauded—publicly.

In February, 1956, the Vice-Premier of Communist China, Li Hsien-nien, said that the Soviet Union was "preparing" to set up a 6,500-kilowatt experimental atomic reactor in China "to help Chinese scientists and technicians in the peaceful uses of atomic energy." Li also boasted that China would soon be able to master "the world's most advanced scientific technique—within a short period of time."

Fifteen months later, the Chinese press again mentioned that the Russians had promised "an experimental atomic pile (reactor) with a heat-generating power of 6,500 kilowatts . . . to 10,000 kilowatts and a cyclotron that will accelerate the particle from 12,500,000 up to 25,000,000 volts."

It was not until July, 1959, that P'u Ch'ien-fu, Vice-President of the Chinese Academy of Sciences, finally confirmed in the Shanghai paper *Wen Hui-pao* that the Russians had delivered the atomic reactor they had promised four years before.

In Hong Kong, where Western specialists read the Chinese press very carefully for any hint of China's atomic progress, a French diplomat said: "You can be sure the Russians help the Chinese only very reluctantly. It was only after years of insistent Chinese demands, in public, that the Russians grudgingly gave them one reactor and possibly one cyclotron."

The Chinese realize that, if they want a bomb, they will have to make it themselves.

In Tokyo, Japanese scientists made three important points:

1. Chinese scientific progress has been "astonishing."

2. In the last year the Chinese have built four small atomic reactors and two cyclotrons on their own.

3. Since 1955 the Chinese have been building a great science city in Lanchow, a war-weary town in Kansu Province that has boosted its population in the last ten years from 118,000 to 850,-000.

"It was in Lanchow," a Japanese diplomat remarked with extraordinary understatement, "that a small nuclear device was tested last summer!" Guillain said that he had heard the same report—and, he added, "it was on excellent authority." The Atomic Energy Commission has reported that a 9,200-ton underground nuclear blast took place in December, 1956, near Lanchow—supposedly under Soviet auspices. This is likely, because it is believed that the Chinese did possess sufficient skill in 1956 to set off a nuclear device. Everyone says that 1959 is another matter.

This tightly guarded secret, if true, lends weight to the predictions of a small group of French scientists who recently returned from a tour of China. In Paris they talked about China's "mighty" and "impressive" strides in modern science; and one of them reportedly told a friend, "I see no reason why China could not explode a nuclear bomb on its own by the end of 1962."

A recent American survey, published in June, 1959, said that there was no longer any scientific secret about making an atomic bomb. Twelve nations were said to have the scientific and technological capacity to produce atomic weapons. In another five years, the survey continued, twelve other nations would have this capacity.

It is expensive to produce a bomb, but China can apparently afford the expense. Moreover, China knows that an atomic explosion would have significant advantages in foreign and domestic policy that would justify any cost. Recently, an American scientist speculated in New York that China could make a small atomic bomb for about $50,000,000—"maybe less, if she really does have three or four, or more, atomic reactors producing plutonium as a by-product." Another American scientist said: "Once you know it can be done, there are all kinds of short cuts you can take—and get to the same end. I should think the Chinese could have their bomb in 1961—at the latest."

He may have exaggerated when he added, "The tick-tock of the Chinese clock must sound like a time bomb in Moscow"; but there seems to be no question that Russia has become deeply concerned by China's unrelenting drive toward big-power status.

Russia is in the shadow of a dragon.

* * *

If the Russians are disturbed by the rising threat of a Chinese Goliath, bristling with atomic weapons and big with dreams of world power and status, so is Washington. Not too long ago, despite the hot-and-cold Kremlin attitude toward Washington, the Defense Department organized a special Committee, which has thus far been kept secret, to examine the possibilities of a strategic rapprochement with the Soviet Union in the face of the mounting challenge of the new China.

CHAPTER FIFTEEN Wrap-Up

April, 1960

ON SEPTEMBER 30, 1959, NIKITA KHRUSHCHEV, FRESH FROM A historic journey to the United States, hotbed of world capitalism, arrived in Peking to celebrate the tenth anniversary of the Chinese People's Republic. To the handful of Western reporters who were permitted to "cover" the festivities, there seemed to be a noticeable freeze in Russian-Chinese relations. The Soviet leader had seemed more at ease with Wall Street monopolists than with Chinese revolutionaries.

Peking newspapers did not banner-headline Khrushchev's arrival, although they did mention it. Mao Tse-tung was at the airport to greet him. After a ceremonial handshake, Khrushchev told the Chinese that he was very pleased with the outcome of his American visit. "The talks that took place there," the Russian said, "were most useful. They without doubt should lead to an improvement between our countries and to a relaxation of international tensions."

Did this prospect please the Chinese? Apparently not.

A few days earlier, Liu Shao-chi had launched a bitter attack against the United States at a mass meeting in Peking. Liu stated that "United States imperialists" must "curb" their "aggression." They "occupy our territory, Taiwan," he went on. "We absolutely cannot tolerate" this situation. "We Chinese people are determined to liberate our territory of Taiwan, Penghu, Quemoy and Matsu." To safeguard peace, Liu added, "we must curb aggression."

As Khrushchev talked peace, Peking talked war—especially against the United States. Liu's attack was soon echoed by Foreign Minister Chen Yi, who wrote in *Izvestia* that the "United States has not renounced its policy of aggression and war." Chen pulled no punches. "We firmly demand," he said, "that American troops pull out of the Taiwan area: Taiwan is Chinese territory, and the Chinese people are determined to liberate it." In the past ten years, Chen continued, "the United States imperialists have carried out a series of aggressive acts and war threats against new China, fully revealing that they are the enemy of the Chinese people."

On October 1, 1959, Khrushchev attended a mass rally in Peking's Square of Heavenly Peace. Seven hundred thousand Chinese cheered Mao Tse-tung. Chinese-built jets roared over the square. Marshal Lin Piao, newly appointed Defense Minister, shook his fist at American "imperialism." And, according to official Peking reports, six "huge portraits" "decorated" the square. They were portaits of Mao, Sun Yat-sen, Marx, Engels, Lenin, and *Stalin.* There were no portraits of Khrushchev.

As the Soviet leader silently watched this mass spectacle, fate seemed to play an ironic trick on him. One hundred doves of peace were released. Khrushchev, who has tried to make "peace" his middle name, spotted one of the graceful doves arcing toward him. In London, Washington and, of course, Moscow, it would not have been surprising if he had snatched the peace dove. In Peking, he grabbed for it—but missed.

Khrushchev remained in the Chinese capital for four days. Although he frequently spoke at rallies and banquets, he never mentioned the communes; and, although he heard the Chinese leaders attack the United States and call for the "forceful recovery" of Formosa, he never once repeated this theme. In fact, he seemed to want to restrain Mao. "We must reason realistically," he warned, "and correctly understand the present situation, and this certainly does not mean that since we are so strong we should test the stability of the capitalist system by force. This would be wrong. The peoples would never understand and would never support those who took into their heads to act in this way. We have always been against predatory wars."

His visit was unsatisfactory. No communiqué was signed. At the airport, Khrushchev shook hands with Mao, Chou, and Liu. He then thanked them and wished them success. They applauded politely. Mao, the Oriental sphinx, said nothing. Khrushchev, the loquacious Slav, smiled weakly, and departed.

* * *

In the last six months, there have been many illustrations of the major divisive issue in the Russian-Chinese alliance—the issue of war or peace.

First, the Sino-Indian border dispute, which erupted suddenly upon the world's stage. On December 18, 1959, a Soviet diplomat in Geneva reportedly expressed his government's "concern" and "embarrassment." He said he hoped that the Chinese-Indian border dispute would not create new East-West tensions. He described Chinese actions along the Indian border as "more than untimely"; they "would be inopportune at any time." He was asked whether the Soviet government was trying to restrain Peking. "It is difficult to say," he answered, "but I am sure they are not happy about the situation." The West must understand, he cautioned, that China "is a very young country, which feels it must assert itself as a great power." It was significant that these remarks were made against the backdrop of President Eisenhower's successful trip to India—a trip that made friends for America while Russia, ally of belligerent China, was losing friends throughout Asia.

Second, on December 21, 1959, the eightieth anniversary of Stalin's birth, *Pravda* and *People's Daily* published long critiques of the late Soviet dictator. *Pravda* bitterly attacked Stalin, stressing his "errors" and "shortcomings." *People's Daily* described his "errors" as "secondary," stressing his "greatness" and "staunchness" in the fight against "imperialism and warmongers." The varying assessments of Stalin were illustrative of the differences in Moscow and Peking approaches to the United States.

Third, on December 30, 1959, Moscow Radio broadcast an extremely unusual message to the United States about the Russian-Chinese alliance. There was "no single international problem of any moment," Moscow said, on which Russia and China did not agree. *"We can see no threat to ourselves or other nations from China.* China supports every peace effort of the Soviet government. . . ." Moscow charged that some Western leaders were trying to "drive a wedge between the Soviet Union and the People's Republic of China. But they have always failed, thanks to our firm friendship." Then Moscow added the key sentence: "We already have socialism and are marching toward Communism, whereas the Chinese are just building socialism, which is the first phase of Communism."

Fourth, on December 31, 1959, Moscow celebrated New Year's Eve with vodka, champagne, and gifts. Restaurants sported beautifully decorated fir trees. Moscow Radio beamed a New Year's message of joy and peace to its North American listeners, and, for the first time since 1956, Premier Khrushchev invited Western reporters to the Kremlin for a lavish party. Reuters described the New Year's celebrations in Peking with this sentence: "The New Year came quietly to the Chinese capital without any street celebrations as midnight struck."

Fifth, the Chinese-Indonesian dispute over alien Chinese merchants in rural areas of Java. As Peking and Jakarta argued over jurisdiction, plunging their relations to new depths, Premier Khrushchev journeyed to the far-flung Indonesian archipelago in February, 1960, after a brief visit to India. He promised President Sukarno Russia's warm friendship and understanding and a $250-000,000 loan for economic development. In both India and Indonesia, Khrushchev deliberately refused to comment on Communist China, his "great ally," although in a private conversation with Sukarno, as reported in the *New York Times,* he did say that he disapproved of the "heavy cost in human life" involved in the industrialization of China. Thus, once again, as *Pravda* praised Indonesia, a valuable, neutralist, underdeveloped nation, *People's Daily* attacked Indonesia for its "oppression" of Chinese aliens.

Moreover, First Deputy Premier Anastas Mikoyan implicitly criticized China's defense of overseas Chinese capitalists in a comment on Cuban Premier Castro's policy of expropriation of foreign holdings. In Oslo, en route to Moscow after a "business trip" to Havana, Mikoyan reached into history for a parallel to the Castro situation—a parallel with surprising innuendoes for Peking. It is significant that his quote was published in *Izvestia,* which is carefully read in China. "At one time in China, in Harbin," Mikoyan lectured, "there were Russian capitalists. We said to them: Either you return to Russia or take Chinese citizenship, since we will not be able to defend you here. Why did we do this? Are not our compatriots dear to us? *The fact is that this would have been a source of conflict. For example, some capitalist does something in Harbin, and our consul would have to defend him.* There you have a conflict. At the present time, neither the Soviet Union, nor any Soviet citizen, has any property abroad."

Sixth, in February, 1960, at a meeting of Warsaw Pact nations in Moscow, the Soviet delegate raised a toast to peaceful coexistence, universal disarmament, and economic prosperity. The other delegates cheered the toast and drained their glasses. One observer did not cheer. He was Kang Sheng, the delegate from Peking. He, too, favored economic prosperity; but he had grave doubts about peaceful coexistence. He viciously attacked the United States. "The actions of the United States," he exclaimed, "fully prove that its imperialist nature cannot be changed. American imperialism is still the principal enemy of world peace. . . . While being compelled to make certain peace gestures, the U.S. ruling circles are still intensively carrying out arms expansion and war preparation, expanding vigorously their intercontinental missile program. . . ." On universal disarmament, he said, "The Chinese government has to declare *to the world* that a general international disarmament agreement and all other international agreements which are arrived at without the formal participation of the Chinese People's Republic and the signature of its delegates cannot, of course, have any binding force on China." In the light of Chinese atomic development, this statement by Kang Sheng should be made must reading at Geneva.

Seventh, on April 1, 1960, *Pravda* and *People's Daily* compared notes on Lenin, the "great man" of Russian Communism—and again they differed in their assessment. *Pravda* credited Lenin with having conceived of the idea of "peaceful coexistence," while *People's Daily* stressed the "Leninist" theory of the "class struggle." The Chinese newspaper quoted Lenin as having said: "To repudiate civil war, or to forget about it, would be sinking into extreme opportunism and renouncing the Soviet Revolution." This interpretation differed from Khrushchev's thesis that nuclear weapons have made war unthinkable as a national policy. Mao disagrees, holding that "the inevitability of revolutions in the imperialist countries is an objective law of history and independent of human will." Mao adds—possibly for Khrushchev's benefit—"We oppose war. We are against it. But we are not afraid of it. The First World War was followed by the birth of the Soviet Union with a population of 200,000,000. World War Two was followed by the emergence of the socialist camp with a population of 900,-000,000. If the imperialists should insist on launching a third world war, it is certain that several hundred million more will turn to socialism."

Helsinki, September 7, 1960

These exchanges proved to be the dramatic backdrop for a summer of bitter ideological debate. Once again, the Russians and the Chinese were arguing about war. Was war between socialism and capitalism inevitable, as Lenin had believed? Or could war be avoided?

Quoting Lenin, the Chinese said that the nature of imperialism had not changed; therefore, war was inevitable. After all, *Hung-chi,* a Chinese magazine, said on June 16, 1960: "A wolf is a wolf, and its man-eating nature will never change."

Quoting Lenin, too, the Russians argued that the "objective conditions" of the world had changed so much that socialism need no longer be faced with the "dialectical necessity" of fighting capitalism. In Bucharest, Rumania, on June 21, 1960, Premier Nikita Khrushchev warned: "In our day only madmen and maniacs launch calls for a new world war."

The Chinese, who barely concealed their contempt for the Soviet leader, found justification for their view in the same "objective conditions." First, they noted a toughening Western position on Berlin and concluded that the stillborn Paris summit of May, 1960, would not produce any beneficial results. On April 26th, in *Peking Review,* an English-language periodical, they wrote: "The fact is that even after the Camp David talks and even on the eve of the East-West summit conference, we see no change at all in substance in the United States imperialist war policy, in the policy carried out by the United States Government and by Eisenhower personally."

The U-2 reconnaissance plane, shot down by the Russians over Sverdlovsk on May 1, 1960, gave the Chinese an excellent opportunity to say "I told you so." In Wuhan, on May 16, 1960, Mao Tse-tung, who rarely expresses a personal view on a current topic, told a gathering of Communist leaders: "This incident demonstrates the *true* nature of American imperialism, which is preparing for an aggressive war." Warming up to his theme, Mao continued: "One cannot entertain any illusions about imperialism; this would be to lack realism." Those "who described Eisenhower as a man of peace," he said, should now know better.

The Chinese, who were excluded from the Paris conference, were pleased that Premier Khrushchev chose to break up the summit, but the Chinese do not appear to have had much influence on Khrushchev's decision. The Soviet leader may have taken Mao's attitude into consideration, but, in the final analysis, China's wishes proved to be less important than Russia's domestic and diplomatic needs.

Nevertheless, Khrushchev's tougher line encouraged the Chinese to think that he might rush to East Berlin and, as a gesture of defiance, sign a separate peace treaty with the East German Communists. Once again, the Chinese were disappointed. The Soviet leader did rush to East Berlin. The West waited. But Khrushchev did not sign a separate treaty; he merely postponed the deadline for "another six to eight months" until the election of a new American President. To the Chinese, this seemed to be a lame excuse, since there really was no difference between either of the two "bourgeois" candidates for the office. For, as the Russians cheered this postponement, and Khrushchev continued to appeal for "peaceful coexistence," Peking hardened its ideological position. Even the violently anti-American demonstrations in Japan, forcing the postponement of the Eisenhower visit, did not change Khrushchev's mind about coexistence. In magazines and newspapers, the Chinese intensified their attacks against "revisionists" in the "world Communist movement" who were "damaging" the "purity" of Marxism-Leninism by suggesting that a world war could bring about the destruction of socialism as well as that of capitalism.

"The result will certainly not be the annihilation of mankind," the Chinese stressed. "In the debris of dead imperialism, the victorious people would very quickly create a civilization thousands of times higher than the capitalist system, and a truly beautiful future for themselves."

The Russians, who had been very circumspect in their official reactions to these pointed attacks, began to bristle openly in mid-June. *Pravda* took advantage of the fortieth anniversary of the publication of a pamphlet by Lenin, called *Left-Wing Communism—An Infantile Disorder,* to sharpen its attack on certain unnamed "contemporary leftists." Echoing Khrushchev's theory that "peaceful coexistence" made good sense even after the U-2 flight, *Pravda* charged: "Contemporary leftists consider the *slightest* aggravation of the international situation as a justification of their sectarian convictions."

There was also an unconfirmed report that this argument raged during the eleventh Session of the General Council of the World Federation of Trade Unions, which opened in Peking on June 6th. The report included the threat of a Soviet walkout unless the Chinese called off their anti-coexistence campaign.

As this debate became more bitter, attracting world attention, Premier Khrushchev decided to act. He informed his Communist colleagues that he intended to lead the Soviet delegation to the third Congress of the Roumanian Communist Party, and he suggested that they follow his example. Unsurprisingly, they did; and on June 20, 1960, when the congress opened in Bucharest, Khrushchev and many other Communist Party leaders were present. Khrushchev was accompanied, among others, by Boris Ponomarev and Pyotr Pospelov, two of Russia's leading theoreticians. The Chinese sent Peng Chen, mayor of Peking and a member of the Politburo of the CCP.

On June 21st Khrushchev addressed the congress—and made a simple point. The world has changed since Lenin's time, he said, and contemporary Communists can no longer simply quote Lenin to justify their actions; they must extract the ideological nectar of Leninism and apply it to today's problems. "If Lenin could get up from his grave," he said, "he would take such people by the ear and he would teach them how one should understand the essence of the issue." The only justifiable course, Khrushchev concluded, is peaceful coexistence. "Those who do not believe in this idea do not understand socialism."

The Chinese sniffed a "revisionist." Peng Chen ignored Khrushchev's injunction and lashed out at "imperialists," who were preparing a new war, and "Bernsteinians," who were ready to "revise" the sacred Leninist text.

It soon became clear that neither Khrushchev nor Peng wanted to yield an inch; nevertheless, both Communist leaders realized that they would have to compromise for the sake of bloc unity. Significantly, the Chinese were the first to back down. Mme. Soong Ching-ling, Vice-President of Communist China and widow of Dr. Sun Yat-sen, founder of the Chinese Republic, said on June 27, 1960: "China is willing to coexist with anyone, even imperialism. In fact, we have to coexist with it. Imperialism exists as an objective reality. Socialist states also exist as objective realities."

This concession led to the Bucharest communiqué, signed by twelve ruling Communist parties on June 28, 1960. This communiqué, which has become the official yardstick for measuring ideological conformity on this issue, restated Khrushchev's policy of peaceful coexistence; but it also stated the diluted Maoist idea that "it is also necessary to proceed from the possibility of the working class gaining a victory for the socialist revolution by non-peaceful means."

Shortly after the Bucharest Congress, a plenum of the Central Committee of the Communist Party of the Soviet Union met in Moscow and declared its support of the communiqué. At the same time, the Chinese are believed to have held a meeting of their Central Committee, led by Mao. No public statement was made, although it is now considered likely that the Chinese repudiated the pledge made at Bucharest.

When word of this likelihood reached Moscow, the Russians immediately began to circulate two memorandums, delineating the Russian-Chinese dispute over war and peace: one went to local Party cells within the Soviet Union; the other went to Communist parties all over the world. Supporting this offensive, Moscow unleashed some of its sharpest ideological pens. The press suddenly blossomed with "antidogmatist" articles. Hardly a day passed without a scathing attack against unnamed "sectarians" who violated the "purity" of Marxism-Leninism.

And this attack carried a new and important twist. For the first time, the Russians warned China by name that it might become isolated from the rest of the socialist bloc if it insisted on maintaining its "dogmatic" approach to "objective conditions." The warning appeared in five provincial newspapers: in Baku and Riga on August 16th; in Tashkent on August 21st; and in Kaunas and Stalinabad on August 24th. It was written by S. Titarenko, a specialist on ideology for the Central Committee, and it raised the question of whether a large nation, such as China, could build socialism "successfully" if it "were to find itself in an isolated position —not able to rely on the cooperation and mutual aid of all other socialist countries." By implication, the Russians were saying that China could find itself alone if it insisted on pursuing its "dogmatism."

The Chinese did not need much time to reply. On August 23rd, in *Peking Review,* Li Fu-chun, a Deputy Premier, wrote: "Since 1958, the modern revisionists have launched movements in an effort to isolate us, but they will succeed only in isolating themselves."

These were serious charges, and they were reflected in the image of China that was developing in Moscow in the summer of 1960. First, one rarely saw Chinese delegations. In the past, they were as conspicuous as Khrushchev portaits. Suddenly, they disappeared. Second, two Russian-language magazines dealing with China, *Druzhba* and *Kitai* (*Friendship* and *China*), did not appear on Moscow kiosks after late June. Third, news about China dwindled down to nothing. In fact, there was considerably more news about the United States, the Sudan, or Ceylon in the Soviet press than about China, Russia's biggest ally. Fourth, there was not a single Chinese scholar or any other Chinese representative at the International Orientalists' Congress held in Moscow in early August, nor was Chinese one of the four official languages at the congress. Fifth, this writer never heard a favorable comment about the Chinese from any Russian, whether during an official interview or during an informal chat. On the contrary, he heard either neutral comments or hostile comments. Most frequently, he heard Russians say: "I don't know; I just don't like them."

Russian-Chinese tension seemed to be increased by the announcement that Premier Khrushchev would head the Soviet delegation to the fifteenth session of the General Assembly of the United Nations. Chinese Communist newspapers in Hong Kong tended to ignore Khrushchev's journey, though the *New Evening Post* did state in an editorial, on September 3, 1960, that it would be a waste of time. For their part, the Russians, who published congratulatory cables from many Communist parties, published nothing from the Chinese—an indication that they had received nothing.

Something had to be done. When Khrushchev arrived in New York to participate in the plenary sessions of the General Assembly, he began by playing the role of the flaming revolutionary. In barricade style he assailed the "imperialists, led by the United States." People's China, he argued, must be admitted to the United Nations; the "corpse of Chiang Kai-shek" must be thrown into the "dustbin of history."

The Soviet leader tirelessly quoted Asian and African neutralists, extended de facto recognition to the Algerian provisional government, and uncompromisingly trumpeted Peking's cause. Mao himself could not have done a better job.

Apparently it had a wholesome effect upon the Russian-Chinese alliance. In early November, 1960, the representatives of eighty-one Communist parties, including Liu Shao-chi of Communist China, arrived in Moscow at Khrushchev's invitation. Ostensibly, they were there to participate in the celebration of the forty-third anniversary of the Bolshevik Revolution; actually, they were there to participate in a Communist summit meeting.

On November 10th, these representatives disappeared behind

the walls of the Kremlin, and for three weeks, in an atmosphere of Byzantine secrecy, they debated the ideological merits of peaceful coexistence. Finally, on November 30th, after one of the most important conclaves in Communist history, they emerged in the snowy twilight, an ideological formula in their hip pockets acceptable to all shades of opinion in the Communist world.

To a chorus of "Long live the Russian-Chinese Alliance" Liu journeyed to Leningrad and Minsk, where he made ceremonial speeches supporting peaceful coexistence. When he returned to Moscow, the Russians staged a giant friendship rally in the Lenin Stadium. Again, peaceful coexistence. On December 7th, the eve of Liu's departure for Peking, they threw a lavish party in the Kremlin for the spare Chinese leader. Again, peaceful coexistence. On November 9th, *Pravda* summarized: "Russian-Chinese friendship is as firm and indestructible as the Himalayas, as deep as the Pacific, as vast as the Yangtze and the Volga."

The theme of Chinese acceptance of the Khrushchev doctrine of peaceful coexistence ran through a major statement of Communist global strategy and an "appeal to the workers of the world" that was published within ten days after the conclusion of the summit meeting. But the statement and the "appeal" also contained several ringing Communist clichés with a decidedly Peking edge, and many diplomats were convinced that the strength and substance of these documents would be tested in the policy that Russia and China would follow—especially in their respective attitudes toward the Kennedy administration.

* * *

Despite the apparent accommodation at the Moscow summit, there is still reason to believe that it has not reconciled the major Sino-Soviet differences in theory and mood. It appears that Mao is unwilling to see the world through Khrushchev's eyes. The Soviet leader apparently believes that a smile will advance the cause of Communism more rapidly than a frown. He realizes that there are important differences among the Western powers, and he has used a flexible policy of alternating smiles and frowns to exploit these differences. And he uses the smile to get at the West "through the back door"—on the old Leninist assumption that without the markets and raw materials of the underdeveloped nations of the world, the West cannot maintain its high-consumption levels and will sink into an abyss of depression and civil strife, the most fertile soil for Communism. Khrushchev apparently feels that, for the time being, these underdeveloped areas need not go Communist; his aim is that they become "friendly neutrals." Krushchev is certain that eventually all of these "friendly neutrals" will slip into the "socialist camp." And so, although a devout Communist—and this is a fact that requires repetition—Khrushchev feels that Communism can defeat capitalism without first hurling the world into a cataclysmic war that could destroy all civilization.

Although Mao apparently agrees with Khrushchev's goal, he disagrees with Khrushchev's tactics and pace. Mao does not believe that Communism needs a smile or a frown; Communism depends only on economic statistics and class warfare. In his raw, fundamentalist view, the United States is the symbol of capitalist evil; and the United States must be constantly opposed, bullwhipped, and humiliated. Mao does not feel that a socialist nation should "coddle" Wall Street into defeat; nor, for that matter, does he believe that it is possible. Moreover, he feels that now is as good a time as any for a direct expansion of Communist power in shaky areas, such as Iraq, Algeria, or Southeast Asia. Mao knows that one of the possible consequences of a "hard" Communist policy is war, but he is not afraid of war. As he stated on April 1, 1960, if the world should be thrown into war, only capitalism can lose. The corollary of this premise is that only socialism can win. Mao does not fear war, because Mao commands a huge population and a broadly dispersed industry. He apparently does not feel that China can "lose" an atomic war.

Thus, Mao and Khrushchev disagree on the potential destructiveness of nuclear war, and this disagreement has posed an extraordinarily difficult problem for Khrushchev. The Soviet leader is concerned that Mao's truculence may accidentally or deliberately touch off an atomic war—one that could destroy Russia's abundance and Communism's hope. This fear has forced Khrushchev into the uncomfortable position where he feels he must overlook China's psychological and ideological haughtiness and try to maintain closer relations with Peking. A warmer alliance might then help Khrushchev to exercise a moderating influence over Chinese behavior.

This is Khrushchev's hope; this is also Khrushchev's dilemma. For he is afraid that Soviet economic and military assistance may help develop China into so powerful a nation that he will lose the restraining influence over Peking's policies that he so desperately desires. Already he can see three areas in which China's potential is clearly and frighteningly visible.

First, in economic strength. Khrushchev knows that China's total industrial and agricultural output in 1959 grew by 31 per cent over 1958 levels. This statistic is easy to write and easy to say, but its implications are enormous, posing the greatest problems for Russia. Assuming an upward bias in Chinese bookkeeping, it still means that China will become the third ranking industrial power in the world sometime in the 1960's. Experts feel that this prospect is likely—even if China merely doubles its industrial production in this decade. At its present rate of growth, this can be accomplished in three or four years!

China's economic growth can have serious repercussions throughout the world; certainly, at a minimum, it will radically alter the balance of power. For, at that time, Washington's attention will be forced to focus on China, because American economic and diplomatic interests in the Far East will be affected by China's every action. In similar fashion, so will Soviet interests. As China grows stronger, Peking will become increasingly less dependent on Soviet aid; and Moscow will lose its most important lever for influencing Chinese behavior.

So, where does China stand now vis-à-vis Russia in the output of steel, coal, electricity, and cement?

Steel: Russia—59.9 million metric tons; China—13.35.
Coal: Russia—506.5 million metric tons; China—347.8.
Electricity: Russia—264 billion kilowatt hours; China—41.5.
Cement: Russia—38.8 million metric tons; China—12.3.

For Khrushchev, the chilling fact about these statistics is that China's *rate* of economic growth is virtually unparalleled in world history. At a similar stage in Soviet development, Russia's rate of growth was less than half of China's current rate of growth; and, if Washington is having sleepless nights over Soviet economic progress, it will be in for rougher times in the near future over China's projected growth.

Second, in ideological terms. Khrushchev knows that Chinese journals portray Mao Tse-tung as the "world's greatest contemporary theoretician of Marxism-Leninism." Indeed, during the winter of 1959–1960, a major campaign was launched in Communist China to propagandize the alleged infallibility of Maoism as a blueprint for social and economic revolution in the underdeveloped areas of the world. Soviet journals would rather pin that glowing epithet on Khrushchev, but they rarely do. Instead, they praise his "creative application" of Marxism-Leninism to the "concrete tasks of the moment," and it appears that the Soviet leader feels more comfortable as a "doer" than as a "thinker." This is the image that he has sought to spread throughout the Soviet Union, and to a large extent he has succeeded. Even in eastern Europe, Khrushchev's reputation is based on his ability to apply the broadest limits of established Marxist-Leninist dogma to current problems—not on his ability to conceive new dogmas. Thus, in February, 1959, when Khrushchev announced his "new theory" on the simultaneous admission of all socialist states to Communism "more or less at the same time," it was not taken seriously in Russia or eastern Europe. In China, it received only passing mention.

The two leading figures in the Communist world have encouraged different images of themselves. Khrushchev—the miner, peasant, agronomist, and footloose diplomat. Mao—the poet, writer, recluse, and soil-bound philosopher. Khrushchev—the doer. Mao—the thinker. This difference is vitally important in a Marxist context, because theory is the lifeblood of the Communist movement. Communists believe in Communism. They absorb their ideas and concepts from the Marxist classics. When Stalin lived, he was the "greatest theoretician." Since his death, Mao has slowly acquired the status of "top thinker," though Khrushchev for understandable reasons has been tardy in acknowledging Mao's new position. Thus, Hsia Yen, Peking's Vice-Minister of Culture, can proclaim: "Comrade Mao Tse-tung has creatively developed the Marxist-Leninist theory of art and literature and *solved problems that Marx, Lenin, and Stalin failed to solve.*"

Mao's creativity has helped to win the allegiance of the Southeast Asian CP's to Peking's example of revolution. It is certain that Khrushchev himself realizes the significance of the Chinese example in Asia and Africa. During his October, 1959, visit to Peking, he made a major ideological concession to Mao. With only a modest application of Marxist double talk, he said: "The tumultuous growth of the socialist countries has become an inescapable fact, and scares the capitalist bosses. They admit that the example of the successful advance of the great People's Republic of China—in the sphere of the development of agriculture, industry, and culture—is exerting an immense influence on the countries of Asia and Africa. *This example can inspire peoples* with the desire to follow suit, in order to score equally great successes. . . . The peoples of Asia and Africa see along what path, under what system, the talents and creative forces of the peoples can really burst forth. . . ."

This concession must have pleased Mao, for it seemed to underline two vital factors—first, that Mao's "creativity" has been "acknowledged," and, second, that Khrushchev was wise enough to bend with the ideological pressures that Mao's pronouncements have produced in the Communist world. The question now looming before the Kremlin seems to be: How does Mao's enhanced stature as a "creative thinker"—possibly, the greatest "creative thinker" in the Marxist world—affect the Russian-Chinese alliance? Does this mean that the entire socialist bloc now looks toward Peking for ideological leadership? Does this mean that Moscow has forfeited its right to make ideological pronouncements? Most important, if this really was a concession, is it not possible that it portends a series of concessions that could eventually strip the Soviet Union of its "leading role" in the socialist bloc? These are questions with which Khrushchev must grapple; for it seems likely that, if he does not, other Soviet leaders who oppose him will seize upon them to force a change in the Kremlin hierarchy.

Third, in military matters. Khrushchev knows that at the moment Peking has a standing professional army of 2,500,000 men, equipped with the latest weapons of war and supported by a home guard of 30,000,000. The air force is relatively small but modern, and it is nourished by a minimum of thirty jet fighters and bombers produced every month in China. The navy is small; but, once again, it is modern; and it has lately begun to accelerate the production of submarines—some, it is believed, atomic-powered, missile-launching submarines.

* * *

Thus, it is clear that for economic, ideological, and military reasons the Russian-Chinese alliance has been plagued in recent years by a rash of disagreements and anxieties. Both Moscow and Peking seem to realize that they are bound by a common ideology which gives them strength, purpose, and direction; yet they have been unable to reduce the intensity and frequency of their disputes.

For example, it was reasonable to assume in February, 1959, that Russia and China were prepared to bury the hatchet on the commune issue after Russia had announced a new $1,250,000,000 loan and a new theory that all socialist nations would enter the heaven of Communism "more or less at the same time." Yet, five months later, Krushchev chose to attack the communes in the unusual setting of a Poznań farm run by Catholic peasants. It was equally reasonable to assume that the Chinese might have abandoned the belligerency in their foreign policy after signing border agreements with Burma and Nepal in early 1960 and accepting Nehru's invitation to discuss the Sino-Indian border dispute in New Delhi. Still, on April 1, 1960, the Chinese decided to publish their strongest disagreement with Khrushchev's policy of "peaceful coexistence," adopting a tougher, harder line on over-all foreign policy than they had followed in 1959.

These peculiar developments, among others, indicate that strong disruptive pressures do exist in the Russian-Chinese alliance. Some of these have already come to the surface; others are still disguised behind cozy clichés. Nevertheless, it would be supreme folly to anticipate a dissolution of the alliance owing to these pressures. Indeed, it is highly likely that for the immediate future the Russian-Chinese axis will continue to function as a viable and powerful political, economic, and diplomatic force.

However, the key phrase in this evaluation is *for the immediate future,* for when China explodes a nuclear bomb it is possible that Russia may have to discard many of its ideas about China. Certainly, the alliance will have entered a new stage—one that is pregnant with danger for Russia and the United States. At that time, China will have added the big weapon to its already formidable arsenal of manpower, strength, dedication, and zeal; and the world will never be the same again. No disarmament agreement will be worth a headline without China's signature. No nuclear ban will be worth a broadcast without China's approval.

The time is near—perhaps only two years away!

For Russia, it will be a time for decision. Possibly, tensions between Moscow and Peking will force a rupture in their alliance. For example, China may unilaterally decide that the time has come to seize Formosa. Peking may brandish its bombs and manpower, and threaten the outbreak of a world war in deadly earnestness. Russia may warn China that the United States is committed to defend Chiang Kai-shek—or lose face before the world. China may again express its disdain for "paper tiger" America and declare war against Chiang—in effect, against Washington. According to the terms of the Moscow-Peking alliance, Russia should leap to China's defense in a war against America—one that almost inevitably would lead to the use of nuclear weapons against Russia, China, and America. If Russia should balk at supporting China, raising some kind of legalistic smoke screen, and if China should insist on Russian aid, according to their treaty, the alliance would be dissolved.

The same possibility exists if China should suddenly lay claim to some area in Southeast Asia—such as Laos. Here, another factor is involved: Would the United States be prepared to go to war against China for the sake of "little" Laos, "which is so far way"?

Would we be able to mobilize popular support in a major war to defend an Asian nation that is of little strategic value to the United States? If we would, then the immediacy of global war would hinge on Russia's willingness to help China. If Russia were unwilling to help China, then the alliance would again be jeopardized—and for the same reason as the one mentioned in the Formosa example.

In some circumstances, the alliance need not be openly ruptured by disagreement; it may simply be reduced to an ineffectual agreement between two suspicious partners. For example, it is conceivable that a China with atom bombs may deliberately antagonize Russia's ideological and nationalistic sensibilities. China may swagger and strut across the world's stage as though it "ran" the Communist world. It may *openly* proclaim itself the ideological leader of the socialist bloc. It may brazenly demand a commanding voice in bloc decisions. It may refuse to co-operate with Russia. Any of these possibilities is real, and any may dissuade Russia from confiding in China and from aligning its policies with China's.

Of course, in a broad consideration of possibilities, it must be recognized that Khrushchev, a proud and intelligent pragmatist, may decide to meet Peking's peacock posturing with another strategy—one that may initially appear to sacrifice Russian interests but that, in the long run, may prove to benefit them. He may feel that Moscow's long-range strategy would best be served by agreeing to Chinese demands—so long as they do not involve a surrender of national power—while hoping to moderate Chinese policy or banking on a change in Chinese policy. Thus, he may again acknowledge China's value to world Communism as a good example for Asia and Africa. He may even be pressed to "relinquish" Outer Mongolia as a Russian sphere of influence, although this may be farfetched.

In any case, if he were asked for an explanation by some of his more finicky associates, he could explain these decisions or concessions as expedient maneuvers to save the alliance—hopeful at the same time that either the Chinese would change their tough tactics and mesh their policies with Russia's or that his opponents would finally agree that the interests of world Communism demand a major readjustment of the Russian-Chinese relationship to take account of Peking's new power position. It would seem that Khrushchev would try to follow this latter policy, since he probably believes that a relatively united front between Russia and China may be all he needs to tip the scales of the world in Communism's favor forever.

* * *

When China develops its own atomic bombs, the United States will have reached a crossroads in its history. For Washington, it will also be a time for decision, big decisions upon which may rest the future of American democracy. China has made no secret of the fact that it wishes to destroy the United States. With nuclear weapons and with the possibility of implicating Russia, China may decide to force America out of the Far East. Peking feels it represents the "middle kingdom," and the "middle kingdom" cannot tolerate the continued presence of American troops and influence in Korea, Formosa, Vietnam, and Thailand. Since it is unlikely that we would simply abandon these nations, the strong possibility exists that we would be dragged into a major war against China.

As if this prospect were not sobering enough, it should be added that this war might also involve the employment of Soviet military power. The Chinese in the Far East. The Russians in Europe and the Middle East. We would be fighting a war on two fronts against two enemies that together seem to have the capacity to wipe the United States off the face of the map. It would be little consolation if in the process we destroyed the Soviet Union.

If the Soviet Union managed to stay out of the war, then we would still have an extremely formidable foe in Communist China. Even if we were victorious, we would be a tired, battered nation, unable to withstand the probable economic and political assault of the Soviet Union in the rest of the world.

So, in either case, the challenge is direct; and the challenge is mortal. Therefore, we should adopt a highly flexible foreign policy aimed at exploiting the divisive pressures in the alliance so that Moscow and Peking will be deprived of the opportunity of facing the United States as a united team. For we would be playing with our national survival if we based our policy on the assumption that Russia and China will inevitably break away from each other.

This is a big job, since it requires the seizure of the diplomatic initiative from the Communists; but it is possible. In this light, I should like to make a few suggestions.

First, recognition. We may not like the idea that China is ruled by a dedicated fistful of fanatic Communists who hate us; we may not like what they have done to China. Similarly, we may not like the idea that Russia has been governed by Communists—no matter how mellow they may appear in their middle age—nor may we like what they have done to Russia. But in 1933 we recognized Moscow because we felt that recognition would increase our ability to deal with the Soviet Union. It is for this reason that we should recognize Peking.

Second, admission to the United Nations. Again, we may not like the idea of Peking sitting in the United Nations, an international organization that condemned Peking as an "aggressor" for its role in the Korean War. Still, we—not Russia—should propose before the General Assembly that Communist China be admitted to membership in the United Nations, to sit alongside Nationalist China in the General Assembly, and that Chiang's seat on the Security Council be given to India. Our proposal to seat Communist China should be coupled with our recognition of Peking.

This proposal is advanced because it is my feeling that it would have a number of salutary by-products for United States diplomacy. We may dislike a regime, but we can no longer afford the luxury of substituting emotion for policy. In my view, this proposal would show the uncommitted third of the world that we do not "fear" Communist China—a story that is heard in Asia and Africa. Second, it would rid us of our barren policy of nonrecognition, freeing our hands and minds for some imaginative diplomatic offensives. We should never forget that the image of American democracy throbs throughout Africa, that the message of the American Revolution beats in colonial countries, and that the concept of a United States of America, or of Europe, or of Africa, is inspiring. We have great, enviable weapons; we should use them skillfully to show our greatness. Finally, this kind of proposal would place the Communists on the defensive for the first time in many years. Moscow and Peking would be puzzled by our change in attitude; and Moscow would be placed in the uncomfortable position of either antagonizing India by rejecting our proposal or offending China by accepting it. Peking, it should be added, would probably reject the proposal, because Peking does not accept the idea of two Chinas. Neither does Chiang. But this proposal, boldly, almost defiantly, proclaimed by Washington, would create major problems for Moscow and Peking and deepen the tensions in their alliance.

Third, we should recognize the government of Outer Mongolia. We know that there is a quiet competition between Moscow and Peking for this remote Asian nation—a nation that fervently desires to break out of its diplomatic isolation. We should play on this desire by extending not only diplomatic recognition but also economic aid; and, if possible, we should begin an exchange of students and officials with Outer Mongolia.

Once again, Ulan Bator may not want our recognition, but Ulan Bator will then be faced with internal dissension. For American recognition is not to be treated lightly, even in Ulan Bator. Thus, this concept would show Moscow and Peking that just as they can invade the American sphere of influence in Cuba, exacerbating tensions between Washington and Havana, so we can invade their sphere of influence by establishing a working relationship with Outer Mongolia.

Fourth, we should make every effort to begin a program of exchanges with Communist China—even if Peking chooses to ignore our recognition-and-admission proposal. We should not accept Peking's rejection as an insult, since China has its reasons for rejection just as we have our reasons for making the proposal. Transient considerations should play only a minor role in the formulation of our national policy. We should realize that it is vitally important that we get newspapermen, television reporters, students, and tourists into Communist China. They would serve as our emissaries of good will. They would try to convince the

Chinese Communists that they can get along with America and that it is possible to "coexist" with capitalism, since American capitalism wants nothing from China. These emissaries may fail, but in that case we have at least tried.

Fifth, we should try to find areas where our interests coincide with Russia's and, if possible, embark on joint Soviet-American projects—such as economic-aid programs for Africa, Asia, and the Middle East—always within the context of the United Nations. Hopefully, this would encourage the "peace and co-operation" faction within the Soviet Communist Party that opposes the Chinese view that war with imperialism is inevitable.

Sixth, we should begin a massive education program throughout the United States—with federal funds, if necessary—to prepare the American people for the bitter, desperate struggle that we surely face with China—whether China remains allied to Russia or not. This program should stress language and area training. We need specialists on China as much as we need peace; and, oddly, in this case, the two go hand in hand.

* * *

On February 21, 1960, Robert D. Murphy, former Under-Secretary of State, skilled in trouble-shooter diplomacy, addressed a luncheon of the American Bar Foundation in Chicago. His topic was the Russian-Chinese alliance, which he described as the "major element weighing on our foreign policy today." He said there was "reason to believe that a certain cleavage may exist"; that a good deal of "distrust and dislike" divide Russia and China. When asked what the United States might do, he answered: "We are doing little to nothing to exploit the differences between the two. No doubt it is the part of wisdom to let these differences grow naturally, as inevitably it seems to me they must. At times, it is necessary in diplomacy to await the turn of the cycle of events."

The "turn" is two years away, when China begins to produce atomic bombs. Perhaps, in this case, it would be wiser not to await the "turn"; for, when it comes, it may be too late.

Index